LADIES' HomeJournal®

Quick & Easy *favorites*

Meredith® Consumer Marketing
Des Moines, Iowa

Ladies' Home Journal® Quick & Easy Favorites, Vol. 1

Meredith® Corporation Consumer Marketing
Vice President, Consumer Marketing: Janet Donnelly
Consumer Product Marketing Director: Steve Swanson
Consumer Product Marketing Manager: Wendy Merical
Business Director: Ron Clingman
Senior Production Manager: George Susral

Waterbury Publications, Inc.
Editorial Director: Lisa Kingsley
Creative Director: Ken Carlson
Associate Editors: Tricia Laning, Mary Williams
Associate Design Directors: Doug Samuelson, Bruce Yang
Production Assistant: Mindy Samuelson
Cover Photographer: Jason Donnelly
Cover Food Stylist: Charles Worthington
Cover Prop Stylist: Sue Mitchell
Contributing Copy Editors: Terri Fredrickson, Peg Smith
Contributing Indexer: Elizabeth T. Parson

Ladies' Home Journal® **Magazine**
Editor-in-Chief: Sally Lee
Creative Director: Jeffrey Saks
Food and Entertaining Editor: Tara Bench
Assistant Food Editor: Khalil A. Hymore

Meredith Publishing Group
President: Tom Harty
Vice President, Manufacturing: Bruce Heston

Meredith Corporation
Chairman and Chief Executive Officer: Stephen M. Lacy

In Memoriam: E.T. Meredith III (1933–2003)

Pictured on the front cover:
Sautéed Chicken with Garlicky Pasta
(recipe on page 131)

Night after night and bite after bite, families agree that nothing beats the flavor of a fresh home-cooked meal. Busy cooks who pull off the dinnertime challenge with ease admit that some of their best, most-requested family meals require only a handful of ingredients and a couple of easy prep steps.

Thumb through the pages of *Quick & Easy Favorites* and discover some of the slickest ways to throw together dinner, even on the days when you have little time or energy to cook. This book is bursting with recipes, including easy and versatile pastas, quick-to-grill meats, toss-and-serve salads, and fix-and-forget slow cooker meals. Recipe ingredient lists call for familiar supermarket basics: fresh and prepared foods as well as convenience items. Along with that, nearly all of these recipes have the cook out of the kitchen in fewer than 30 minutes. And because health is paramount to our readers, look for the ♥ icon throughout the book. This "healthy" icon means that the recipe meets the following guidelines: 10 or fewer grams of fat per serving, less than 900 milligrams of sodium per serving, and 2 or more grams of fiber per serving.

Spend a few minutes on the weekend selecting recipes for the upcoming week. Write each night's menu, do the shopping, and post the menu list on the fridge. Check the list throughout the week to jog your memory for important steps, such as thawing meat or allowing time in the morning to toss ingredients in a slow cooker. The more you follow your plan, the easier it becomes to whip together a weeknight meal, come to the table with a smile, and say, "Dinner is served!"

Contents

CHAPTER 1 /

Soups & Sandwiches

7

French Onion and Beef Soup

2 cups coarsely chopped cabbage
  (about ⅓ of a small head)
½ cup chopped tomato (1 medium)
  Black pepper
  Sour cream (optional)

1. Place beef roast and juices in a large saucepan. Add undrained beets and beef broth. Bring to boiling, breaking up meat with a spoon. Add cabbage and tomato. Simmer, covered, for 5 minutes. Season to taste with pepper. If desired, serve with sour cream. **MAKES 4 SERVINGS.**

Per serving: 222 cal., 9 g total fat (4 g sat. fat), 64 mg chol., 1,014 mg sodium, 13 g carbo., 3 g fiber, 26 g pro.

Quick Meatball Minestrone

Start to Finish: 25 minutes

1 12- to 16-ounce package frozen cooked Italian-style meatballs
3 14.5-ounce cans lower-sodium beef broth
1 15- to 16-ounce can Great Northern beans or white kidney (cannellini) beans, rinsed and drained
1 14.5-ounce can diced tomatoes with basil, garlic, and oregano, undrained
1 10-ounce package frozen mixed vegetables
1 cup dried small pasta (such as macaroni, small shell, mini penne, or rotini)
1 teaspoon sugar
  Finely shredded Parmesan cheese (optional)

1. In a 4-quart Dutch oven stir together meatballs, beef broth, beans, undrained tomatoes, and frozen vegetables. Bring to boiling. Stir in pasta. Return to boiling; reduce heat. Simmer, uncovered, about 10 minutes or until pasta is tender and meatballs are heated through. Stir in sugar. If desired, sprinkle servings with Parmesan cheese. **MAKES 6 TO 8 SERVINGS.**

Per serving: 413 cal., 15 g total fat (7 g sat. fat), 40 mg chol., 1,242 mg sodium, 47 g carbo., 8 g fiber, 24 g pro.

French Onion and Beef Soup

Start to Finish: 25 minutes

3 tablespoons butter or margarine
1 medium onion, thinly sliced and separated in rings
2 10.5-ounce cans condensed French onion soup
2½ cups water
2 cups cubed cooked beef (10 ounces)
4 1-inch slices French bread
½ cup shredded Gruyère or Swiss cheese (2 ounces)

1. Preheat broiler. In a large skillet melt butter over medium heat. Add onion; cook about 5 minutes or until tender. Stir in soup, the water, and beef. Bring to boiling, stirring occasionally.

2. Meanwhile, place the bread slices on a baking sheet. Broil 4 inches from the heat about 1 minute or until toasted on one side. Top the toasted sides of bread slices with shredded cheese; broil about 1 minute more or until cheese is melted.

3. To serve, ladle soup into soup bowls. Top with bread slices, cheese sides up. **MAKES 4 SERVINGS.**

Per serving: 465 cal., 21 g total fat (10 g sat. fat), 82 mg chol., 1,701 mg sodium, 40 g carbo., 3 g fiber, 28 g pro.

Easy Beef Borscht

Start to Finish: 18 minutes

1 17-ounce package refrigerated cooked beef roast au jus
1 15-ounce can julienne beets, undrained
3 cups reduced-sodium beef broth

Quick
Meatball
Minestrone

Beef, Orzo,
and Escarole
Soup

Quick Hamburger Soup
Start to Finish: 30 minutes

8 ounces extra-lean ground beef
8 ounces uncooked ground turkey breast
1 cup finely chopped onions (2 medium)
1 cup coarsely shredded carrots (2 medium)
1 cup sliced celery (2 stalks)
2 cloves garlic, minced
6 cups reduced-sodium beef broth
2 14.5-ounce cans diced tomatoes, undrained
1 tablespoon snipped fresh sage or
  1 teaspoon dried sage, crushed
2 teaspoons snipped fresh thyme or
  1 teaspoon dried thyme, crushed
1 teaspoon snipped fresh rosemary or
  1/2 teaspoon dried rosemary, crushed
1/4 teaspoon salt
1/4 teaspoon black pepper
2 chopped potatoes (2 medium)
  Fresh sage (optional)

1. In a Dutch oven combine beef, turkey, onions, carrots, celery, and garlic; cook until meat is brown and onion is tender. Drain off fat. Stir broth, undrained tomatoes, sage, thyme, rosemary, salt, and pepper into beef mixture in Dutch oven. Bring to boiling; stir in potatoes. Reduce heat. Cover and simmer for 10 to 15 minutes or until vegetables are tender. If desired, garnish with additional fresh sage. **MAKES 12 SERVINGS.**

Per serving: 103 cal., 2 g total fat (1 g sat. fat), 19 mg chol., 418 mg sodium, 10 g carbo., 1 g fiber, 10 g pro.

Quick Hamburger Soup

Beef, Orzo, and Escarole Soup ♡
Prep: 5 minutes **Cook:** 25 minutes

12 ounces lean ground beef
1 small fennel bulb, chopped (about 2/3 cup)
1/2 cup chopped onion (1 medium)
2 cloves garlic, minced
4 cups beef broth
2 cups water
1 teaspoon dried oregano, crushed
2 bay leaves
1/4 teaspoon cracked black pepper
1/2 cup orzo pasta
4 cups shredded escarole, curly endive, and/or spinach
3 ounces Parmesan cheese with rind, cut into 4 wedges (optional)

1. In a large saucepan combine beef, fennel, onion, and garlic. Cook, uncovered, over medium-high heat for 5 minutes or until meat is browned and vegetables are nearly tender, stirring occasionally. Drain off fat, if necessary.
2. Stir in broth, the water, oregano, bay leaves, and pepper. Bring to boiling; reduce heat. Simmer, covered, for 10 minutes. Remove bay leaves; discard.

3. Add orzo. Return to boiling; reduce heat. Boil gently, uncovered, for 10 minutes or just until pasta is tender, stirring occasionally. Remove from heat; stir in escarole.
4. If desired, place a wedge of cheese in each of 4 soup bowls. Ladle hot soup into bowls. **MAKES 4 SERVINGS.**

Per serving: 262 cal., 10 g total fat (4 g sat. fat), 54 mg chol., 873 mg sodium, 22 g carbo., 7 g fiber, 21 g pro.

Quick Pork-Bean Soup

Prep: 15 minutes **Cook:** 15 minutes

- 12 ounces lean boneless pork
- 1 cup chopped onion (1 large)
- 2 tablespoons vegetable oil
- 2 cups water
- 1 11.5-ounce can condensed bean with bacon soup
- 1 1/2 cups sliced carrots (3 medium)
- 1 teaspoon Worcestershire sauce
- 1/4 teaspoon dry mustard

1. Cut pork into thin bite-size strips. In a large skillet cook pork and onion in hot oil for 3 to 4 minutes or until pork is browned. Stir in the water, soup, carrots, Worcestershire sauce, and dry mustard.

2. Bring to boiling; reduce heat. Cover and simmer for 15 minutes. **MAKES 4 SERVINGS.**

Per serving: 312 cal., 13 g total fat (3 g sat. fat), 52 mg chol., 678 mg sodium, 23 g carbo., 6 g fiber, 24 g pro.

Speedy Beef Stew

Start to Finish: 25 minutes

- 1 17-ounce package refrigerated cooked beef roast au jus
- 2 10.75-ounce cans condensed beefy mushroom soup
- 1 16-ounce package frozen stew vegetables
- 1 1/2 cups milk
- 4 teaspoons snipped fresh basil or 1 1/2 teaspoons dried basil, crushed

1. Cut beef into bite-size pieces if necessary. In a 4-quart Dutch oven combine beef and juices, soup, frozen vegetables, and dried basil, if using. Bring to boiling; reduce heat.

Cover and simmer for 10 minutes. Stir in milk and fresh basil, if using. Heat through. **MAKES 4 SERVINGS.**

Per serving: 386 cal., 15 g total fat (7 g sat. fat), 80 mg chol., 1,688 mg sodium, 33 g carbo., 5 g fiber, 33 g pro.

Chunky Chipotle Pork Chili

Start to Finish: 30 minutes

- 1 tablespoon vegetable oil
- 1/3 cup chopped onion (1 small)
- 2 teaspoons bottled minced garlic (4 cloves)
- 12 ounces pork tenderloin, cut into 3/4-inch cubes
- 2 teaspoons chili powder
- 2 teaspoons ground cumin
- 1 yellow or red sweet pepper, cut into 1/2-inch pieces
- 1 cup beer or beef broth
- 1/2 cup bottled picante sauce or salsa
- 1 to 2 tablespoons finely chopped canned chipotle chile peppers in adobo sauce*
- 1 15-ounce can small red beans or pinto beans, rinsed and drained
- 1/2 cup sour cream
  Fresh cilantro or flat-leaf parsley sprigs (optional)

1. In a large saucepan heat oil over medium-high heat. Add onion and garlic; cook about 3 minutes or until tender.

2. In a medium bowl toss pork with chili powder and cumin; add to saucepan. Cook and stir until pork is browned. Add sweet pepper, beer, picante sauce, and chipotle chile peppers. Bring to boiling; reduce heat. Cover and simmer about 5 minutes or until pork is tender. Stir in beans; heat through. Top each serving with sour cream. If desired, garnish with cilantro. **MAKES 4 SERVINGS.**

Per serving: 328 cal., 11 g total fat (4 g sat. fat), 65 mg chol., 625 mg sodium, 29 g carbo., 7 g fiber, 26 g pro.

*Note Because chile peppers contain volatile oils that can burn your skin and eyes, avoid direct contact with them as much as possible. When working with chile peppers, wear plastic or rubber gloves. If your bare hands do touch the peppers, wash your hands and nails well with soap and warm water.

Freeze extra chiles

Chipotle chile peppers in adobo sauce are generally sold in cans that hold more than the 1 or 2 tablespoons you need for most recipes. Divide any remaning chipotle peppers and sauce among small freezer bags. Label the bags and freeze to use later. Because it's a small amount, the chiles will thaw quickly—in less than an hour at room temperature. Or thaw them in the refrigerator for several hours.

Chunky Chipotle Pork Chili

Spicy Red Beans and Sausage Soup

Spicy Red Beans and Sausage Soup

Start to Finish: 30 minutes

- 6 ounces uncooked chorizo sausage or uncooked turkey Italian sausage links, casings removed
- 3/4 chopped green sweet pepper (1 medium)
- 1/2 cup thinly sliced green onions (4)
- 1 clove garlic, minced
- 2 15- to 16-ounce cans kidney beans, rinsed and drained
- 1 14.5-ounce can diced tomatoes, undrained
- 1 14.5-ounce can reduced-sodium chicken broth
- 1 cup water
- 3 cups coarsely chopped fresh kale or spinach
- 1/3 cup no-salt-added tomato paste
- 1/2 teaspoon dried thyme, crushed

1. In a 4- to 6-quart Dutch oven cook sausage until brown, stirring to break it up as it cooks. Drain off fat. Add sweet pepper, green onions, and garlic to sausage. Cook for 3 to 5 minutes or just until sweet pepper is tender, stirring occasionally.

2. Add kidney beans, undrained tomatoes, broth, the water, kale (if using), tomato paste, and thyme to Dutch oven. Bring to boiling; reduce heat. Simmer, covered, for 10 minutes. Stir in spinach (if using); heat through. **MAKES 6 SERVINGS.**

Per serving: 295 cal., 12 g total fat (4g sat. fat), 25 mg chol., 900 mg sodium, 35 g carbo., 11 g fiber, 20 g pro.

Quick Tip If you are watching fat intake, you can reduce the amount of fat in your food by cooking and then rinsing ground meats such as sausage in a colander under hot running tap water. Just be sure it has completely drained before proceeding with your recipe.

Chilly Ham and Cucumber Bisque

Chilly Ham and Cucumber Bisque

Start to Finish: 17 minutes

- 8 ounces cubed cooked ham
- 1 English cucumber, cut up
- 3 cups buttermilk
  Salt and black pepper
- 1 cup packaged shredded fresh carrots
- 1/2 cup chopped red sweet pepper, chopped

1. In a large nonstick skillet cook ham on medium-high heat for 4 to 5 minutes or until light brown. Set aside.

2. In a blender combine cucumber and buttermilk; blend until smooth. Season to taste with salt and pepper. Ladle cucumber mixture into 4 soup bowls. Divide ham, carrots, and sweet pepper evenly among the bowls. **MAKES 4 SERVINGS.**

Per serving: 196 cal., 7 g total fat (3 g sat. fat), 40 mg chol., 1,099 mg sodium, 18 g carbo., 2 g fiber, 17 g pro.

Winter Vegetable Soup

Start to Finish: 30 minutes

- 6 ounces kielbasa or smoked sausage, halved lengthwise and sliced
- 1/3 cup chopped onion (1 small)
- 2 14.5-ounce cans chicken broth
- 2 cups water
- 1/2 of a small (8 ounces) butternut squash, peeled, seeded, and cubed (about 1 1/3 cups)
- 1 cup sliced carrots (2 medium)
- 1/8 to 1/4 teaspoon black pepper
- 1 cup dried ditalini or orzo pasta
- 1 15- to 16-ounce can red kidney beans, rinsed and drained
- 2 cups prewashed baby spinach leaves

1. In a 4-quart Dutch oven cook kielbasa and onion over medium-high heat for 5 minutes or until onion is tender, stirring occasionally. Add broth, the water, squash, carrots, and pepper. Cover; bring to boiling. Reduce heat. Simmer, covered, for 5 minutes.

2. Stir in pasta and drained beans. Return to boiling; reduce heat. Cover and boil gently for 6 minutes or until pasta and vegetables are tender, stirring occasionally. Stir in spinach. Serve immediately. **MAKES 6 SERVINGS.**

Per serving: 350 cal., 12 g total fat (4 g sat. fat), 28 mg chol., 1,598 mg sodium, 48 g carbo., 7 g fiber, 15 g pro.

Chicken-Lime Chili

Start to Finish: 15 minutes

- 1/2 cup chopped onion (1 medium)
- 1 tablespoon vegetable oil
- 1 15- to 16-ounce can hominy, rinsed and drained
- 1 15- to 16-ounce can Great Northern beans, rinsed and drained
- 1 14.5-ounce can reduced-sodium chicken broth
- 1 9-ounce package frozen cooked chicken breast strips
- 1/4 cup lime juice
- 2 tablespoons snipped fresh cilantro
- 1/4 teaspoon ground cumin
- 1/4 teaspoon black pepper
- 1/2 cup shredded Colby and Monterey Jack cheese, Monterey Jack, or cheddar cheese (2 ounces)
  Bottled green salsa
  Corn tortilla chips
  Fresh cilantro leaves

1. In a large saucepan cook onion in hot oil over medium heat for 3 minutes. Stir in drained hominy, drained beans, broth, frozen chicken, lime juice, the 2 tablespoons cilantro, cumin, and pepper. Cover and bring to boiling over high heat, stirring occasionally. Serve topped with cheese, salsa, tortilla chips, and fresh cilantro. **MAKES 4 SERVINGS.**

Per serving: 434 cal., 14 g total fat (5 g sat. fat), 58 mg chol., 1,001 mg sodium, 48 g carbo., 9 g fiber, 31 g pro.

Sausage Soup

Prep: 30 minutes **Cook:** 1 hour + 30 minutes

- 1 pound bulk Italian sausage
- 1 cup chopped onion (1 large)
- 1/2 cup chopped carrot (1 medium)
- 1/2 cup chopped celery (1 stalk)
- 8 cups chicken broth
- 1 14.5-ounce can diced tomatoes, undrained
- 1 8-ounce can tomato sauce
- 1 clove garlic, minced
- 2 teaspoons dried Italian seasoning, crushed
- 1 bay leaf
- 1/2 cup dried orzo pasta or finely broken capellini pasta
  Finely shredded Parmesan cheese (optional)

1. In a 4-quart Dutch oven cook sausage, onion, carrot, and celery over medium heat until sausage is brown. Drain well.

2. Add broth, undrained diced tomatoes, tomato sauce, garlic, Italian seasoning, and bay leaf to sausage mixture in Dutch oven. Bring to boiling; reduce heat. Cover and simmer for 1 hour. Add uncooked pasta. Return to boiling; reduce heat. Cook, uncovered, for 30 minutes more. Discard bay leaf. If desired, serve with shredded Parmesan cheese. **MAKES 8 SERVINGS.**

Per serving: 285 cal., 18 g total fat (6 g sat. fat), 46 mg chol., 1,600 mg sodium, 17 g carbo., 1 g fiber, 11 g pro.

A warming bowl of soup is a simple and satisfying dinner. When it's broth-based and packed with vegetables, it's healthful too.

Chicken-
Vegetable
Soup

Chicken-Vegetable Soup ♡

Start to Finish: 25 minutes

- 1   16-ounce package frozen Italian vegetables (zucchini, carrots, cauliflower, lima beans, and Italian beans)
- 1   14.5-ounce can Italian-style stewed tomatoes, undrained
- 1   12-ounce can vegetable juice
- 1   cup chicken broth
- 1½   cups chopped cooked chicken or turkey (about 8 ounces)

1. In a large saucepan combine frozen vegetables, undrained tomatoes, vegetable juice, and broth.

2. Bring to boiling; reduce heat. Cover and simmer about 10 minutes or until vegetables are tender. Stir in chicken. Heat through. **MAKES 4 SERVINGS.**

Per serving: 186 cal., 4 g total fat (1 g sat. fat), 47 mg chol., 888 mg sodium, 17 g carbo., 5 g fiber, 18 g pro.

Curry Lentil Soup ♡

Prep: 10 minutes   **Cook:** 22 minutes

- 2   teaspoons vegetable oil
- ½   cup chopped onion (1 medium)
- 1   teaspoon curry powder
- ½   teaspoon cumin
- ¾   chopped red sweet pepper (1 medium)
- 1   clove garlic, minced
- 4   cups water
- 1   cup red or yellow lentils
- 1   teaspoon salt

1. In a large saucepan heat oil over medium-high heat. Stir in onion, curry powder, and cumin, and cook 4 minutes. Stir in red pepper and garlic, and cook 3 minutes more.

2. Stir in the water, lentils, and salt. Bring to a boil. Reduce heat; simmer until lentils are soft, about 15 minutes. **MAKES 4 SERVINGS.**

Per serving: 207 cal., 3 g total fat (1 g sat. fat), 0 mg chol., 886 mg sodium, 33 g carbo., 7 g fiber, 14 g pro.

Chicken Tortilla Soup

Chicken Tortilla Soup

Start to Finish: 25 minutes

- 2   14.5-ounce cans chicken broth with roasted garlic
- 1   14.5-ounce can Mexican-style stewed tomatoes, undrained
- 2   cups chopped cooked chicken (about 10 ounces)
- 2   cups frozen sweet pepper and onion stir-fry vegetables
      Tortilla chips
      Sliced fresh jalapeño peppers (optional) (see note, page 12)
      Lime wedges (optional)

1. In a large saucepan combine chicken broth, undrained tomatoes, chicken, and frozen vegetables. Bring to boiling; reduce heat. Cover and simmer for 5 minutes.

2. To serve, ladle soup into warm soup bowls. Serve with tortilla chips. If desired, top with sliced jalapeño chile peppers and serve with lime wedges. **MAKES 4 SERVINGS.**

Per serving: 266 cal., 9 g total fat (2 g sat. fat), 65 mg chol., 1,260 mg sodium, 22 g carbo., 1 g fiber, 24 g pro.

Corn Chowder

2. Meanwhile, pat whole kernel corn dry with paper towels. Line a 15×10×1-inch baking pan with foil. Spread corn in the baking pan and drizzle with olive oil; toss to coat. Broil 4 to 5 inches from the heat for 5 to 8 minutes or until light brown, stirring once; set aside.
3. Add chicken, cream-style corn, and whole kernel corn to Dutch oven. Heat through. Season to taste with pepper. Ladle into 6 bowls. Top each serving with shredded smoked Gouda cheese. **MAKES 6 SERVINGS.**

Per serving: 307 cal., 8 g total fat (2 g sat. fat), 88 mg chol., 1,304 mg sodium, 40 g carbo., 2 g fiber, 20 g pro.

White Bean-Turkey Chili with Corn Bread Dumplings

Start to Finish: 22 minutes

1 pound cooked turkey
1 16-ounce jar chunky salsa
1 15-ounce can cannellini beans (white kidney beans), rinsed and drained
1 teaspoon chili powder
1 8.5-ounce package corn bread mix
1 egg
1/4 cup shredded cheddar cheese (1 ounce) (optional)
Slivered green onions (optional)
Chili powder (optional)

1. Chop turkey. In a 4-quart Dutch oven combine turkey, salsa, beans, chili powder, and 2/3 cup water. Bring to boiling.
2. Meanwhile, for dumplings, in a medium bowl mix together corn bread mix, egg, and 1/4 cup water. Drop batter by large spoonfuls into boiling turkey chili.
3. Cover; reduce heat and simmer for 10 to 15 minutes or until a wooden pick inserted into a dumpling comes out clean. Ladle into 4 bowls. If desired, top each serving with cheese, green onions, and chili powder.
MAKES 4 SERVINGS.

Per serving: 555 cal., 15 g total fat (4 g sat. fat), 140 mg chol., 1,618 mg sodium, 64 g carbo., 11 g fiber, 47 g pro.

Quick Tip If you can't find cannellini beans, any white bean including Great Northern and navy beans works fine in this chili.

Corn Chowder

Start to Finish: 20 minutes

1 8-ounce tub cream cheese with chives and onions
1 14.75-ounce can cream-style corn
2 cups milk
8 ounces smoked turkey breast, chopped
1 cup frozen peas
Black pepper

1. In a medium saucepan heat cream cheese over medium heat to soften; blend in corn and milk. Add turkey and peas; heat through. Season to taste with black pepper.
MAKES 4 SERVINGS.

Per serving: 397 cal., 23 g total fat (15 g sat. fat), 88 mg chol., 1,159 mg sodium, 27 g carbo., 3 g fiber, 19 g pro.

Smoky Corn and Chicken Noodle Soup

Start to Finish: 30 minutes

4 14.5-ounce cans chicken broth
1 8-ounce package frozen egg noodles
1 cup frozen whole kernel corn, thawed
1 tablespoon olive oil
2 cups chopped cooked chicken (about 10 ounces)
1 14.75-ounce can cream-style corn
Black pepper
Shredded smoked Gouda cheese or mozzarella cheese

1. In a 4- to 6-quart Dutch oven bring chicken broth to boiling. Add noodles and cook, uncovered, for 20 minutes.

White Bean-Turkey Chili with Corn Bread Dumplings

Creamy
Tomato and
Shrimp
Chowder

Creamy Tomato and Shrimp Chowder

Start to Finish: 18 minutes

- 1 tablespoon olive oil
- 1 cup chopped celery (2 stalks)
- ½ cup chopped onion (1 medium)
- 2 14.5-ounce cans diced tomatoes with basil, garlic, and oregano, undrained
- 8 ounces peeled and deveined cooked medium shrimp
- ½ cup whipping cream
- ½ cup water
  Black pepper
  Slivered fresh basil (optional
  Focaccia, cut in wedges (optional)

1. In a large saucepan heat olive oil over medium heat. Add celery and onion; cook just until tender.
2. Stir in undrained tomatoes; heat through. Add shrimp, whipping cream, and the water. Cook over medium heat just until heated through. Season to taste with pepper. If desired, top with basil and serve with focaccia wedges. **MAKES 4 SERVINGS.**

Per serving: 245 cal., 15 g total fat (8 g sat. fat), 152 mg chol., 1,056 mg sodium, 14 g carbo., 2 g fiber, 15 g pro.

Soba Noodles in Broth

Start to Finish: 20 minutes

- 8 ounces fresh or frozen shrimp in shells
- 6 ounces soba (buckwheat noodles) or dried vermicelli
- 2 cups reduced-sodium chicken broth
- ¼ cup mirin (Japanese sweet rice wine)
- ¼ cup reduced-sodium soy sauce
- 2 teaspoons sugar
- ½ teaspoon instant dashi granules (dried tuna-and-seaweed-flavor soup stock)
- ¼ cup thinly bias-sliced green onions (2)

1. Thaw shrimp, if frozen. Peel and devein shrimp, leaving tails intact. Rinse shrimp; pat dry with paper towels; set shrimp aside. In a large saucepan cook soba noodles in boiling water about 4 minutes or until tender.

Soba Noodles in Broth

2. Meanwhile, in a medium saucepan combine chicken broth, mirin, soy sauce, sugar, and dashi granules. Bring to boiling; reduce heat. Add shrimp; simmer, uncovered, about 2 minutes or until shrimp are opaque.
3. Drain noodles; divide noodles between 2 soup bowls. Pour the shrimp mixture over the noodles. Sprinkle with green onions. **MAKES 2 SERVINGS.**

Per serving: 515 cal., 2 g total fat (0 g sat. fat), 129 mg chol., 2,698 mg sodium, 93 g carbo., 4 g fiber, 35 g pro.

Thai Coconut-Shrimp Soup

Start to Finish: 25 minutes

- 12 ounces fresh or frozen medium shrimp, peeled and deveined
- 3 cups reduced-sodium chicken broth
- 1 14-ounce can unsweetened light coconut milk
- 1 tablespoon fish sauce (nam pla)
- 2 teaspoons grated fresh ginger
- 1 teaspoon red curry paste
- 1 clove garlic, minced
- ½ teaspoon kosher salt
- 1 cup green beans, cut in 1-inch pieces (4 ounces)
- ¼ cup thinly sliced green onions (2)
  Lime wedges (optional)

1. Thaw shrimp, if frozen. In a large saucepan combine chicken broth, coconut milk, fish sauce, ginger, curry paste, garlic, and salt. Bring to boiling; reduce heat.
2. Add green beans; cook for 2 minutes. Add shrimp; cook about 5 minutes or until shrimp turn opaque. Sprinkle servings with green onions. If desired, serve with lime.
MAKES 5 SERVINGS.

Per serving: 160 cal., 7 g total fat (3.5 g sat. fat), 103 mg chol., 656 mg sodium, 9 g carbo., 1 g fiber, 18 g pro.

Smoky Cheese and Corn Chowder

Black Bean and Corn Soup

Start to Finish: 20 minutes

- 2 tablespoons vegetable oil
- 1/2 cup chopped red onion (1 medium)
- 2 15-ounce cans black beans, rinsed and drained
- 1 14.5-ounce can chicken broth
- 1 11-ounce can whole kernel corn, drained
- 1 cup bottled chunky salsa
- 1 tablespoon fresh lime juice
- 1/2 teaspoon salt
- 1/8 teaspoon black pepper

1. In a large saucepan heat oil over medium heat. Add onion; cook until tender. Mash 1 cup of the beans with a potato masher or fork.

2. Add mashed beans, whole beans, chicken broth, corn, salsa, lime juice, salt, and pepper to saucepan. Bring to boiling; reduce heat. Simmer, uncovered, about 10 minutes or until heated through. If desired, serve with sour cream and lime wedges. **MAKES 6 SERVINGS.**

Per serving: 191 cal., 7 g total fat (1 g sat. fat), 2 mg chol., 1,171 mg sodium, 25 g carbo., 7 g fiber, 8 g pro.

Broccoli-Beer-Cheese Soup

Start to Finish: 30 minutes

- 3 slices bacon, chopped
- 1/2 cup chopped onion (1 medium)
- 2 tablespoons all-purpose flour
- 1/4 teaspoon black pepper
- 2 3/4 cups chicken broth
- 2 cups bite-size broccoli florets
- 2/3 cup beer
- 12 ounces smoked turkey breast, chopped
- 6 ounces process Swiss cheese, torn
- 1/3 cup half-and-half or light cream

1. In a large saucepan cook bacon and onion until bacon is crisp and onion is tender, stirring occasionally. Stir in flour and pepper until well combined. Add chicken broth, broccoli, and beer. Bring to boiling; reduce heat. Simmer, uncovered, for 3 to 5 minutes or until broccoli is nearly tender. Add turkey, cheese, and half-and-half. Cook and stir until cheese is melted. **MAKES 4 SERVINGS.**

Per serving: 386 cal., 22 g total fat (11 g sat. fat), 97 mg chol., 2,048 mg sodium, 13 g carbo., 2 g fiber, 31 g pro.

Smoky Cheese and Corn Chowder ♡

Start to Finish: 25 minutes

- 1 10-ounce package frozen whole kernel corn (2 cups)
- 1/2 cup chopped onion (1 medium)
- 1/2 cup water
- 1 teaspoon instant chicken bouillon granules
- 1/4 teaspoon black pepper
- 2 1/2 cups milk
- 3 tablespoons all-purpose flour
- 1 cup shredded smoked process cheddar cheese (4 ounces)
- 1 tablespoon chopped pimiento, drained
Fresh chives (optional)
Chopped pimiento (optional)

1. In a large saucepan combine corn, onion, the water, bouillon granules, and pepper. Bring to boiling; reduce heat. Simmer, covered, about 4 minutes or until corn is tender.

2. Stir together 1/2 cup of the milk and the flour; add to corn mixture along with the remaining milk. Cook and stir until slightly thickened and bubbly. Add cheese and the 1 tablespoon pimiento; heat and stir until cheese is melted.

3. If desired, garnish with chives and additional pimiento. **MAKES 4 SERVINGS.**

Per serving: 283 cal., 13 g total fat (8 g sat. fat), 42 mg chol., 462 mg sodium, 28 g carbo., 2 g fiber, 15 g pro.

Black Bean and Corn Soup

Pumpkin Soup with Spiced Croutons

Pumpkin Soup with Spiced Croutons ♡

Start to Finish: 30 minutes

2 medium carrots, sliced
2 tablespoons butter
1 medium onion, finely chopped
1 stalk celery, finely chopped
1 clove garlic, minced
2 15-ounce cans pumpkin
1 32-ounce package reduced-sodium chicken broth
½ cup half-and-half or light cream
½ cup water
3 tablespoons maple syrup
1 teaspoon pumpkin pie spice
1 recipe Spiced Croutons
   Celery leaves (optional)

1. In a large saucepan cook carrots in hot butter on medium heat for 2 minutes; add onion, celery, and garlic. Cook 8 to 10 minutes or until vegetables are tender.
2. Stir in pumpkin, broth, half-and-half, the water, maple syrup, and pumpkin pie spice. Heat through. Season with salt and black pepper.
3. To serve, top soup with Spiced Croutons and, if desired, celery leaves.

Spiced Croutons In a bowl toss 3 cups of 1-inch bread cubes with 2 teaspoons pumpkin pie spice. In a large skillet cook bread cubes in 2 tablespoons hot butter for 8 minutes or until toasted, turning occasionally. **MAKES 8 SERVINGS.**

Per serving: 200 cal., 9 g total fat (5 g sat. fat), 21 mg chol., 537 mg sodium, 28 g carbo., 4 g fiber, 5 g pro.

Quick Tip If you don't have 1 teaspoon of pumpkin pie spice, stir together ½ teaspoon ground cinnamon, ¼ teaspoon ground ginger, ¼ teaspoon ground allspice, and ⅛ teaspoon ground nutmeg.

Broccoli-Potato Soup with Greens

Broccoli-Potato Soup with Greens

Start to Finish: 20 minutes

2 medium red potatoes, chopped
1 14.5-ounce can reduced-sodium chicken broth
3 cups small broccoli florets
2 cups milk
3 tablespoons all-purpose flour
2 cups smoked Gouda cheese, shredded (8 ounces)
2 cups torn winter greens (such as curly endive, chicory, romaine, escarole, or spinach)
   Smoked Gouda cheese, shredded (optional)

1. In a large saucepan combine potatoes and broth. Bring to boiling; reduce heat. Simmer, covered, for 8 minutes. Mash slightly. Add broccoli and milk; bring just to simmering.
2. In a medium bowl toss flour with cheese; gradually add to soup, stirring cheese until melted. Season to taste with black pepper. Ladle soup into 4 bowls. Divide the greens evenly among the bowls. If desired, sprinkle with additional smoked Gouda cheese.
MAKES 4 SERVINGS.

Per serving: 365 cal., 18 g total fat (11 g sat. fat), 74 mg chol., 782 mg sodium, 28 g carbo., 4 g fiber, 23 g pro.

Roast Beef and Red Pepper Sandwiches

Barbecue Beef Wrap ♡

Start to Finish: 10 minutes

 8 ounces leftover roast beef, shredded
    (¹/₃ cup)
 4 7- to 8-inch flour tortillas
 ¹/₄ cup bottled barbecue sauce
 ¹/₂ cup shredded Monterey Jack cheese
    (2 ounces)
 ¹/₂ cup packaged shredded broccoli (broccoli
    slaw mix)

1. Arrange beef on the tortillas. Drizzle with barbecue sauce and top with cheese and broccoli; roll up. Serve immediately or wrap tightly in plastic wrap and chill for up to 24 hours. **MAKES 4 WRAPS.**

Per wrap: 280 cal., 13 g total fat (6 g sat. fat), 57 mg chol., 367 mg sodium, 17 g carbo., 1 g fiber, 21 g pro.

Meat Loaf Open-Facers

Start to Finish: 18 minutes

 4 ¹/₂-inch slices eggplant
 2 tablespoons olive oil
    Salt and black pepper
 1 17-ounce package refrigerated meat loaf
    with tomato sauce
 ¹/₂ cup no-salt-added tomato sauce
 4 1-inch diagonal slices Italian bread,
    toasted
 ¹/₄ cup finely shredded Parmesan cheese
    (1 ounce) (optional)

1. Preheat broiler. Brush oil on both sides of eggplant. Sprinkle with salt and pepper. Place eggplant slices on the unheated rack of broiler pan. Broil 3 to 4 inches from heat for 2 to 3 minutes per side or until browned.
2. Meanwhile, slice meat loaf; place slices in a large skillet. Pour sauce from package and tomato sauce over slices. Cook over medium-high heat about 6 minutes or until heated through.
3. Place meat loaf slices on toast; top with eggplant, any remaining sauce, and cheese, if desired. **MAKES 4 SANDWICHES.**

Per sandwich: 327 cal., 16 g total fat (5 g sat. fat), 64 mg chol., 707 mg sodium, 21 g carbo., 2 g fiber, 27 g pro.

Roast Beef and Red Pepper Sandwiches ♡

Start to Finish: 25 minutes

 ¹/₃ cup light mayonnaise or mayonnaise
 ¹/₃ cup Dijon mustard
 2 to 4 tablespoons prepared horseradish
 6 6- to 7-inch rustic Italian sandwich breads
12 ounces thinly sliced cooked roast beef
 1 12-ounce jar roasted red sweet peppers,
    drained and cut into ¹/₄-inch-wide strips
 6 ounces thinly sliced Monterey Jack cheese
 2 cups fresh watercress, tough stems
    removed
 2 cups fresh spinach

1. In a small bowl combine mayonnaise, mustard, and horseradish. Using a serrated knife, slice bread in half horizontally.
2. For each sandwich, spread 1 bread half with mayonnaise mixture. Top each with roast beef, peppers, cheese, watercress, spinach, and remaining half of bread. To serve, cut each sandwich in half. **MAKES 12 SERVINGS (¹/₂ SANDWICH EACH).**

Per ¹/₂ sandwich: 303 cal., 14 g total fat (4 g sat. fat), 41 mg chol., 656 mg sodium, 27 g carbo., 2 g fiber, 20 g pro.

Barbecue
Beef Wrap

Beef and Blue
Cheese Wraps

Beef and Blue Cheese Wraps

Start to Finish: 20 minutes

- 3 tablespoons mayonnaise or salad dressing
- 1 teaspoon dried thyme, crushed
- 2 tablespoons yellow mustard
- 4 8-inch flour tortillas
- 12 ounces thinly sliced deli roast beef
- 1 12-ounce jar roasted red sweet peppers, drained
- 1/3 cup crumbled blue cheese
- 4 cups mixed salad greens
  Olive oil (optional)
  Additional crumbled blue cheese (optional)

1. In a small bowl combine mayonnaise and thyme; remove and set aside 1 tablespoon. Stir mustard into the remaining mayonnaise mixture.

2. Spread one side of each tortilla with mayonnaise-mustard mixture. Evenly divide roast beef, roasted peppers, and the 1/3 cup blue cheese among tortillas. Roll up; brush with reserved mayonnaise-thyme mixture.

3. In an extra-large skillet cook tortilla wraps over medium heat about 2 minutes per side or until lightly browned. Cut each wrap in half. Divide greens among 4 plates. If desired, drizzle greens with olive oil and sprinkle with additional blue cheese; top with halved wraps. **MAKES 4 WRAPS.**

Per wrap: 395 cal., 23 g total fat (7 g sat. fat), 50 mg chol., 1,145 mg sodium, 22 g carbo., 3 g fiber, 21 g pro.

Beef and Cabbage Wraps

Beef and Cabbage Wraps

Start to Finish: 20 minutes **Oven:** 350°F

- 8 8-inch flour tortillas
- 12 ounces lean ground beef
- 1/2 cup chopped onion (1 medium)
- 1 cup frozen whole kernel corn
- 1/2 to 2/3 cup bottled barbecue sauce
- 2 cups packaged shredded cabbage with carrots (coleslaw mix)

1. Preheat oven to 350°F. Wrap tortillas tightly in foil; place on baking sheet. Heat in oven about 10 minutes or until heated through.

2. Meanwhile, in large skillet cook beef and onion over medium heat until beef is browned and onion is tender. Drain off fat. Stir in corn and 1/3 cup of the barbecue sauce. Cook and stir until heated through.

3. To serve, spread one side of tortillas with the remaining barbecue sauce. Spoon about 1/2 cup beef mixture on each tortilla. Add shredded cabbage. Roll up.

MAKES 4 SERVINGS. (2 wraps each).

Per serving (2 wraps): 391 cal., 14 g total fat (4 g sat. fat), 54 mg chol., 535 mg sodium, 46 g carbo., 3 g fiber, 21 g pro.

Reuben Sandwiches

Prep: 10 minutes **Cook:** 8 minutes

- 3 tablespoons butter or margarine, softened
- 8 slices dark rye or pumpernickel bread
- 3 tablespoons bottled Thousand Island or Russian salad dressing
- 6 ounces thinly sliced cooked corned beef
- 4 slices Swiss cheese (3 ounces)
- 1 cup sauerkraut, well drained

1. Spread butter on 1 side of each bread slice and salad dressing on the other. With the buttered sides down, top 4 slices with meat, cheese, and sauerkraut. Top with remaining bread slices, dressing sides down.
2. Preheat a large skillet over medium heat. Reduce heat to medium-low. Cook 2 sandwiches at a time on medium-low heat for 4 to 6 minutes or until the bread is toasted and the cheese melts, turning once. Repeat with remaining sandwiches.
MAKES 4 SANDWICHES.

Per sandwich: 404 cal., 22 g total fat (10 g sat. fat), 64 mg chol., 2,508 mg sodium, 34 g carbo., 8 g fiber, 20 g pro.

Beef and Sweet Pepper Tortilla Wraps ♡

Start to Finish: 15 minutes

- 3 7- or 8-inch flour tortilla wraps
- 1/2 of a 8-ounce tub light cream cheese with chives and onion or roasted garlic
- 18 to 24 fresh basil leaves
- 1/2 of a 7-ounce jar roasted red sweet peppers, well-drained and cut into 1/4-inch strips
- 4 ounces thinly sliced cooked beef, ham, and/or turkey
- 1 tablespoon light mayonnaise or salad dressing

1. Spread each tortilla with one-third of the cream cheese. Cover each with basil leaves, leaving a 1-inch border. Arrange pepper strips on basil leaves. Top with sliced meat. Spread mayonnaise on meat.
2. Tightly roll up each tortilla into a spiral; cut each wrap in half crosswise. **MAKES 6 WRAPS.**

Per wrap: 135 cal., 6 g total fat (3 g sat. fat), 24 mg chol., 186 mg sodium, 10 g carbo., 1 g fiber, 8 g pro.

Beef and Cucumber Stacks

Start to Finish: 15 minutes

- 8 slices dark rye bread
- 1/4 cup mayonnaise or salad dressing
- 8 ounces thinly sliced deli roast beef
- 1 small cucumber, very thinly sliced
- 1/2 cup plain yogurt
- 1/4 cup sliced green onions (2)
- 1/2 teaspoon dried Italian seasoning
  Salt
  Black pepper

1. If desired, toast bread. Place a slice of rye bread on each of 4 plates; spread with mayonnaise. Top with beef and cucumber.
2. In a small bowl combine yogurt, green onions, and Italian seasoning; season to taste with salt and pepper. Spoon over cucumber. Top with remaining bread slices.
MAKES 4 SANDWICHES.

Per sandwich: 377 cal., 15 g total fat (4 g sat. fat), 33 mg chol., 1,286 mg sodium, 37 g carbo., 4 g fiber, 19 g pro.

Quick Tip Greek yogurt, which is thicker and more flavorful than regular plain yogurt, is increasingly available. If you can find it, try it in this recipe. It comes in both light and regular varieties.

A tasty sandwich makes a super-quick supper when you are especially pressed for time. All of these recipes are ready to eat in 15 minutes or less!

Beef and Cucumber Stacks

Thai Chicken-Broccoli Wraps

Thai Chicken-Broccoli Wraps ♡

Start to Finish: 25 minutes

- 12 ounces chicken breast strips for stir-fry
- 1/4 teaspoon garlic salt
- 1/8 teaspoon ground black pepper
  Nonstick cooking spray
- 2 cups packaged shredded broccoli
  (broccoli slaw mix)
- 1/4 teaspoon ground ginger
- 3 10-inch whole wheat flour tortillas (wrap in
  foil and warm in 350°F oven for 10 minutes)
- 1 recipe Peanut Sauce

1. Sprinkle chicken with garlic salt and pepper. Coat a large unheated nonstick skillet with cooking spray. Preheat skillet over medium-high heat. Add chicken; cook and stir for 2 to 3 minutes or until chicken is no longer pink. Remove chicken from skillet; keep warm. Add broccoli and ginger to skillet. Cook and stir for 2 to 3 minutes or until vegetables are crisp-tender.
2. Spread tortillas with Peanut Sauce. Top with chicken mixture. Roll up and cut in half. Serve immediately. **MAKES 6 SERVINGS (1/2 WRAP EACH).**

Peanut Sauce In a small saucepan combine 3 tablespoons creamy peanut butter; 2 tablespoons water; 1 tablespoon reduced-sodium soy sauce; 1 clove garlic, minced; and 1/4 teaspoon ground ginger. Heat over low heat until melted.

Per 1/2 wrap: 191 cal., 6 g total fat (1 g sat. fat), 33 mg chol., 460 mg sodium, 16 g carbo., 2 g fiber, 18 g pro.

Make-Your-Own Garden Tacos

Make-Your-Own Garden Tacos

Start to Finish: 15 minutes

- 1/2 cup mayonnaise or salad dressing
- 3 to 4 tablespoons purchased dried-tomato pesto
- 8 to 12 six-inch corn or 7- to 8-inch flour tortillas
- 2 6-ounce packages refrigerated grilled chicken breast strips
- 2 small yellow summer squash or zucchini (8 ounces), cut into matchstick-size strips
- 1 medium sweet pepper, cut into strips
  Cilantro sprigs (optional)

1. In a bowl stir together mayonnaise and pesto; divide among 4 small bowls. Place tortillas on a microwave-safe plate, cover with paper towels. Microwave on (high) for 30 to 45 seconds or until tortillas are warm.
2. Divide chicken, squash, sweet pepper, and warm tortillas among 4 shallow bowls. Place a bowl of pesto mixture with each bowl. If desired, garnish with cilantro.
MAKES 4 SERVINGS.

Per serving: 481 cal., 30 g total fat (6 g sat. fat), 66 mg chol., 1,021 mg sodium, 30 g carbo., 5 g fiber, 24 g pro.

Spicy Taco Tostadas

Chicken Panini ♡

Start to Finish: 20 minutes

¹⁄₃ cup fat-free mayonnaise or salad dressing
2 cloves garlic, minced
1 teaspoon dried Italian seasoning, crushed
8 ¹⁄₂-inch-thick slices hearty multigrain bread
8 ounces sliced or shredded cooked
   chicken breast
¹⁄₂ cup bottled roasted red sweet peppers,
   drained and cut into strips
1 cup lightly packed fresh basil
4 teaspoons olive oil

1. Preheat an electric sandwich press, a covered indoor grill, grill pan, or skillet. To assemble sandwiches, in a small bowl combine mayonnaise, garlic, and Italian seasoning. Spread 1 side of each bread slice with the mayonnaise mixture. Layer chicken, roasted sweet peppers, and basil leaves on half of the bread slices. Top with the remaining bread slices, spread sides down. Brush top and bottom of each sandwich lightly with oil.
2. Place sandwiches (half at a time, if necessary) in the sandwich press or indoor grill; cover and cook about 6 minutes or until bread is toasted. (If using a grill pan or skillet, place sandwiches on preheated grill pan or skillet. Weight sandwiches down and grill about 2 minutes or until bread is lightly toasted. Turn sandwiches over, weight down, and grill until the remaining side is lightly toasted.) **MAKES 4 SANDWICHES.**

Per sandwich: 312 cal., 9 g total fat (1 g sat. fat), 47 mg chol., 390 mg sodium, 35 g carbo., 9 g fiber, 25 g pro.

Quick Tip If you don't have leftover chicken breast, purchase a rotisserie chicken from the supermarket deli for the breast meat in these sandwiches. Use the thighs and drumsticks for another meal.

Spicy Taco Tostadas

Start to Finish: 15 minutes

1 18-ounce tub refrigerated taco sauce with
   shredded chicken
2 medium tomatoes, chopped
1 to 2 jalapeño peppers, seeded and
   chopped (see note, page 12)
5 tostada shells
3 cups packaged shredded lettuce
   Shredded Mexican cheese blend
   (optional)

1. In a large skillet combine taco sauce with shredded chicken, tomatoes, and jalapeño pepper(s). Cook over medium heat until heated through.
2. Place 4 tostada shells on a serving platter. Top with shredded lettuce. Spoon chicken mixture on the lettuce. Coarsely crush the remaining tostada shell; sprinkle over taco mixture. If desired, sprinkle with cheese. **MAKES 4 TOSTADAS.**

Per tostada: 236 cal., 8 g total fat (2 g sat. fat), 57 mg chol., 1,106 mg sodium, 25 g carbo., 5 g fiber, 15 g pro.

Turkey
Caesar
Sandwiches

Turkey Caesar Sandwiches

Prep: 10 minutes **Grill:** 12 minutes

2 8-ounce turkey tenderloins or 4 skinless, boneless chicken breast halves
1/2 cup bottled Caesar salad dressing
4 teaspoons olive oil
1 clove garlic, minced
4 thick pita bread rounds, split horizontally
   Lettuce leaves
2 medium tomatoes, sliced
1 medium avocado, peeled and sliced (optional)
   Shaved Parmesan cheese

1. Split each turkey tenderloin in half horizontally. Place turkey on the rack of an uncovered grill directly over medium coals. Grill for 12 to 15 minutes or until turkey is tender and no longer pink, turning once. Set aside half of the salad dressing; brush remaining salad dressing on the turkey during the last 5 minutes of grilling.

2. Meanwhile, in a small bowl stir together oil and garlic. Using a pastry brush, brush oil mixture over 1 side of each pita bread. Place pita bread, brushed sides down, on grill rack directly over medium heat. Grill for 2 to 3 minutes or until toasted.

3. To assemble, cut turkey tenderloins crosswise into 1/2-inch slices. Place lettuce leaves on broiled side of 4 pita bread halves. Top with tomato, turkey, and, if desired, avocado; drizzle with reserved salad dressing. Top with shaved Parmesan cheese. Top with remaining pita bread halves.

MAKES 4 SANDWICHES.

Per sandwich: 535 cal., 26 g total fat (5 g sat. fat), 74 mg chol., 823 mg sodium, 37 g carbo., 2 g fiber, 36 g pro.

Tall Turkey Sandwiches

Tall Turkey Sandwiches

Start to Finish: 15 minutes

1/4 cup fat-free plain yogurt
3 tablespoons horseradish mustard
8 slices multigrain bread, toasted
12 lettuce leaves
8 to 12 ounces deli-sliced cooked turkey breast
1 medium tomato, sliced
1 medium yellow sweet pepper, seeded sliced into rings
1 cup fresh pea pods

1. In a small bowl stir together yogurt and horseradish mustard. Spread yogurt mixture on 4 toasted bread slices.

2. Top the remaining bread slices with lettuce, turkey, tomato, sweet pepper, and pea pods. Top with remaining bread slices, spread sides down. **MAKES 4 SANDWICHES.**

Per sandwich: 235 cal., 3 g total fat (0 g sat. fat), 23 mg chol., 1,163 mg sodium, 34 g carbo., 6 g fiber, 22 g pro.

Salmon Salad Sandwiches

Catfish Po'Boys

Start to Finish: 20 minutes

  1 to 1¼ pounds fresh or frozen farm-raised
     catfish fillets
     Salt and black pepper
  ½ cup fine dry bread crumbs
  2 tablespoons olive oil
  2 medium red and/or yellow sweet peppers,
     cored and sliced in rings
  1 cup shredded Monterey Jack cheese with
     jalapeño peppers (4 ounces)
  1 cup deli coleslaw
  4 hoagie buns, split and, if desired, toasted
     Bottled hot pepper sauce (optional)
     Small hot peppers (optional)

1. Thaw fish, if frozen. Cut fish fillets into 3-inch pieces. Lightly sprinkle fish with salt and pepper. Coat fish with the bread crumbs.
2. In an extra-large skillet heat olive oil over medium-high heat. Add fish; cook for 6 to 8 minutes or until golden brown and fish begins to flake when tested with a fork, turning once halfway through cooking.
3. Layer fish, sweet peppers, cheese, and coleslaw in buns. If desired, pass hot pepper sauce and hot peppers. **MAKES 4 SANDWICHES.**

Per sandwich: 675 cal., 30 g total fat (10 g sat. fat), 86 mg chol., 1,004 mg sodium, 67 g carbo., 4 g fiber, 35 g pro.

Salmon Salad Sandwiches

Start to Finish: 20 minutes

  4 sandwich rolls
  ½ cup bottled ranch salad dressing
  2 6-ounce cans skinless, boneless salmon
  2 small tomatoes
  ½ of a medium cucumber
  1 cup coarsely shredded carrots (2) or
     shredded, peeled jicama (¼ of a jicama)

1. Split sandwich rolls. Lightly spread sliced rolls with some of the salad dressing. Drain salmon. Place salmon in a medium bowl and flake with a fork. Add remaining salad dressing to salmon; mix to combine.
2. Thinly slice tomatoes and cucumber. Layer tomato slices on rolls. Top with salmon mixture, cucumber slices, shredded carrots, and roll tops. **MAKES 4 SANDWICHES.**

Per sandwich: 575 cal., 25 g total fat (4 g sat. fat), 64 mg chol., 1,094 mg sodium, 57 g carbo., 4 g fiber, 32 g pro.

Shrimp-
Avocado
Hoagies

Shrimp-Avocado Hoagies

Start to Finish: 15 minutes

1 10- to 12-ounce package frozen peeled, cooked shrimp, thawed and coarsely chopped
2 large avocados, seeded, peeled, and chopped
1/2 cup shredded carrot (1 medium)
1/3 cup bottled coleslaw salad dressing
4 hoagie buns
Lemon wedges (optional)

1. In large bowl combine shrimp, avocados, carrot, and salad dressing.
2. Halve hoagie buns. Using a spoon, slightly hollow bottoms and tops of hoagie buns, leaving 1/2-inch shells. Reserve excess bread for another use. Toast buns.
3. Spoon shrimp mixture into buns. If desired, serve with lemon wedges.
MAKES 4 SANDWICHES.

Per sandwich: 560 cal., 24 g total fat (4 g sat. fat), 144 mg chol., 825 mg sodium, 63 g carbo., 8 g fiber, 25 g pro.

Nutty Hummus Open-Face Sandwiches

Start to Finish: 15 minutes

1 tablespoon olive oil
1/2 cup coarsely chopped walnuts
3/4 cup coarsely chopped bottled roasted red sweet peppers
1/2 of a 7- to 8-ounce container hummus
4 1/2-inch slices round country Italian bread, toasted
1 small cucumber (8 ounces), thinly sliced

1. In a large skillet heat olive oil over medium heat. Add walnuts; cook until toasted. Stir in roasted peppers. Cook and stir until heated through; set aside.
2. Spread hummus on toasted bread slices; arrange on serving plates. Top with cucumber slices and walnut mixture.
MAKES 4 SANDWICHES.

Per sandwich: 264 cal., 17 g total fat (2 g sat. fat), 0 mg chol., 343 mg sodium, 25 g carbo., 4 g fiber, 7 g pro.

Strawberry, Goat Cheese, and Arugula Toasts

Strawberry, Goat Cheese, and Arugula Toasts

Start to Finish: 20 minutes

1 8-ounce baguette, halved crosswise, then each halved lengthwise
1 tablespoon olive oil
1 4-ounce log goat cheese (chèvre)
1 1/2 cups sliced strawberries
1/2 cup arugula
Olive oil
Sea salt or coarse salt
Freshly ground black pepper
Snipped fresh oregano, thyme, rosemary, and/or basil

1. Preheat broiler. Place baguette quarters, cut sides up, on a large baking sheet. Brush with 1 tablespoon olive oil. Broil 3 to 4 inches from heat for 1 1/2 to 2 minutes or until bread is lightly toasted.
2. Slice goat cheese and divide evenly among bread quarters; top with sliced strawberries. Return to broiler; broil for 2 to 3 minutes or until cheese is softened and berries begin to juice out. Remove from broiler; top with arugula. Drizzle with additional olive oil; sprinkle with salt, pepper, and fresh herb.
MAKES 4 SANDWICHES.

Per sandwich: 346 cal., 16 g total fat (7 g sat. fat), 22 mg chol., 616 mg sodium, 37 g carbo., 2 g fiber, 13 g pro.

Fruit and Cheese Pitas

Grilled Formaggio Sandwiches

Start to Finish: 30 minutes

- 4 teaspoons butter or olive oil
- 4 wedges Italian flatbread (focaccia) (about 1 inch thick), split in half horizontally*
- 8 slices Scamorza or provolone cheese (about 8 ounces)
- 12 to 16 fresh spinach leaves, washed and patted dry**
- ¼ cup finely crumbled cooked bacon or turkey bacon

1. Spread 1 teaspoon of the butter on 1 side of each slice of bread. Place 2 slices cheese, 3 to 4 spinach leaves, and 1 tablespoon cooked bacon between the unbuttered sides of the bread.

2. Place 1 sandwich in a large skillet or on a griddle. Cook over medium-high heat for 3 to 4 minutes on each side or until the cheese is melted and the bread is golden brown. If necessary to prevent overbrowning, reduce heat to medium or brush on extra butter.

3. Repeat with remaining sandwiches. **MAKES 4 SANDWICHES.**

Per sandwich: 442 cal., 25 g total fat (14 g sat. fat), 55 mg chol., 657 mg sodium, 33 g carbo., 3 g fiber, 24 g pro.

*Note If using thin focaccia bread, use 2 unsplit wedges to make each sandwich.

**Note Purchase spinach with crisp, dark green leaves that have a fresh fragrance. Avoid leaves that are limp, damaged, or have yellow spots. To wash spinach, remove the stems and place the leaves in a large container of cold water. Swish the leaves using your hands, then let stand for a few minutes to allow any dirt and sand to sink to the bottom. Lift the leaves out of the water. If the spinach is very gritty, wash it a second time.

Fruit and Cheese Pitas ♡

Start to Finish: 20 minutes

- ½ cup low-fat cottage cheese
- ½ cup shredded reduced-fat cheddar cheese (2 ounces)
- 2 kiwifruit, peeled and chopped, or ½ cup small strawberries, hulled and chopped
- ¼ cup drained pineapple tidbits
- 1 large whole wheat or regular pita bread round, halved crosswise
- 4 Bibb lettuce leaves
- 2 tablespoons sliced almonds, pecan pieces, or walnut pieces; toasted, if desired (optional) (see note, page 160)

1. In a small bowl combine cottage cheese, cheddar cheese, kiwifruit, and pineapple. Stir gently to mix. Set aside.

2. Line pita bread halves with Bibb leaves. Spoon some of the fruit and cheese mixture into each half. If desired, sprinkle with almonds. Serve immediately. **MAKES 2 SERVINGS (½ SANDWICH EACH).**

Per ½ sandwich: 271 cal., 8 g total fat (4 g sat. fat), 22 mg chol., 642 mg sodium, 36 g carbo., 5 g fiber, 18 g pro.

Quick Tip These healthful pitas make a terrific lunch. To tote them, keep the bread, lettuce, filling, and almonds separate until it's time to eat to prevent the pita from getting soggy. Refrigerate only the lettuce and filling.

Grilled Formaggio Sandwiches

Eggplant
Panini

Eggplant Panini ♡

Start to Finish: 25 minutes

- 1 cup torn arugula
- 2 teaspoons red wine vinegar
- 1 teaspoon olive oil
- 1/3 cup seasoned fine dry bread crumbs
- 2 tablespoons grated pecorino Romano cheese or Parmesan cheese
- 1 egg
- 1 tablespoon milk
- 2 tablespoons all-purpose flour
- 1/2 teaspoon salt
- 1 medium eggplant, cut crosswise into 1/2-inch slices
- 1 tablespoon olive oil
- 3 ounces fresh mozzarella cheese, thinly sliced
- 6 individual focaccia rolls or one 12-inch plain or seasoned Italian flatbread (focaccia),* halved horizontally
- 1 large tomato, thinly sliced

1. In a small bowl toss together arugula, vinegar, and the 1 teaspoon oil; set aside. In a shallow dish stir together the bread crumbs and Romano cheese. In another shallow dish beat together the egg and milk. In a third shallow dish stir together the flour and salt. Dip the eggplant slices into flour mixture to coat. Dip the eggplant slices into egg mixture; coat both sides with bread crumb mixture.

2. In a 12-inch nonstick skillet heat the 1 tablespoon oil over medium heat. Add eggplant slices; cook for 6 to 8 minutes or until lightly browned, turning once. (Add more oil as necessary during cooking.) Top the eggplant with mozzarella cheese; reduce heat to low. Cook, covered, just until cheese begins to melt.

3. To serve, place the tomato slices on bottom halves of rolls. Top with eggplant slices, cheese sides up, and the arugula mixture. Add top halves of rolls. (Or place tomato slices on bottom half of bread. Top with eggplant slices, arugula mixture, tomato slices, and top half of bread. Cut into wedges.) **MAKES 4 SANDWICHES.**

Per sandwich: 271 cal., 10 g total fat (3 g sat. fat), 53 mg chol., 687 mg sodium, 37 g carbo., 3 g fiber, 12 g pro.

*Note For easy slicing, purchase focaccia that is at least 2 1/2 inches thick.

Bean and Cheese Quesadillas

Prep: 15 minutes **Bake:** 12 minutes
Oven: 400°F

- 1/2 of a 16-ounce can refried beans (3/4 cup)
- 1 8-ounce can whole kernel corn, drained
- 1/4 cup bottled salsa
- 1 canned chipotle chile pepper in adobo sauce, drained and chopped (optional) (see note, page 12)
- 8 8-inch flour tortillas
- 2 tablespoons vegetable oil
- 1 cup packaged shredded broccoli (broccoli slaw mix)
- 1 4- to 4 1/4-ounce can diced peaches, drained
- 1 cup finely shredded Mexican cheese blend (4 ounces)
  Purchased guacamole dip, sour cream, and/or bottled salsa

1. Preheat oven to 400°F. In a small bowl combine refried beans, corn, 1/4 cup salsa, and, if desired, chipotle chile pepper. Brush 1 side of each tortilla with some of the oil. Spread bean mixture over the plain side of 4 tortillas; set aside.

2. In another bowl combine broccoli slaw and peaches and spoon on top of bean mixture. Top with cheese. Top with remaining tortillas, oiled sides up; press down lightly. Place on a large baking sheet.

3. Bake for 12 to 15 minutes or until golden brown and cheese is melted. Cut into quarters. Serve with guacamole dip, sour cream, and/or additional salsa. **MAKES 4 SERVINGS.**

Per serving: 444 cal., 21 g total fat (7 g sat. fat), 25 mg chol., 825 mg sodium, 50 g carbo., 5 g fiber, 14 g pro.

Crisp-fried eggplant on chewy focaccia or creamy refried beans between toasty tortillas? Even meat-eaters will love these meatless sandwiches.

Meatless

Roasted Vegetable Couscous

Roasted Vegetable Couscous ♡

Prep: 20 minutes **Roast:** 45 minutes
Stand: 20 minutes **Oven:** 375°F

Nonstick cooking spray
1 Japanese eggplant or 1 small eggplant, halved lengthwise
1 small sweet onion (such as Walla Walla or Vidalia), halved
1 carrot, halved lengthwise, or 4 ounces packaged peeled baby carrots
1 yellow or red sweet pepper, halved lengthwise and seeded
1 or 2 yellow banana peppers, halved lengthwise and seeded (see tip, page 12)
1 cup water
3/4 cup quick-cooking couscous
1 recipe Balsamic-Mustard Dressing
Butterhead lettuce leaves (optional)

1. Preheat oven to 375°F. Lightly coat a shallow baking pan with cooking spray. Place all vegetables, cut sides down, in prepared baking pan. Roast for 45 to 60 minutes or until tender.
2. Wrap eggplant and peppers in foil; let stand for 20 minutes. Set remaining vegetables aside. Peel eggplant and peppers. Cut all vegetables into bite-size pieces.
3. In a medium saucepan bring the water to boiling. Stir in couscous. Remove from heat; let stand, covered, for 5 minutes.
4. In a large bowl combine vegetables, couscous, and Balsamic-Mustard Dressing. Toss gently to coat. If desired, line a shallow serving bowl with lettuce leaves. Spoon in couscous mixture. Serve chilled or at room temperature. **MAKES 6 SERVINGS.**

Balsamic-Mustard Dressing In a screw-top jar combine 1/4 cup white or regular balsamic vinegar, 1 tablespoon canola oil, 1 1/2 teaspoons Dijon mustard, 1/4 teaspoon black pepper, and 1/4 teaspoon garlic powder. Cover; shake well.

Per serving: 141 cal., 3 g total fat (0 g sat. fat), 0 mg chol., 105 mg sodium, 25 g carbo., 3 g fiber, 4 g pro.

Quick Tip If you like, use half a yellow sweet pepper and half a red sweet pepper.

Ramen Noodles with Vegetables

Start to Finish: 15 minutes

1 3-ounce package ramen noodles (any flavor)
1 tablespoon vegetable oil
6 ounces fresh asparagus, trimmed and cut into 1-inch pieces (1 cup)
1/2 cup shredded carrot (1 medium)
1/4 cup light teriyaki sauce

1. Cook noodles according to package directions (discard seasoning packet or save for another use). Drain noodles and keep warm.
2. Meanwhile, in a large skillet heat oil over medium-high heat. Add asparagus and carrot. Cook and stir for 3 to 5 minutes or until asparagus is crisp-tender. Stir in teriyaki sauce and noodles; toss to coat. **MAKES 2 TO 3 SERVINGS.**

Per serving: 291 cal., 14 g total fat (4 g sat. fat), 0 mg chol., 1,396 mg sodium, 36 g carbo., 3 g fiber, 7 g pro.

Quick Tip Purchase firm, bright green asparagus stalks with tight tips. Choose stalks that are all approximately the same size and thickness—they'll cook more evenly than varying sizes. Generally, the thinner the spear the more tender it will be.

Ramen
Noodles with
Vegetables

Udon Noodles
with Tofu

Farfalle with Spinach and Mushrooms

Udon Noodles with Tofu ♡

Start to Finish: 25 minutes

  8 ounces dried udon noodles or whole
       wheat linguine
  2 6- to 8-ounce packages smoked teriyaki-
       flavor or plain firm tofu (fresh bean curd),
       cut into ½-inch pieces
1½ cups chopped cucumber
  1 large carrot, cut into thin bite-size pieces
  ½ cup sliced green onions (4)
  1 recipe Ginger-Soy Vinaigrette

1. Cook pasta according to package
directions; drain. Cool pasta slightly.
2. Meanwhile, in a large bowl combine tofu,
cucumber, carrot, and green onions. Add
drained pasta; toss gently to mix.
3. Drizzle Ginger-Soy Vinaigrette onto
cooked pasta mixture. Toss salad gently to
coat. **MAKES 6 SERVINGS.**

Ginger-Soy Vinaigrette In a small bowl
whisk together 2 tablespoons rice vinegar or
cider vinegar; 1 tablespoon toasted sesame
oil; 2 teaspoons reduced-sodium soy sauce;
4 cloves garlic, minced; 1 teaspoon grated
fresh ginger; and ¼ teaspoon crushed red
pepper. **MAKES ¼ CUP.**

Per serving: 231 cal., 4 g total fat (0 g sat. fat), 0 mg
chol., 571 mg sodium, 39 g carbo., 3 g fiber, 7 g pro.

Make-Ahead Directions Prepare as
directed. Cover and chill for up to 6 hours.

Farfalle with Spinach and Mushrooms ♡

Start to Finish: 15 minutes

  6 ounces dried farfalle (bow tie) pasta
  1 tablespoon butter
  ½ cup chopped onion (1 medium)
  1 cup sliced portobello mushrooms or other
       fresh mushrooms
  2 cloves garlic, minced
  4 cups thinly sliced fresh spinach or
       2 cups thinly sliced sorrel and 2 cups
       thinly sliced fresh spinach
  1 teaspoon snipped fresh thyme
  ⅛ teaspoon black pepper
  1 tablespoon licorice-flavor liqueur (optional)
  2 tablespoons shredded Parmesan cheese

1. Cook pasta according to package
directions; drain.
2. Meanwhile, in a large skillet melt butter
over medium heat. Add onion, mushrooms,
and garlic; cook and stir for 2 to 3 minutes or
until mushrooms are nearly tender. Stir in
spinach, thyme, and pepper; cook 1 minute
or until heated through and spinach is slightly
wilted. Stir in cooked pasta and, if desired,
liqueur. Toss gently to mix. Sprinkle with
cheese. **MAKES 4 SERVINGS.**

Per serving: 214 cal., 6 g total fat (1 g sat. fat), 39 mg
chol., 127 mg sodium, 33 g carbo., 2 g fiber, 9 g pro.

Bow Tie Pasta with Fresh Mozzarella

Start to Finish: 30 minutes

- 1 16-ounce package dried bow tie pasta
- 3 tablespoons olive oil
- 4 large plum tomatoes, seeded and chopped, or 2 cups cherry tomatoes, halved
- 1 15-ounce can cannellini beans (white kidney beans), rinsed and drained
- 8 ounces fresh mozzarella cheese, cubed
- 1/4 cup finely shredded Parmesan cheese
- 1/4 cup snipped fresh basil or 1 teaspoon dried basil, crushed
- 2 cloves garlic, minced
- 1/4 teaspoon salt

1. In a 5- to 6-quart Dutch oven cook pasta according to package directions; drain and return to pan. Add olive oil and toss with pasta to coat. Add tomatoes, cannellini beans, mozzarella and Parmesan cheeses, basil, garlic, and salt; toss gently to coat. **MAKES 6 SERVINGS.**

Per serving: 513 cal., 17 g total fat (7 g sat. fat), 29 mg chol., 385 mg sodium, 69 g carbo., 6 g fiber, 24 g pro.

Quick Tip If you can find the tiny fresh mozzarella balls (bocconcini in Italian), they're a perfect fit for this dish. There's no cubing needed if they're smaller than 1 inch. If they're slightly larger than that, just cut them in half.

Fusilli with Garlic Pesto and Aged Pecorino

Start to Finish: 35 minutes

- 15 cloves garlic, peeled
- 1/2 cup packed fresh basil leaves
- 1 pound dried fusilli, gemelli, or tagliatelle pasta
- 1/2 cup olive oil
- 1/3 cup pine nuts, toasted (see note, page 160)
- 2 tablespoons finely shredded Pecorino Romano cheese
- 3/4 teaspoon sea salt
- 1/8 teaspoon freshly ground black pepper
- 1 cup small fresh basil leaves
- 1/4 cup finely shredded Pecorino Romano cheese (1 ounce)

1. In a 5- to 6-quart Dutch oven cook garlic cloves in a large amount of boiling salted water for 8 minutes. Using a slotted spoon, transfer garlic to a blender. Add 1/3 cup basil leaves to the boiling water and cook for 5 seconds; remove with slotted spoon and drain well on paper towels. (Do not drain boiling water.) Add basil to blender.

2. Add pasta to the boiling water and cook according to package directions. Before draining pasta, remove 1/2 cup of the hot cooking water and set aside. Drain pasta; return to Dutch oven.

3. Meanwhile, for pesto, add oil, 2 tablespoons of the pine nuts, 2 tablespoons cheese, salt, and pepper to blender. Cover and blend until nearly smooth (pesto will be thin).

4. Add pesto to cooked pasta; toss gently to coat. If necessary, toss in enough of the reserved cooking water to help coat the pasta evenly with pesto. Transfer pasta mixture to a serving bowl. Sprinkle with 1 cup basil leaves, 1/4 cup cheese, and remaining pine nuts. Serve immediately. **MAKES 4 SERVINGS.**

Per serving: 524 cal., 26 g total fat (4 g sat. fat), 5 mg chol., 264 mg sodium, 61 g carbo., 3 g fiber, 13 g pro.

Quick Tip Fresh basil leaves will darken if left on top of the hot pasta very long. To avoid this, serve the pasta right after adding the basil.

Who doesn't love a big bowl of noodles? Toss pasta with vegetables, beans, cheese, and herbs, and you have got a simple meal with universal appeal.

Fusilli with Garlic Pesto and Aged Pecorino

Pasta with Zucchini and Walnuts

Start to Finish: 18 minutes

- 1 9-ounce package refrigerated whole wheat or plain cheese ravioli
- 2 tablespoons olive oil
- 1/2 cup walnuts, coarsely chopped
- 2 medium zucchini, halved lengthwise and sliced
- 6 green onions, diagonally sliced in 1/4-inch pieces
- 1/3 cup milk
- 1 cup finely shredded Parmesan cheese (4 ounces) or grated Parmesan cheese
  Salt and black pepper

1. In a large saucepan cook ravioli in 4 cups boiling lightly salted water for 6 to 8 minutes or until tender; drain.

2. Meanwhile, in a large skillet heat oil over medium heat. Add walnuts; cook for 2 to 3 minutes or until toasted. Using a slotted spoon, remove walnuts from skillet. Add zucchini and green onions; cook and stir for 2 to 3 minutes or until crisp-tender.

3. Add drained ravioli, walnuts, milk, and 3/4 cup of the cheese to skillet; cook and toss for 1 minute. Season to taste with salt and pepper. Transfer to a serving bowl; sprinkle with the remaining 1/4 cup cheese.

MAKES 4 SERVINGS.

Per serving: 466 cal., 29 g total fat (9 g sat. fat), 59 mg chol., 859 mg sodium, 33 g carbo., 6 g fiber, 21 g pro.

Linguini with Tomato Sauce and Basil Garlic Toast ♡

Start to Finish: 20 minutes

- 10 ounces dried linguini
- 3 tablespoons olive oil
- 6 cloves garlic, minced
- 2 English muffins, split
- 2/3 cup fresh basil, chopped
- 2 cups grape tomatoes, halved, or 4 plum tomatoes, chopped
- 1/2 cup chicken broth or pasta water

Linguini with Tomato Sauce and Basil Garlic Toast

- 1 teaspoon sugar
  Salt and black pepper
- 1/2 cup halved, pitted kalamata olives (optional)
  Grated Parmesan cheese (optional)
  Fresh basil (optional)

1. Preheat broiler. Cook pasta following package directions.

2. Meanwhile, in a small bowl combine 1 tablespoon of the oil and 2 cloves of the garlic; brush on cut sides of English muffins. Place on baking sheet. Broil 3 to 4 inches from heat for 2 to 3 minutes or until edges begin to brown and tops are golden. Sprinkle with 1 tablespoon of the basil; set aside.

3. Meanwhile, in a large saucepan heat remaining 2 tablespoons oil over medium-high heat; add remaining 4 cloves garlic, the remaining basil, and the tomatoes. Cook about 2 minutes or until garlic is tender. Add chicken broth and sugar. Cook for 3 to 4 minutes or until tomatoes have softened. Season with salt and pepper. Add drained pasta and, if desired, olives; heat through.

4. Serve pasta with toasted muffins. If desired, sprinkle Parmesan cheese and additional basil. **MAKES 4 SERVINGS.**

Per serving: 450 cal., 12 g total fat (2 g sat. fat), 0 mg chol., 403 mg sodium, 72 g carbo., 3 g fiber, 12 g pro.

Peach and Edamame Soba Salad

Start to Finish: 30 minutes

- 6 ounces dried soba (buckwheat noodles) or multigrain spaghetti
- 2 cups frozen shelled sweet soybeans (edamame), thawed, or one 15-ounce can black beans, rinsed and drained
- 3 medium peaches or nectarines, halved, pitted, and coarsely chopped
- 1 large red sweet pepper, seeded and cut into bite-size strips
- 1/4 cup sliced green onions (2)
- 1/4 cup rice vinegar
- 2 tablespoons reduced-sodium soy sauce
- 1 tablespoon toasted sesame oil
- 2 teaspoons grated fresh ginger
- 1/4 cup sliced almonds, toasted (see note, page 160)

1. In a large saucepan cook soba according to package directions. Drain and rinse with cold water; drain well. In a large bowl toss together soba, edamame, peaches, sweet pepper, and green onions.

2. In a small screw-top jar combine vinegar, soy sauce, sesame oil, and ginger; cover and shake well. Pour over soba mixture. Toss to coat. Sprinkle each serving with almonds. **MAKES 4 SERVINGS.**

Per serving: 368 cal., 11 g total fat (1 g sat. fat), 0 mg chol., 632 mg sodium, 55 g carbo., 9 g fiber, 18 g pro.

Quick Tip Sesame oil is sold two ways. The light-color oil, made from untoasted seeds, has a light, nutty flavor and is used primarily in salad dressings and for sautéeing. Darker Asian-style sesame oil, made from toasted seeds, has more intense flavor. Use it in salad dressings and to add flavor to stir-fries. A little goes a long way!

Pasta with Swiss Chard ♡

Start to Finish: 35 minutes

- 8 ounces dried whole grain bow tie or mostaccioli pasta
- 12 ounces fresh Swiss chard or spinach
- 1 tablespoon olive oil
- 4 cloves garlic, minced
- 2/3 cup light ricotta cheese
- 1/4 cup fat-free milk
- 1/4 cup snipped fresh basil or 1 teaspoon dried basil, crushed
- 1/4 teaspoon salt
- 1/4 teaspoon black pepper
- 1/8 teaspoon ground nutmeg
- 2 medium tomatoes, seeded and chopped
- 1/4 cup shredded Parmesan cheese

1. Cook pasta according to package directions, except omit any oil or salt. Drain well. Return pasta to hot saucepan. Cover and keep warm.

2. Meanwhile, cut out and discard center ribs from Swiss chard or remove stems from spinach. Coarsely chop greens; set aside. In a large nonstick skillet heat oil over medium heat. Add garlic; cook for 15 seconds. Add Swiss chard or spinach. Cook over medium-low heat about 3 minutes or until greens are wilted and tender, stirring frequently. Stir in ricotta cheese, milk, basil, salt, pepper, and nutmeg. Cook and stir for 3 to 5 minutes more or until heated through.

3. Add the ricotta mixture and tomatoes to cooked pasta; toss gently to combine. Sprinkle servings with Parmesan cheese. **MAKES 4 SERVINGS.**

Per serving: 307 cal., 8 g total fat (2 g sat. fat), 14 mg chol., 435 mg sodium, 51 g carbo., 8 g fiber, 14 g pro.

Eating whole grain pasta is a great way to work more fiber into your diet. The toothsome texture and nutty taste is a delicious bonus.

Penne with
Fennel

Penne with Fennel ♡

Start to Finish: 30 minutes

  6 ounces dried penne or mostaccioli
  2 medium fennel bulbs
  1 tablespoon olive oil or vegetable oil
  1 tablespoon butter or margarine
  3 cloves garlic, minced
  ¼ teaspoon crushed red pepper
  1 cup red and/or green sweet pepper cut
     into thin bite-size strips
  1 15-ounce can Great Northern beans,
     rinsed and drained
  ¼ teaspoon dried thyme, crushed
     Black pepper
  ¼ cup shaved or shredded Parmesan
     cheese

1. Cook penne following package directions. Drain penne. Return to pan. Cover; keep warm.

2. Cut off and discard upper stalks from fennel bulbs. If desired, reserve some of the feathery leaves for garnish. Cut fennel bulbs lengthwise in quarters. Remove and discard cores. Cut fennel in thin strips.

3. In a large skillet heat oil and butter over medium-high heat. Add garlic; cook for 30 seconds. Add fennel and crushed red pepper; cook and stir for 5 minutes. Add sweet pepper strips; cook for 3 minutes. Add beans and thyme; cook about 2 minutes or until heated through.

4. To serve, add fennel mixture to hot cooked pasta; toss gently. Season with black pepper. Sprinkle with Parmesan cheese. If desired, garnish with reserved fennel leaves.

MAKES 4 SERVINGS.

Per serving: 349 cal., 9 g total fat (2 g sat. fat), 5 mg chol., 309 mg sodium, 53 g carbo., 4 g fiber, 15 g pro.

Pasta with Three Cheeses

Pasta with Three Cheeses

Start to Finish: 30 minutes

10 ounces dried medium shell macaroni or
    rotini
  2 cups frozen cauliflower, broccoli, and
    carrots or other vegetable combination
  1 cup milk
  1 3-ounce package cream cheese, cut up
  ¼ teaspoon black pepper
  ¾ cup shredded Gouda, Edam, Havarti,
    fontina, cheddar, or Swiss cheese
    (3 ounces)
  ¼ cup grated Parmesan cheese
    Grated Parmesan cheese (optional)

1. In a large saucepan cook pasta following package directions, adding the frozen vegetables the last 5 minutes of cooking. Drain.

2. In the hot saucepan combine milk, cream cheese, and pepper. Cook and stir over low heat until cheese is melted.

3. Return pasta mixture to saucepan. Toss to coat with cream cheese mixture. Gently stir in the shredded cheese and the ¼ cup Parmesan cheese. If desired, sprinkle with additional Parmesan cheese.

MAKES 4 SERVINGS.

Per serving: 598 cal., 25 g total fat (14 g sat. fat), 86 mg chol., 596 mg sodium, 66 g carbo., 3 g fiber, 28 g pro.

Pasta
Rosa-Verde

Smoky Mushroom Stroganoff

Start to Finish: 20 minutes

- 1 8.8-ounce package dried pappardelle (wide egg noodles)
- 1 tablespoon olive oil
- 1½ pounds sliced mushrooms, such as button, cremini, and/or shiitake
- 2 cloves garlic, minced
- 1 8-ounce carton light sour cream
- 2 tablespoons all-purpose flour
- 1½ teaspoons smoked paprika
- ¼ teaspoon black pepper
- 1 cup vegetable broth
   Snipped fresh parsley (optional)

1. Cook pasta according to package directions; drain. Cover and keep warm.
2. In an extra-large skillet heat olive oil over medium-high heat. Add mushrooms and garlic; cook for 5 to 8 minutes or until mushrooms are tender, stirring occasionally. Remove mushrooms with a slotted spoon; cover to keep warm.
3. For sauce, in a small bowl combine sour cream, flour, paprika, and pepper. Stir in broth until smooth. Add to skillet. Cook and stir until thickened and bubbly. Cook and stir for 1 minute more. Serve mushroom mixture and sauce over noodles. If desired, sprinkle with parsley. **MAKES 4 SERVINGS.**

Per serving: 407 cal., 13 g total fat (5 g sat. fat), 72 mg chol., 443 mg sodium, 59 g carbo., 4 g fiber, 17 g pro.

Quick Tip To get the best flavor from pasta, cook it only to al dente, or firm and somewhat chewy. In Italian, al dente means "to the tooth" and describes the doneness of pasta and other foods, such as vegetables. For the best results, follow cooking directions on the package of dried or fresh pasta carefully.

Pasta Rosa-Verde

Start to Finish: 30 minutes

- 8 ounces dried penne or ziti pasta
- 1 tablespoon olive oil
- 1 medium onion, thinly sliced
- 2 cloves garlic, minced
- 4 to 6 medium tomatoes, seeded and coarsely chopped (3 cups)
- 1 teaspoon salt
- ½ teaspoon black pepper
- ¼ teaspoon crushed red pepper (optional)
- 3 cups arugula, watercress, and/or spinach, coarsely chopped
- ¼ cup pine nuts or slivered almonds, toasted
- 2 tablespoons crumbled Gorgonzola or other blue cheese

1. Cook pasta according to package directions; drain. Cover and keep warm.
2. Meanwhile, in a large skillet heat oil over medium heat. Add onion and garlic; cook until onion is tender. Add tomatoes, salt, black pepper, and, if desired, crushed red pepper. Cook and stir over medium-high heat about 2 minutes or until the tomatoes are warm and release some of their juices. Stir in arugula, watercress, and/or spinach and heat just until greens are wilted.
3. To serve, divide pasta among serving bowls. Top with tomato mixture. Sprinkle with pine nuts and cheese. **MAKES 4 SERVINGS.**

Per serving: 352 cal., 11 g total fat (2 g sat. fat), 3 mg chol., 610 mg sodium, 54 g carbo., 2 g fiber, 12 g pro.

Couscous-
Stuffed
Peppers

Couscous-Stuffed Peppers ♡

Prep: 15 minutes **Bake:** 25 minutes
Oven: 350°F

- 1 6-ounce package toasted pine nut couscous mix
- ½ cup shredded carrot (1 medium)
- 2 large or 4 small red, yellow, green, or orange sweet peppers
- ½ cup shredded Italian cheese blend (2 ounces)
- 1½ cups mushroom and olive or tomato basil pasta sauce

1. Preheat oven to 350°F. Prepare couscous mix according to package directions, omitting oil and adding the shredded carrot with the couscous.
2. Meanwhile, cut large peppers in half lengthwise (for small peppers, cut off tops and reserve). Remove seeds and membranes from peppers. Cook peppers (and tops, if using) in boiling water for 5 minutes. Drain on paper towels. Place peppers, cut sides up, in a 2-quart rectangular baking dish. Spoon cooked couscous mixture into peppers.
3. Bake, covered, for 20 to 25 minutes or until filling is heated through and peppers are tender. Sprinkle cheese over peppers. Bake, uncovered, about 5 minutes more or until cheese is melted.
4. Meanwhile, in a small saucepan heat the pasta sauce. Serve peppers with sauce. (For small peppers, place pepper tops on couscous filling.) **MAKES 4 SERVINGS.**

Per serving: 259 cal., 6 g total fat (3 g sat. fat), 10 mg chol., 801 mg sodium, 42 g carbo., 7 g fiber, 11 g pro.

Fontina-Topped Angel Hair and Vegetables ♡

Start to Finish: 25 minutes

- 1 tablespoon olive oil
- 1 pound fresh asparagus spears, trimmed and cut into 1-inch pieces (3 cups)
- 1½ cups assorted sliced fresh mushrooms, such as button, shiitake, or oyster
- 1 small red onion, thinly sliced
- 2 cloves garlic, minced
- ¼ cup dry white wine or chicken broth
- 8 ounces dried angel hair pasta, broken in half
- 2 medium tomatoes, coarsely chopped (2 cups)
- 1 tablespoon snipped fresh oregano
- ½ cup shredded fontina cheese (2 ounces)
  Coarsely ground black pepper

1. In a large skillet heat oil over medium heat. Add asparagus, mushrooms, onion, and garlic; cook for 3 to 4 minutes or until tender. Carefully stir in wine. Bring to boiling; reduce heat. Simmer, uncovered, about 3 minutes or until liquid is almost evaporated.
2. Meanwhile, cook pasta according to package directions; drain. Add drained pasta to asparagus mixture in skillet. Stir in tomatoes and oregano, tossing to coat.
3. Transfer pasta and asparagus mixture to a serving platter. Top with fontina and sprinkle with black pepper. Serve immediately.
MAKES 4 SERVINGS.

Per serving: 242 cal., 6 g total fat (2 g sat. fat), 11 mg chol., 83 mg sodium, 36 g carbo., 2 g fiber, 10 g pro.

Cheesy Tortellini and Vegetables

Start to Finish: 20 minutes

- 1 6-ounce package dried cheese-filled tortellini
- 1 16-ounce package frozen broccoli, cauliflower, and carrots
- 1¼ cups milk
- ½ of a 1.8-ounce envelope white sauce mix (about 3 tablespoons)
- 6 ounces Havarti cheese with dill, cubed

1. Cook tortellini according to package directions, adding the frozen vegetables for the last 5 minutes of cooking. Drain well. Return tortellini mixture to hot pan; cover to keep warm.
2. Meanwhile, for the sauce, in a small saucepan whisk together milk and white sauce mix. Bring to boiling; reduce heat. Cook and stir for 1 minute. Remove from heat. Add cheese, stirring until melted. Pour sauce over tortellini mixture. Toss lightly.
MAKES 4 SERVINGS.

Per serving: 453 cal., 24 g total fat (1 g sat. fat), 59 mg chol., 1,004 mg sodium, 38 g carbo., 4 g fiber, 22 g pro.

Prep your pantry

Keeping your pantry and freezer full of long-keeping staples is a smart strategy for whipping up quick, delicious dinners with minimal planning and shopping time. Items such as dried pasta, canned chicken broth, jarred pasta sauce, dried white sauce mix, flavored and plain couscous mixes, and frozen vegetables stand at the ready. Add a few fresh vegetables, herbs, cheeses, and/or meat and you have one-dish meals in no time.

Vegetable
Medley
au Gratin

Vegetable Medley au Gratin

Prep: 20 minutes **Bake:** 65 minutes
Oven: 300°F/375°F

- 1 10.75-ounce can condensed cream of chicken and mushroom soup
- ¹/₂ cup sour cream
- ¹/₂ teaspoon dried dill, crushed
- 2 16-ounce packages frozen broccoli, cauliflower, and carrots, thawed
- ²/₃ cup crushed stone-ground wheat crackers (about 15 crackers)
- ¹/₃ cup finely chopped walnuts
- ¹/₄ cup shredded Parmesan cheese
- 2 tablespoons butter, melted

1. Preheat oven to 300°F. In a large bowl combine soup, sour cream, and dill; stir in thawed vegetables. Transfer mixture to an ungreased 2-quart rectangular baking dish.
2. In a small bowl combine crackers, walnuts, cheese, and melted butter. Cover and chill until needed.
3. Bake, covered, for 50 minutes. Increase oven temperature to 375°F. Sprinkle crumb mixture over vegetable mixture. Bake, uncovered, about 15 minutes more or until topping is golden brown. **MAKES 5 SERVINGS.**

Per serving: 314 cal., 20 g total fat (8 g sat. fat), 32 mg chol., 904 mg sodium, 22 g carbo., 6 g fiber, 10 g pro.

Broccoli Rabe and Penne ♡

Start to Finish: 25 minutes

- 1 pound broccoli rabe
- 8 ounces dried multigrain penne pasta
- 2 tablespoons extra virgin olive oil
- 6 cloves garlic, minced (1 tablespoon)
- ¹/₄ to ¹/₂ teaspoon crushed red pepper
- ¹/₄ cup grated Parmesan cheese
- 1 tablespoon lemon juice
  Salt and black pepper
- ¹/₃ cup shredded Parmesan cheese

1. Trim tough stems from broccoli rabe; discard stems. Coarsely chop the broccoli rabe leaves. In a Dutch oven cook broccoli rabe in a large amount of boiling salted water for 5 to 7 minutes or until tender. Drain; submerse broccoli rabe into a large bowl of ice water to cool quickly. When cool, drain well.
2. Meanwhile, cook pasta according to package directions. Drain pasta, reserving ³/₄ cup of the cooking water.
3. In a large skillet heat olive oil over medium heat. Add garlic and red pepper; cook for 1 minute. Add broccoli rabe; toss to coat with oil. Add the drained pasta, reserved pasta cooking water, grated Parmesan cheese, and lemon juice. Cook and stir until heated through. Season to taste with salt and black pepper. Sprinkle each serving with shredded Parmesan cheese. **MAKES 6 SERVINGS.**

Per serving: 238 cal., 7 g total fat (2 g sat. fat), 6 mg chol., 263 mg sodium, 30 g carbo., 5 g fiber, 12 g pro.

Broccoli Rabe and Penne

Black Bean
Cakes
with Salsa

Black Bean Cakes with Salsa

Start to Finish: 25 minutes

1½ cups prepared salsa
  1 jalapeño (see note, page 12)
  2 15-ounce cans black beans, rinsed and drained
  1 8.5-ounce package corn muffin mix
  3 teaspoons chili powder
  2 tablespoons olive oil
  ½ cup sour cream
  ½ teaspoon chili powder

1. In a colander drain ½ cup of the salsa. Seed and finely chop half the jalapeño; thinly slice remaining half. In a large bowl mash beans with vegetable masher or fork. Stir in muffin mix, drained salsa, 2½ teaspoons of the chili powder, and the chopped jalapeño.
2. In an extra-large skillet heat 1 tablespoon of the olive oil over medium-high heat. Add four ½-cup mounds bean mixture to skillet. Flatten mounds with spatula to 3½-inch-round cakes. Cook about 3 minutes on each side or until browned. Remove bean cakes from skillet. Repeat with remaining olive oil and bean mixture.
3. In a small bowl combine sour cream and ½ teaspoon chili powder. Top cakes with remaining salsa, sliced jalapeño, and seasoned sour cream. **MAKES 4 SERVINGS (2 CAKES PER SERVING).**

Per serving: 519 cal., 19 g total fat (4 g sat. fat), 11 mg chol., 1,553 mg sodium, 79 g carbo., 12 g fiber, 20 g pro.

Lentil and Veggie Tostadas

Lentil and Veggie Tostadas ♡

Start to Finish: 25 minutes

1¾ cups water
  ¾ cup dry red lentils, rinsed and drained
  ¼ cup chopped onion
  1 to 2 tablespoons snipped fresh cilantro
  1 clove garlic, minced
  ½ teaspoon salt
  ½ teaspoon ground cumin
  4 tostada shells
  2 cups chopped assorted fresh vegetables (such as broccoli, tomato, zucchini, and/or yellow summer squash)
  ¾ cup shredded Monterey Jack cheese (3 ounces)

1. In a medium saucepan stir together the water, lentils, onion, cilantro, garlic, salt, and cumin. Bring to boiling; reduce heat. Simmer, covered, for 12 to 15 minutes or until lentils are tender and most of the liquid is absorbed. Use a fork to mash the cooked lentils.
2. Preheat broiler. Place tostada shells on a large baking sheet. Spread the lentil mixture on tostada shells; top with vegetables and cheese. Broil 3 to 4 inches from the heat about 2 minutes or until cheese is melted. Serve the tostadas immediately.
MAKES 4 TOSTADAS.

Per tostada: 288 cal., 11 g total fat (5 g sat. fat), 20 mg chol., 497 mg sodium, 34 g carbo., 7 g fiber, 16 g pro.

Red Lentil Rice

Red Lentil Rice ♡

Start to Finish: 35 minutes

 1 tablespoon olive oil
 1/2 cup chopped onion (1 medium)
 2 cloves garlic, minced
 1 teaspoon cumin seeds, crushed
 1/2 teaspoon salt
 1/8 teaspoon cayenne pepper
 1 1/3 cups basmati rice or long grain rice
 2 14.5-ounce cans vegetable broth or chicken broth
 1/2 cup water
 1 cup frozen peas
 1/2 cup dry red lentils, rinsed
 1/4 cup snipped fresh mint
 1 teaspoon garam masala
 1 recipe Yogurt Raita

1. In a 4-quart Dutch oven heat olive oil over medium heat. Add onion, garlic, cumin seeds, salt, and cayenne pepper. Cook and stir for 2 minutes. Add rice; cook and stir for 1 minute more. Remove from heat. Carefully add broth and the water. Bring to boiling; reduce heat. Simmer, covered, for 10 minutes.
2. Stir in peas and lentils. Return to boiling; reduce heat. Simmer, covered, for 8 to 10 minutes or just until lentils are tender. Remove from heat; stir in mint and garam masala. Let stand, covered, for 5 minutes before serving. Serve with Yogurt Raita.

Yogurt Raita In a medium bowl combine one 6-ounce carton plain yogurt; 3/4 cup seeded, chopped cucumber; 1 medium tomato, seeded and chopped; 1 tablespoon snipped fresh mint; 1/8 teaspoon salt; and a dash of black pepper. **MAKES 6 SERVINGS.**

Per serving: 274 cal., 3 g total fat (1 g sat. fat), 3 mg chol., 827 mg sodium, 50 g carbo., 4 g fiber, 10 g pro.

Quick Rice and Black Beans

Start to Finish: 25 minutes

 1 1/4 cups uncooked instant brown rice
 1 14.5-ounce can reduced-sodium chicken broth
 1 15-ounce can black beans, rinsed and drained
 1 1/2 cups frozen whole kernel corn
 1 cup salsa
 2 tablespoons snipped fresh cilantro
 1 cup shredded Monterey Jack or cheddar cheese (4 ounces)
   Thinly sliced jalapeños (optional) (see note, page 12)

1. In a large saucepan combine rice, chicken broth, beans, corn, and salsa. Bring to boiling; reduce heat. Simmer, covered, for 10 minutes.
2. Remove from heat. Stir in cilantro and half of the cheese. Let stand, covered, for 5 minutes.
3. Top with remaining cheese and, if desired, jalapeño slices. **MAKES 4 SERVINGS.**

Per serving: 411 cal., 12 g total fat (6 g sat. fat), 25 mg chol., 1,188 mg sodium, 62 g carbo., 10 g fiber, 22 g pro.

Quick Rice
and
Black Beans

Spicy Vegetable Fried Rice

Open-Face Veggie Burgers

Start to Finish: 20 minutes

- 2 tablespoons olive oil
- 1 large sweet onion, halved and thinly sliced (about 3 cups)
- 1 10-ounce package refrigerated or frozen meatless burger patties
- 2 tablespoons mayonnaise or salad dressing
- 1 teaspoon yellow mustard
- 4 ½-inch-thick slices ciabatta, toasted
- 1 cup fresh baby spinach
- 2 tablespoons steak sauce

1. In a large skillet heat olive oil on medium-high heat. Add onion; cook for 8 to 10 minutes or until very tender, stirring frequently.

2. Meanwhile, prepare patties according to package microwave directions.

3. In a small bowl combine mayonnaise and mustard; spread on 1 side of each bread slice. Top with spinach and a patty. Stir steak sauce into cooked onion. Spoon onion mixture over patties. **MAKES 4 BURGERS.**

Per burger: 329 cal., 20 g total fat (3 g sat. fat), 3 mg chol.,688 mg sodium, 21 g carbo., 5 g fiber, 18 g pro.

Quick Tip Types of sweet onions include Vidalia, Maui, and Walla Walla—any of them work beautifully in this recipe. As sweet onions cook, their sugars condense and caramelize, and they get even sweeter!

Spicy Vegetable Fried Rice ♡

Start to Finish: 30 minutes

- 4 eggs
- 2 tablespoons water
  Nonstick cooking spray
- 1 tablespoon olive oil
- 1 tablespoon finely chopped, peeled fresh ginger
- 2 cloves garlic, minced
- 2 cups chopped Chinese cabbage
- 1 cup coarsely shredded carrot
- 1 cup fresh pea pods, trimmed
- 2 cups cooked brown rice
- ⅓ cup sliced green onions
- 2 tablespoons reduced-sodium soy sauce
- 1 to 2 teaspoons Sriracha chile sauce
- 2 tablespoons snipped fresh cilantro
  Lime slices or wedges

1. In a small bowl whisk together eggs and the water. Coat an unheated very large nonstick skillet with cooking spray. Preheat skillet on medium heat. Pour in egg mixture. Cook, without stirring, until mixture begins to set on the bottom and around edges. With a spatula or large spoon, lift and fold the partially cooked eggs so the uncooked portion flows underneath. Continue cooking for 2 to 3 minutes or until egg mixture is cooked through but is still glossy and moist, keeping eggs in large pieces. Carefully transfer eggs to a medium bowl; set aside.

2. In the same skillet heat oil over medium-high heat. Add ginger and garlic; cook for 30 seconds. Add cabbage, carrot, and pea pods; cook and stir for 2 minutes. Stir in cooked eggs, brown rice, green onions, soy sauce, and chile sauce; cook and stir about 2 minutes or until heated through. Top with cilantro. Serve with lime slices.

MAKES 4 SERVINGS.

Per serving: 250 cal., 9 g total fat (2 g sat. fat), 212 mg chol., 367 mg sodium, 31 g carbo., 4 g fiber, 11 g pro.

Pumpkin-Bean
Soup

package directions; stir rice mixture into skillet. Stir in beans.

2. In a large bowl combine eggs, milk, salt, and pepper; pour into skillet. Continue to cook over medium heat. As mixture sets, run a spatula around the edge of the eggs, lifting egg mixture so uncooked portion flows underneath. Cook just until egg mixture is set. Sprinkle with cheese. **MAKES 4 SERVINGS.**

Per serving: 510 cal., 26 g total fat (9 g sat. fat), 343 mg chol., 1,127 mg sodium, 43 g carbo., 7 g fiber, 26 g pro.

Bean and Potato Chowder

Start to Finish: 20 minutes

- 1 20-ounce package refrigerated diced potatoes with onions
- 1 14.5-ounce can vegetable broth
- 1 cup shredded Swiss cheese (4 ounces)
- 1/3 cup all-purpose flour
- 3 cups milk
- 1 teaspoon dried Italian seasoning, crushed
- 1 15-ounce can navy beans, rinsed and drained
  Salt and black pepper
  Bottled roasted red sweet peppers (optional)
  Snipped fresh Italian (flat-leaf) parsley (optional)
- 8 slices toasted Italian bread with shredded Swiss cheese (optional)

1. In a 4-quart Dutch oven combine potatoes and vegetable broth. Cover and bring to boiling; reduce heat. Simmer, covered, for 4 minutes.

2. In a large bowl toss together cheese and flour until cheese is coated. Gradually stir in milk until combined. Add cheese mixture and Italian seasoning to potato mixture in Dutch oven. Cook and stir over medium heat until thickened and bubbly. Stir in beans; cook and stir for 1 minute more. Season to taste with salt and pepper. If desired, top servings with roasted pepper and parsley and serve with toasted cheese-topped bread.

MAKES 4 SERVINGS.

Per serving: 494 cal., 12 g total fat (7 g sat. fat), 41 mg chol., 1,344 mg sodium, 70 g carbo., 9 g fiber, 25 g pro.

Pumpkin-Bean Soup

Start to Finish: 15 minutes

- 1 15-ounce can pumpkin
- 1 14-ounce can unsweetened coconut milk
- 1 15-ounce can white kidney (cannellini) beans, rinsed and drained
- 1 14.5-ounce can vegetable broth
- 1 teaspoon dried leaf sage, crushed
  Salt and black pepper
  Cracked black peppercorns (optional)
  Fresh lime slices (optional)

1. In a medium saucepan combine pumpkin, coconut milk, beans, vegetable broth, and sage. Heat through.

2. Season to taste with salt and pepper. If desired, sprinkle with cracked peppercorns and serve with lime. **MAKES 4 SERVINGS.**

Per serving: 285 cal., 19 g total fat (17 g sat. fat), 0 mg chol., 729 mg sodium, 28 g carbo., 8 g fiber, 9 g pro.

Rice and Bean Frittata

Start to Finish: 20 minutes

- 2 tablespoons vegetable oil
- 1 large yellow summer squash, halved lengthwise and sliced
- 1 8.8-ounce pouch cooked long grain and wild rice
- 1 15-ounce can navy beans, red beans, or garbanzo beans (chickpeas), rinsed and drained
- 6 eggs, lightly beaten
- 1/4 cup milk
- 1/4 teaspoon salt
- 1/4 teaspoon black pepper
- 1 cup shredded Colby and Monterey Jack cheese, cheddar cheese, or Swiss cheese (4 ounces)

1. In a large skillet heat oil over medium heat. Add summer squash; cook until crisp-tender. Meanwhile, microwave rice following the

Bean and Potato Chowder

Poached Eggs with Polenta and Black Beans

Start to Finish: 35 minutes

- 3 medium plum tomatoes, seeded and chopped
- 1/2 cup canned black beans, rinsed and drained
- 2 tablespoons chopped red onion
- 1 fresh jalapeño, seeded and finely chopped (see note, page 12)
- 1 tablespoon snipped fresh cilantro
- 2 teaspoons balsamic vinegar
- 1 teaspoon olive oil
- 1/8 teaspoon salt
- 1/8 teaspoon black pepper
- 1 16-ounce tube refrigerated plain cooked polenta
- 1 tablespoon olive oil
- 4 eggs
- 2 teaspoons snipped fresh cilantro
  Lime wedges

1. For salsa, in a small bowl combine tomatoes, black beans, red onion, jalapeño, the 1 tablespoon cilantro, the balsamic vinegar, the 1 teaspoon oil, the salt, and black pepper. Set aside until ready to serve.

2. Unwrap the polenta and cut into 12 slices. In an extra-large nonstick skillet heat the 1 tablespoon olive oil over medium heat. Add polenta; cook for 14 to 16 minutes or until polenta is browned and crisp, turning once halfway through cooking.

3. Meanwhile, to poach eggs, fill a large skillet half full with water. Bring to boiling; reduce heat to simmering (bubbles begin to break the surface of the water). Break 1 egg into a measuring cup. Carefully slide egg into simmering water, holding the lip of the cup as close to the water as possible. Repeat with remaining eggs, allowing each egg an equal amount of space. Simmer, uncovered, for 3 to 5 minutes or until the egg whites are completely set and yolks begin to thicken but are not hard. Using a slotted spoon, remove eggs.

4. To serve, divide polenta slices among 4 plates. Top with salsa and poached eggs. Sprinkle eggs with additional salt and black pepper. Sprinkle with the 2 teaspoons cilantro. Serve with lime wedges. **MAKES 4 SERVINGS.**

Per serving: 254 cal., 10 g total fat (2 g sat. fat), 213 mg chol., 768 mg sodium, 29 g carbo., 6 g fiber, 11 g pro.

Quick Tip If you have trouble keeping poached eggs intact, add about 1 teaspoon of vinegar to the boiling water, then slip in the eggs. Vinegar helps the eggs keep their shape by quickly firming up and congealing the edges.

Italian Mozzarella Salad ♡

Start to Finish: 30 minutes

- 1/4 cup red wine vinegar
- 1/4 cup olive oil
- 1 1/2 teaspoons snipped fresh basil or 1/2 teaspoon dried basil, crushed
- 1 teaspoon Dijon mustard
- 1/4 teaspoon crushed red pepper
- 1 clove garlic, minced
- 1 15-ounce can black beans or garbanzo beans (chickpeas), rinsed and drained
- 1 15-ounce can butter beans or Great Northern beans, rinsed and drained
- 1 small cucumber, quartered lengthwise and sliced (1 cup)
- 1 8-ounce round or log fresh mozzarella cheese or part-skim Scamorza, thinly sliced
- 2 red and/or yellow tomatoes, thinly sliced
- 1/2 cup thinly sliced green onions (4)
  Fresh basil sprigs (optional)

1. For dressing, in a screw-top jar combine vinegar, olive oil, snipped basil, mustard, crushed red pepper, and garlic. Cover and shake well.

2. In a large bowl combine beans, cucumber, and the dressing; toss to mix. Divide among 4 plates. Arrange cheese and tomato slices alternately on bean mixture. Sprinkle with green onions. If desired, garnish with basil sprigs. **MAKES 4 SERVINGS.**

Per serving: 433 cal., 23 g total fat (8 g sat. fat), 32 mg chol., 834 mg sodium, 36 g carbo., 11 g fiber, 26 g pro.

The New Chef's Salad ♡

Start to Finish: 25 minutes

- 1/3 cup fat-free mayonnaise or salad dressing
- 1/3 cup light sour cream
- 2 teaspoons white wine vinegar
- 2 cloves garlic, minced
- 1 1/2 teaspoons snipped fresh marjoram or 1/2 teaspoon dried marjoram, crushed
- 1/4 teaspoon dry mustard
- 1/8 teaspoon salt
- 3 tablespoons fat-free milk
- 2 cups Boston or Bibb lettuce
- 2 cups torn fresh spinach
- 1 15-ounce can reduced-sodium kidney beans or garbanzo beans (chickpeas), rinsed and drained
- 1 cup shredded red cabbage
- 1 cup thinly sliced zucchini (1 small)
- 1 cup shredded reduced-fat cheddar cheese (4 ounces)
- 1 small green or red sweet pepper, cut into thin bite-size strips
- 1/2 cup thinly sliced radishes
- 1/2 cup halved cherry tomatoes
- 1 hard-cooked egg, sliced

1. For dressing, in a small bowl combine mayonnaise, sour cream, vinegar, garlic, marjoram, mustard, and salt. Stir in the milk.

2. In a large salad bowl toss together lettuce, spinach, kidney beans, cabbage, zucchini, cheddar cheese, sweet pepper, radishes, and tomatoes. Pour the dressing over all; toss to coat. Divide mixture among 4 plates. Arrange egg slices on salad. **MAKES 4 SERVINGS.**

Per serving: 275 cal., 8 g total fat (4 g sat. fat), 76 mg chol., 740 mg sodium, 34 g carbo., 7 g fiber, 20 g pro.

Mediterranean Beans and Greens Salad ♡

- 8 cups mixed salad greens, such as torn or small whole leaves romaine lettuce, baby spinach, and/or arugula
- 1/4 cup small fresh basil leaves
- 1/2 of a medium cucumber, thinly sliced
- 1 15-ounce can cannellini beans (white kidney beans), rinsed and drained
- 1 15-ounce can black beans, rinsed and drained
- 3 medium plum tomatoes, cored and cut into wedges
- 1/2 cup reduced-calorie balsamic vinaigrette salad dressing
- 1 teaspoon finely shredded orange peel
- 6 slices baguette-style sourdough bread, toasted
- 2 ounces soft goat cheese (chèvre)
- 1 tablespoon snipped fresh basil

1. Arrange salad greens and 1/4 cup basil on a large serving platter. Arrange cucumber and beans over greens. Top with tomato wedges.

2. In a small bowl combine salad dressing and orange peel. Drizzle over salad. Spread toasted bread with goat cheese and sprinkle with snipped basil. Serve with salad.
MAKES 6 SERVINGS.

Per serving: 238 cal., 6 g total fat (2 g sat. fat), 4 mg chol., 809 mg sodium, 40 g carbo., 9 g fiber, 15 g pro.

Kale-Goat Cheese Frittata

Start to Finish: 25 minutes

- 2 cups coarsely torn fresh kale
- 1 medium onion, halved and thinly sliced
- 2 teaspoons olive oil
- 6 eggs
- 4 egg whites
- 1/4 teaspoon salt
- 1/8 teaspoon black pepper
- 1/4 cup drained oil-packed dried tomatoes, thinly sliced
- 1 ounce goat cheese, crumbled

1. Preheat broiler. In a large ovenproof nonstick skillet cook and stir kale and onion in oil over medium heat for 10 minutes or until onion is tender.

2. Meanwhile, in a medium bowl whisk together eggs, egg whites, salt, and pepper. Pour over kale mixture in skillet. Cook over medium-low heat. As egg mixture sets, run a spatula around the edge of the skillet, lifting egg mixture so the uncooked portion flows underneath. Continue cooking and lifting edge until egg mixture is almost set but still glossy and moist.

3. Sprinkle egg mixture with dried tomatoes and goat cheese. Broil 4 to 5 inches from the heat for 1 to 2 minutes or until eggs are set. Cut into wedges to serve. **MAKES 6 SERVINGS.**

Per serving: 145 cal., 9 g total fat (3 g sat. fat), 216 mg chol., 242 mg sodium, 6 g carbo., 1 g fiber, 11 g pro.

Quick Tip If you drop a bit of shell into the bowl when cracking eggs, use half an empty shell to scoop it out. The shell acts to attract the piece of broken shell.

Try eggs in the evening. In the form of a frittata or omelet, one of nature's most perfect foods makes one of the simplest kinds of suppers.

Kale-Goat
Cheese Frittata

Caprese Salad
Sandwiches

Vegetarian Cream Cheese and Bagels ♡

Start to Finish: 30 minutes

- 1/2 of a 8-ounce tub light cream cheese (1/2 cup)
- 1 tablespoon snipped fresh dill or 1 teaspoon dried dill
- 1/4 teaspoon salt
- 1/8 teaspoon black pepper
- 4 whole wheat bagel halves, toasted, or 4 slices whole wheat bread, toasted
- 1/2 of a medium cucumber, thinly sliced
- 1/2 of a medium red onion, thinly sliced
- 1/2 of a medium avocado, halved, seeded, peeled, and thinly sliced
- 3/4 cup bottled roasted red sweet peppers, drained and cut into thin strips
  Fresh dill sprigs (optional)

1. In a small bowl stir together cream cheese, snipped or dried dill, salt, and black pepper. Spread bagel halves with the cream cheese mixture. Top with cucumber slices, onion slices, avocado slices, and red pepper strips. If desired, top with fresh dill sprigs.

MAKES 4 SERVINGS.

Per serving: 222 cal., 8 g total fat (3 g sat. fat), 13 mg chol., 301 mg sodium, 31 g carbo., 5 g fiber, 9 g pro.

Quick Tip Instead of making your own flavored cream cheese, you can use prepared herb-garlic or chive cream cheese on this bagel sandwich.

Caprese Salad Sandwiches ♡

Start to Finish: 30 minutes

- 1 10-ounce loaf baguette-style French bread
- 1/2 cup yellow or red pear tomatoes, cherry tomatoes, and/or grape tomatoes, quartered
- 1/4 cup coarsely chopped cucumber
- 1/4 of a red, yellow, or green sweet pepper, seeded and cut into thin strips
- 1 ounce fresh mozzarella cheese, cubed
- 2 tablespoons chopped green onion (1)
- 2 tablespoons snipped fresh basil
- 1 tablespoon red wine vinegar or cider vinegar
- 1 teaspoon olive oil
- 1/8 teaspoon black pepper
- 3/4 cup mixed spring greens

1. Cut baguette crosswise into 4 equal portions to create 4 mini baguettes. Cut a thin horizontal slice from the top of each portion. Using a knife, carefully remove bread from the centers of the mini baguettes, leaving 1/4-inch-thick shells. Set aside. (Reserve the center baguette pieces for another use.)

2. In a small bowl combine tomatoes, cucumber, sweet pepper, mozzarella cheese, green onion, basil, vinegar, oil, and black pepper. Line bottoms of the baguette pieces with mixed spring greens. Fill baguette pieces with the tomato mixture. Replace tops. If desired, wrap each sandwich in plastic wrap and chill for up to 2 hours before serving.

MAKES 4 SERVINGS.

Per sandwich: 244 cal., 4 g total fat (2 g sat. fat), 5 mg chol., 489 mg sodium, 42 g carbo., 2 g fiber, 10 g pro.

Spinach-Stuffed Flank Steak

Spinach-Stuffed Flank Steak ♡

Start to Finish: 30 minutes

¼ cup dried tomatoes (not oil-packed)
1 pound beef flank steak or top round steak
⅛ teaspoon salt
⅛ teaspoon black pepper
1 10-ounce package frozen chopped spinach, thawed and well drained
2 tablespoons grated Parmesan cheese
2 tablespoons snipped fresh basil
Cooked polenta (optional)

1. In a small bowl soak dried tomatoes in enough hot water to cover for 10 minutes. Drain. Snip into small pieces.
2. Meanwhile, trim fat from steak. Score both sides of steak in a diamond pattern by making shallow diagonal cuts at 1-inch intervals. Place meat between 2 pieces of plastic wrap. Working from center to edges, pound with flat side of a meat mallet to a 12×8-inch rectangle. Discard plastic wrap. Sprinkle meat with salt and pepper.
3. Spread spinach on the steak. Sprinkle with the softened tomatoes, Parmesan cheese, and basil. Roll up the steak from a short side. Secure with wooden toothpicks at 1-inch intervals, starting ½ inch from an end. Cut between the toothpicks into eight 1-inch slices.

4. Preheat broiler. Place slices, cut sides down, on unheated rack of a broiler pan. Broil 3 to 4 inches from heat for 12 to 16 minutes for medium (160°F). Remove toothpicks. If desired, serve with cooked polenta.
MAKES 4 SERVINGS.

Per serving: 213 cal., 9 g total fat (4 g sat. fat), 47 mg chol., 303 mg sodium, 5 g carbo., 3 g fiber, 28 g pro.

Jerk Steaks with Zucchini Salad and Couscous

Start to Finish: 30 minutes

2 tablespoons olive oil
½ cup chopped onion (1 medium)
2 cloves garlic, minced
½ teaspoon salt
1 teaspoon curry powder
1 10- to 12-ounce package quick-cooking couscous
1 teaspoon olive oil
4 beef cube steaks (1¼ pounds)
½ teaspoon salt
⅓ cup prepared Jamaican jerk sauce
2 tablespoons olive oil
⅓ cup snipped fresh mint
1½ teaspoons finely shredded lemon peel
1 teaspoon salt
¼ teaspoon freshly ground black pepper
3 medium zucchini (1½ pounds), cubed
Fresh mint sprigs (optional)
Lemon wedges (optional)

1. For couscous, in a medium saucepan heat 2 tablespoons olive oil over medium heat. Cook onion, garlic, and ½ teaspoon salt in hot oil about 6 minutes or until onion is tender. Add curry powder; cook for 30 seconds more. Stir in couscous and the amount of boiling water specified in the package directions. Remove from heat; cover and set aside.
2. Meanwhile, for the steaks, heat a large grill pan over medium-high heat; brush with 1 teaspoon olive oil. Sprinkle steaks with ½ teaspoon salt; transfer to grill pan. Brush tops of steaks with half of the jerk sauce; cook for 2 to 3 minutes. Turn steaks over; brush steaks with remaining jerk sauce and cook for 2 to 3 minutes more for medium-rare (145°F).

3. For zucchini salad, in a large bowl combine 2 tablespoons olive oil, mint, lemon peel, 1 teaspoon salt, and pepper. Add zucchini and toss to coat.
4. Fluff couscous with a fork. Divide couscous and zucchini salad among 4 serving plates. Top couscous with steaks. If desired, garnish with mint sprigs and lemon wedges.
MAKES 4 SERVINGS.

Per serving: 681 cal., 24 g total fat (5 g sat. fat), 81 mg chol., 1,157 mg sodium, 70 g carbo., 6 g fiber, 45 g pro.

Sautéed Sirloin and Mushrooms

Start to Finish: 30 minutes

1 to 1¼ pounds boneless beef top sirloin steak, ¾ inch thick
¾ teaspoon cracked black pepper
1 tablespoon butter or margarine
¾ cup beef broth
1 tablespoon teriyaki sauce, soy sauce, or hoisin sauce
1¾ cups packaged sliced fresh mushrooms
1 small onion, cut into very thin wedges

1. Trim fat from steak. Cut steak in 4 serving-size portions. Sprinkle both sides of steaks with cracked pepper; pat pepper into meat with fingers. In a large skillet melt butter over medium-high heat. Add steaks; reduce heat to medium. Cook steaks for 9 to 11 minutes for medium-rare (145°F) to medium (160°F). Remove steaks from skillet, reserving drippings; cover steaks to keep warm.
2. Carefully add beef broth and teriyaki sauce to drippings in skillet. Cook until bubbly, stirring to scrape up browned bits. Stir in mushrooms and onion. Cook, uncovered, over medium heat for 8 to 10 minutes or until most of the liquid has evaporated. Transfer steaks to dinner plates; top with mushroom mixture. **MAKES 4 SERVINGS.**

Per serving: 191 cal., 8 g total fat (3 g sat. fat), 62 mg chol., 403 mg sodium, 3 g carbo., 1 g fiber, 26 g pro.

Sautéed
Sirloin and
Mushrooms

Peppered Steak with Mushroom Sauce

Start to Finish: 30 minutes

- 6 beef tenderloin steaks, cut 1 inch thick (about 1 1/2 pounds total)
- 1/2 teaspoon coarsely ground black pepper
- 1 teaspoon dried thyme or oregano, crushed
- 1/4 teaspoon salt
  Nonstick cooking spray
- 1/2 teaspoon instant beef bouillon granules
- 3/4 cup sliced fresh shiitake mushrooms
- 3/4 cup milk
- 2 tablespoons all-purpose flour
- 2/3 cup sour cream

1. Trim fat from steaks. Rub steaks with pepper, 1/2 teaspoon of the thyme, and the salt. Coat a large nonstick skillet with cooking spray. Heat over medium-high heat. Add steak; reduce heat to medium. Cook until desired doneness, turning once. Allow 12 to 14 minutes for medium-rare (145°F) or 15 to 18 minutes for medium (160°F). Remove steaks from skillet; keep warm.

2. Add 1/3 cup water and bouillon granules to skillet. Bring to boiling. Add mushrooms; cook until tender. Stir together milk, flour, and the remaining 1/2 teaspoon thyme; add to mushroom mixture. Cook and stir until bubbly. Stir in sour cream; heat through (do not boil). Serve with steak. **MAKES 6 SERVINGS.**

Per serving: 268 cal., 14 g total fat (6 g sat. fat), 81 mg chol., 252 mg sodium, 8 g carbo., 1 g fiber, 26 g pro.

Hot Italian Beef Salad

Start to Finish: 20 minutes

- 12 ounces beef flank steak, cut 1 inch thick
- 3 teaspoons olive oil or salad oil
- 1 medium red or green sweet pepper, cut into bite-size strips
- 1/2 cup bottled Italian salad dressing
- 6 cups torn mixed salad greens

1. Trim fat from steak. Cut steak into thin strips. In a large skillet heat 2 teaspoons of the oil over medium-high heat; add sweet pepper. Cook and stir until crisp-tender.

Upside-Down Pizza Casserole

2. Add the remaining 1 teaspoon oil to skillet; add steak strips. Cook and stir for 2 to 3 minutes or until desired doneness. Add salad dressing to skillet. Cook and stir until heated through. Serve beef mixture over salad greens. Sprinkle with coarsely ground black pepper. **MAKES 4 SERVINGS.**

Per serving: 317 cal., 24 g total fat (5 g sat. fat), 34 mg chol., 284 mg sodium, 7 g carbo., 2 g fiber, 20 g pro.

Upside-Down Pizza Casserole

Prep: 20 minutes **Bake:** 15 minutes
Oven: 400°F

- 1 1/2 pounds lean ground beef
- 1 15-ounce can Italian-style tomato sauce
- 1 1/2 cups shredded mozzarella cheese (6 ounces)
- 1 10-ounce package refrigerated biscuits (10 biscuits)

1. Preheat oven to 400°F. In a large skillet cook ground beef over medium heat until brown. Drain off fat. Stir in tomato sauce; heat through. Transfer beef mixture to a 2-quart rectangular baking dish or 10-inch deep-dish pie plate. Sprinkle with cheese. Flatten each biscuit with your hands; arrange the biscuits on top of cheese.

2. Bake, uncovered, about 15 minutes or until biscuits are golden. **MAKES 5 SERVINGS.**

Per serving: 642 cal., 40 g total fat (16 g sat. fat), 116 mg chol., 1,102 mg sodium, 30 g carbo., 2 g fiber, 34 g pro.

Herbed
Tenderloin
Steaks and
Vegetables

5 minutes. Turn steaks and asparagus spears; add tomatoes to grill. Grill until steaks are desired doneness. Allow 3 to 7 minutes more for medium-rare (145°F) or 7 to 10 minutes more for medium (160°F). Grill vegetables until asparagus is crisp-tender and tomatoes are hot (do not turn). (For a gas grill, preheat grill. Reduce heat to medium. Place steaks and asparagus (on foil) on rack. Cover and grill as above, adding tomatoes for the last 4 to 5 minutes.) **MAKES 4 SERVINGS.**

Per serving: 245 cal., 14 g total fat (4 g sat. fat), 65 mg chol., 322 mg sodium, 6 g carbo., 2 g fiber, 24 g pro.

Chipotle Steak and Tomatoes
Prep: 10 minutes **Grill:** 10 minutes

  2 6- to 8-ounce beef shoulder petite
    tenders or beef ribeye steaks
    Salt and black pepper
  1 canned chipotle pepper in adobo sauce,
    finely chopped, plus 2 teaspoons adobo
    sauce
  1/4 cup olive oil
  1/4 cup vinegar
  3 medium tomatoes, thickly sliced (1 pound)
  2 medium avocados, halved, seeded,
    peeled, and sliced
  1/2 of a small red onion, thinly sliced

1. Trim fat from steaks. Sprinkle steaks lightly with salt and black pepper. Spread each with 1 teaspoon of the adobo sauce.
2. For a charcoal grill, grill steaks on the rack of an uncovered grill directly over medium coals until desired doneness, turning once. Allow 10 to 12 minutes for medium-rare (145°F) or 12 to 15 minutes for medium (160°F). (For a gas grill, preheat grill. Reduce heat to medium. Place steaks on grill rack. Cover and and grill as above.)
3. Meanwhile, for dressing, in a screw-top jar combine the chopped chipotle pepper, olive oil, and vinegar. Shake to combine.
4. Slice steaks. Arrange steak, tomatoes, and avocados on 4 plates. Top with onion slices; drizzle with dressing. **MAKES 4 SERVINGS.**

Per serving: 421 cal., 33 g total fat (6 g sat. fat), 50 mg chol., 221 mg sodium, 13 g carbo., 7 g fiber, 20 g pro.

Herbed Tenderloin Steaks and Vegetables
Prep: 15 minutes **Grill:** 8 minutes

  2 cloves garlic
  1/4 cup loosely packed fresh basil leaves
  2 tablespoons fresh thyme leaves
  1 tablespoon fresh rosemary
  1 tablespoon fresh mint leaves
  2 tablespoons olive oil
  1/2 teaspoon salt
  1/2 teaspoon black pepper
  4 4- to 5-ounce beef tenderloin steaks, cut
    1 inch thick
  2 large yellow tomatoes, halved crosswise
  1 pound fresh asparagus spears, trimmed

1. For herb mixture, in a food processor or blender process or blend garlic until finely chopped. Add basil, thyme, rosemary, and mint. Cover and process or blend until herbs are chopped. With food processor or blender running, add oil in a thin, steady stream through feed tube or opening in lid. (When necessary, stop food processor or blender and use a rubber scraper to scrape the sides of bowl or container.) Stir in salt and pepper.
2. Trim fat from steaks. Spread some of the herb mixture evenly on both sides of the steaks and cut sides of tomatoes; set aside. Fold an 18×12-inch piece of heavy foil in half to make a 12×9-inch double thickness of foil. Place asparagus in the center of the foil. Add remaining herb mixture, turning asparagus to coat evenly.
3. For a charcoal grill, place steaks and asparagus (on foil) on rack of an uncovered grill directly over medium coals. Grill for

Chipotle
Steak and
Tomatoes

Jalapeño
Beef Kabobs

Jalapeño Beef Kabobs

Prep: 15 minutes **Grill:** 12 minutes

 1 10-ounce jar jalapeño pepper jelly
 2 tablespoons lime juice
 1 clove garlic, minced
 4 small purple or white boiling onions or
   8 very small red onions
 4 baby pattypan squash, halved crosswise,
   if large
 1 pound boneless beef sirloin steak, cut
   1-inch thick
 4 fresh tomatillos, husked and cut into
   quarters
 1/2 of a medium red and/or green sweet
   pepper, cut into 1-inch squares
   Hot cooked polenta (optional)

1. For glaze, in a small saucepan combine the jalapeño jelly, lime juice, and garlic. Cook and stir over medium heat until jelly is melted. Remove from heat.

2. In a small covered saucepan cook onions in a small amount of boiling water for 3 minutes. Add squash; cook for 1 minute more; drain. Trim fat from steak. Cut steak into 1-inch cubes. On eight 6- to 8-inch metal skewers alternately thread onions, squash, steak, tomatillos, and sweet pepper, leaving 1/4-inch space between pieces.

3. For a charcoal grill, grill kabobs on the rack of an uncovered grill directly over medium coals for 12 to 14 minutes for medium (160°F), turning once and brushing occasionally with glaze during the last 5 minutes of grilling. (For a gas grill, preheat grill. Reduce heat to medium. Place kabobs on grill rack over heat. Cover and grill as above.)

4. Serve kabobs with any remaining glaze and, if desired, polenta. **MAKES 4 SERVINGS.**

Per serving: 444 cal., 11 g total fat (4 g sat. fat), 76 mg chol., 71 mg sodium, 61 g carbo., 2 g fiber, 27 g pro.

Beef Tenderloin with Lemon-Dijon Cream

Beef Tenderloin with Lemon-Dijon Cream

Prep: 15 minutes **Grill:** 4 minutes

 1 cup low-fat cottage cheese
 1/4 cup whipping cream
 1 tablespoon lemon juice
 1 tablespoon Dijon mustard
 1 teaspoon snipped fresh thyme or oregano
 1 to 1 1/2 pounds beef tenderloin
   Salt and black pepper
   Snipped fresh watercress or chives
   (optional)

1. For lemon-Dijon cream, in a food processor or blender combine cottage cheese, whipping cream, lemon juice, mustard, and thyme. Cover and process or blend until smooth. Cover and set aside until ready to serve (up to 30 minutes).

2. Trim fat and silverskin from meat. Using a very sharp knife, cut tenderloin* across the grain into 1/4- to 1/2-inch slices. Sprinkle meat slices with salt and pepper.

3. For a charcoal grill, grill beef slices on the rack of an uncovered grill directly over hot coals for 4 minutes for medium-rare (145°F), turning once halfway through grilling. (For a gas grill, preheat grill. Place beef on grill rack over high heat. Cover and grill as above.)

4. Serve meat with lemon-Dijon cream. If desired, garnish with watercress.

MAKES 4 TO 6 SERVINGS.

Per serving: 282 cal., 15 g total fat (7 g sat. fat), 92 mg chol., 523 mg sodium, 3 g carbo., 0 g fiber, 32 g pro.

*Note Partially freeze beef for easy slicing.

Beef Satay with Peanut Sauce

Quick Tip **Quick Tip** Look for flank steak that has a bright red color and even thickness. For the most tender meat, be sure to slice flank steak perpendicular to the grain of the meat.

Beef and Broccoli with Plum Sauce ♡

Start to Finish: 30 minutes

12 ounces beef top round steak
³/₄ cup water
¹/₂ cup bottled plum sauce
 2 tablespoons reduced-sodium soy sauce
 1 tablespoon cornstarch
 1 teaspoon grated fresh ginger
 1 tablespoon vegetable oil
 1 cup broccoli florets
 1 small onion, cut into 1-inch pieces
 2 cloves garlic, minced
 3 cups lightly packed, coarsely chopped bok choy
 2 medium plums, pitted and cut into thin wedges
    Hot cooked Chinese egg noodles, fine egg noodles, or rice

1. If desired, partially freeze steak for easier slicing. Trim fat from steak. Thinly slice steak across the grain into bite-size strips. Set aside. For the sauce, in a small bowl stir together the water, plum sauce, soy sauce, cornstarch, and ginger. Set sauce aside.
2. In a nonstick wok or large skillet heat oil over medium-high heat. (Add more oil as necessary during cooking.) Add broccoli, onion, and garlic; stir-fry for 3 minutes. Remove broccoli mixture from wok. Add beef to hot wok. Cook and stir for 2 to 3 minutes or until brown. Push beef from center of wok. Stir sauce. Add sauce to center of wok. Cook and stir until thickened and bubbly.
3. Return broccoli mixture to wok. Add bok choy and plums. Stir all ingredients together to coat with sauce. Cover and cook about 2 minutes more or until heated through. Serve over hot cooked noodles.
MAKES 4 SERVINGS.

Per serving: 413 cal., 10 g total fat (3 g sat. fat), 74 mg chol., 533 mg sodium, 54 g carbo., 4 g fiber, 26 g pro.

Beef Satay with Peanut Sauce ♡

Prep: 25 minutes **Marinate:** 30 minutes
Broil: 4 minutes

 1 1- to 1¹/₄-pound beef flank steak
¹/₃ cup light teriyaki sauce
¹/₂ teaspoon bottled hot pepper sauce
¹/₂ of a red onion, cut into thin wedges
 4 green onions, cut into 1-inch pieces
 1 red or green sweet pepper, cut into ³/₄-inch chunks
 3 tablespoons peanut butter
 3 tablespoons water
 2 tablespoons light teriyaki sauce

1. Trim fat from steak. Cut steak crosswise into thin slices. For marinade, in a bowl combine ¹/₃ cup teriyaki sauce and ¹/₄ teaspoon of the hot pepper sauce. Add steak; toss to coat. Cover; marinate in refrigerator for 30 minutes.

2. Drain steak, reserving marinade. On skewers, alternately thread steak strips (accordion style), red onion, green onions, and sweet pepper. Brush with reserved marinade. Discard any remaining marinade.
3. Place skewers on the unheated rack of a broiler pan. Broil 4 to 5 inches from the heat about 4 minutes or until steak is slightly pink in center, turning once.
4. For peanut sauce, in a small saucepan combine peanut butter, the water, the 2 tablespoons teriyaki sauce, and the remaining ¹/₄ teaspoon hot pepper sauce. Cook and stir over medium heat just until smooth and heated through. Serve satay with warm peanut sauce. **MAKES 5 SERVINGS.**

Per serving: 230 cal., 10 g total fat (3 g sat. fat), 38 mg chol., 730 mg sodium, 10 g carbo., 2 g fiber, 24 g pro.

Beef and Broccoli with Plum Sauce

Mexican
Beef Hash
with Eggs

Mexican Beef Hash with Eggs

Start to Finish: 30 minutes

- ¼ cup thinly sliced green onions (2)
- 2 fresh jalapeño or serrano peppers, seeded and finely chopped (see note, page 12)
- 2 cloves garlic, minced
- 2 tablespoons vegetable oil
- 8 ounces cooked beef, chopped
- 1 teaspoon ground cumin
- ¼ teaspoon finely shredded lime peel
- 1 tablespoon lime juice
- 8 eggs
- 1 tablespoon water
  Salt and black pepper
- ¼ cup sour cream
- ¼ cup shredded cheddar cheese (1 ounce)
  Snipped fresh cilantro

1. In a large nonstick skillet cook onions, jalapeños, and garlic in 1 tablespoon of the hot oil over medium heat until tender. Stir in beef, cumin, lime peel, and lime juice. Cook and stir until heated through. Divide beef mixture among 4 plates; keep warm.

2. In the same skillet heat the remaining 1 tablespoon oil over medium heat. Carefully break 4 eggs into skillet. When whites are set, add the water. Cover skillet and cook until desired doneness (3 to 4 minutes for soft-set yolks or 4 to 5 minutes for firm-set yolks). Remove from skillet; keep warm. Repeat with remaining eggs.

3. Top each serving of beef mixture with 2 fried eggs. Season to taste with salt and black pepper. Top with sour cream, shredded cheese, and cilantro. **MAKES 4 SERVINGS.**

Per serving: 366 cal., 24 g total fat (8 g sat. fat), 475 mg chol., 374 mg sodium, 3 g carbo., 1 g fiber, 32 g pro.

Weeknight Steak with Vegetables

Weeknight Steak with Vegetables

Start to Finish: 30 minutes

- 2 tablespoons olive oil
- 2 medium zucchini and/or yellow summer squash, cut into 1-inch pieces
- 1 large red onion, cut into thick wedges
- 2 stalks celery, cut into 1-inch-thick slices
- 3 cloves garlic, sliced
- 1 teaspoon dried rosemary, crushed
- 1 pound boneless beef sirloin steak, cut ½ to ¾ inch thick
  Salt and black pepper
- ½ cup dry red wine
- 1 14½-ounce can diced tomatoes with basil, oregano, and garlic, undrained

1. In a large skillet heat 1 tablespoon of the oil over medium heat. Add zucchini and/or yellow summer squash, onion, celery, garlic, and rosemary; cook for 6 to 8 minutes or just until vegetables are crisp-tender, stirring occasionally. Remove from skillet.

2. Cut beef into 4 serving-size pieces. Sprinkle with salt and pepper. Add remaining 1 tablespoon oil to skillet. Add beef to hot skillet. Cook over medium heat about 4 minutes on each side or until desired doneness (145°F for medium-rare or 160°F for medium). Remove meat from skillet; cover and keep warm.

3. Carefully add wine to skillet, scraping up brown bits from bottom of skillet. Add undrained tomatoes. Bring to boiling. Boil gently, uncovered, about 5 minutes or until slightly thickened. Return vegetable mixture to skillet. Cook and stir just until heated through. Spoon vegetable sauce over beef. **MAKES 4 SERVINGS.**

Per serving: 294 cal., 11 g total fat (2 g sat. fat), 69 mg chol., 691 mg sodium, 16 g carbo., 3 g fiber, 27 g pro.

Pan-Fried Garlic Steak and Potatoes
Start to Finish: 30 minutes

- 12 cloves garlic
- 1 pound tiny new potatoes, scrubbed
- 4 6-ounce boneless beef ribeye or beef strip steaks
- 2 tablespoons olive oil
- 1 cup grape or cherry tomatoes
  Fresh oregano (optional)

1. Using the side of large chef's knife smash garlic; discard skins. Halve any large potatoes. Place potatoes in microwave-safe bowl. Cover with vented plastic wrap and cook on high for 5 minutes. Stir in garlic. Cover; cook about 5 minutes more or until tender, stirring once. Drain.

2. Meanwhile, heat 1 tablespoon of the olive oil in a large skillet over medium-high heat. Season steak with salt and pepper. Cook steaks, half at a time, 8 minutes for ribeye or 4 minutes for strip (145°F for medium-rare or 160°F for medium), turning once halfway through cooking. Keep steaks warm while cooking remaining steaks.

3. Add remaining 1 tablespoon oil to skillet. Add potatoes, garlic, and tomatoes. Season with salt and pepper. Cook about 5 minutes or until potatoes are golden and tomatoes begin to wilt, stirring occasionally. Serve potato mixture with steak. If desired, sprinkle with fresh oregano. **MAKES 4 SERVINGS.**

Per serving: 434 cal., 20 g total fat (6 g sat. fat), 99 mg chol., 247 mg sodium, 25 g carbo., 3 g fiber, 38 g pro.

Blackened Beef Stir-Fry ♡
Start to Finish: 25 minutes

- 12 ounces packaged beef stir-fry strips
- 2¼ teaspoons blackened steak seasoning
- ⅔ cup water
- 2 tablespoons tomato paste
- 2 teaspoons cornstarch
- ½ teaspoon instant beef bouillon granules
- 1 tablespoon vegetable oil
- 1 16-ounce package frozen stir-fry vegetables (any combination)

1. Sprinkle steak strips with 2 teaspoons of the blackened steak seasoning; toss to coat well. Set aside.

2. For sauce, in a small bowl stir together the remaining ¼ teaspoon blackened steak seasoning, the water, tomato paste, cornstarch, and bouillon granules. Set aside.

3. In a large skillet or wok heat oil over medium-high heat. Add frozen stir-fry vegetables; cook and stir for 2 to 3 minutes or until crisp-tender. Remove vegetables from skillet. Add beef strips to hot skillet. (Add more oil as necessary during cooking.) Cook and stir for 2 to 3 minutes or until meat is slightly pink in center.

4. Push meat from center of skillet. Stir sauce; add to center of skillet. Cook and stir until thickened and bubbly. Return vegetables to skillet. Stir together to coat all ingredients with sauce. Heat through. **MAKES 4 SERVINGS.**

Per serving: 190 cal., 6 g total fat (2 g sat. fat), 40 mg chol., 373 mg sodium, 10 g carbo., 3 g fiber, 21 g pro.

Quick Tip If you can't find precut beef stir-fry strips in the meat section of your supermarket, it's easy to cut your own. Flank steak is a good cut to use for stir-fry. To make it easy to cut thin slices, place the steak in the freezer for 30 to 45 minutes or until it's partially frozen—then cut. You'll get nice, neat slices.

Microwaving the potatoes cooks them quickly—then a short turn in a hot pan with a little olive oil turns them golden-brown and crisp.

Spicy
Beef-Noodle
Bowl

Spicy Beef-Noodle Bowl

Start to Finish: 20 minutes

1 tablespoon vegetable oil
1 pound boneless beef sirloin steak, cut into thin bite-size strips
2 14.5-ounce cans reduced-sodium beef broth
1/3 cup bottled peanut sauce
1 1/2 cups medium egg noodles (3 ounces)
2 cups broccoli florets
1/4 cup bias-sliced green onions (2) (optional)

1. In a Dutch oven heat oil over medium-high heat. Add beef strips; cook until browned.
2. Add beef broth and peanut sauce to meat in Dutch oven; bring to boiling. Stir in noodles; reduce heat. Simmer, uncovered, for 4 minutes, stirring occasionally. Add broccoli; return to boiling. Reduce heat; simmer, uncovered, for 3 to 4 minutes more or just until noodles are tender, stirring occasionally.
3. Divide beef and noodle mixture among 4 bowls. If desired, sprinkle with green onions. **MAKES 4 SERVINGS.**

Per serving: 316 cal., 12 g total fat (3 g sat. fat), 60 mg chol., 762 mg sodium, 18 g carbo., 2 g fiber, 31 g pro.

Quick curry

Curry paste is one of three basic types—red, green, or yellow. Most of the curry paste you see on your grocery store shelves is Thai-style curry. Green curry is based on fresh green chiles and herbs; red curry is based on dried red chiles; and yellow curry is based on dried red chiles and curry powder. Just a smidgeon of any type creates great flavor fast.

Beef Paprikash

Start to Finish: 30 minutes

1 12-ounce package egg noodles
2 tablespoons vegetable oil
1 1/2 pounds beef strips for stir-fry (top round)
1 teaspoon salt
1/2 teaspoon black pepper
2 medium onions, sliced
1 8-ounce package sliced fresh mushrooms
3 cups beef broth
1 8-ounce container sour cream
3 tablespoons paprika
2 tablespoons Dijon mustard
2 tablespoons tomato paste
1/2 teaspoon dried thyme

1. Cook noodles according to package directions. Drain and keep warm.
2. Meanwhile, in a large skillet heat 1 tablespoon of the oil over medium-high heat. (Add more oil as necessary during cooking.) Sprinkle beef with 1/2 teaspoon of the salt and 1/8 teaspoon of the pepper. In batches, add beef to skillet; cook and stir for 2 to 3 minutes or to desired doneness. Remove beef strips to a plate and keep warm.
3. Add the remaining 1 tablespoon oil to the skillet. Add onions; cook over high heat for 5 minutes, stirring frequently. Add mushrooms; cook for 6 to 7 minutes or until heated through.
4. In a small bowl whisk together 1 cup of the broth, sour cream, paprika, and mustard until smooth.
5. Add the remaining 2 cups broth, the tomato paste, thyme, and the remaining 1/2 teaspoon salt and remaining pepper to onion mixture in skillet. Bring to simmering, stirring to combine. Stir in sour cream mixture and reserved beef strips. Gently heat through for 3 minutes, stirring occasionally. Do not let mixture come to simmering.
5. Place hot noodles in a large bowl. Pour beef mixture over noodles; gently stir to combine. Tent with foil; let stand for 5 minutes before serving. **MAKES 6 SERVINGS.**

Per serving: 523 cal., 22 g total fat (7 g sat. fat), 133 mg chol., 1,100 mg sodium, 43 g carbo., 4 g fiber, 38 g pro.

Thai Beef with Couscous

Start to Finish: 15 minutes

1 tablespoon green curry paste
1 pound beef plate skirt steak or flank steak, cut crosswise into 4 pieces
3/4 teaspoon salt
1 1/2 teaspoons vegetable oil
1/2 teaspoon green curry paste
1 cup unsweetened coconut milk
1 cup water
1/2 teaspoon salt
1 10-ounce package couscous
1 10-ounce package frozen peas, thawed
2 tablespoons snipped fresh cilantro
Fresh cilantro leaves (optional)

1. Rub 1 tablespoon curry paste onto both sides of the steak; sprinkle with salt. In an extra-large skillet heat 1/2 teaspoon of the oil over medium-high heat. Add steak; cook for 6 to 8 minutes for medium-rare (145°F), turning once halfway through cooking.
2. Meanwhile, in a 2-quart saucepan heat the remaining 1 teaspoon oil over medium heat. Add 1/2 teaspoon curry paste; cook, stirring, for 30 seconds. Add coconut milk, the water, and salt; bring to boiling. Stir in couscous. Cover and remove from heat; let stand for 5 minutes. Fluff couscous with a fork. Stir in peas and snipped cilantro; cover and let stand for 1 minute more.
3. Thinly slice steak. Divide steak and couscous among 4 serving plates. If desired, garnish with cilantro leaves.
MAKES 4 SERVINGS.

Per serving: 615 cal., 25 g total fat (14 g sat. fat), 44 mg chol., 1,051 mg sodium, 67 g carbo., 6 g fiber, 30 g pro.

Bail-Out Beef Stroganoff

Bail-Out Beef Stroganoff

Start to Finish: 30 minutes

  3 cups dried wide noodles
  3 cups broccoli florets (12 ounces)
$^1/_2$ cup light sour cream
1$^1/_2$ teaspoons prepared horseradish
$^1/_2$ teaspoon snipped fresh dill
  1 pound beef ribeye steak
  1 small onion, cut into $^1/_2$-inch slices
  1 clove garlic, minced
  1 tablespoon vegetable oil
  4 teaspoons all-purpose flour
$^1/_2$ teaspoon black pepper
  1 14.5-ounce can beef broth
  3 tablespoons tomato paste
  1 teaspoon Worcestershire sauce

1. Cook noodles according to package directions, adding broccoli the last 5 minutes of cooking. Drain well. Return noodle mixture to hot pan; cover to keep warm.

2. Meanwhile, in a small serving bowl stir together the sour cream, horseradish, and dill; cover and chill until serving time.

3. Trim fat from beef. Cut beef into bite-size strips. In a large skillet cook and stir half of the beef, the onion, and garlic in hot oil until onion is tender and beef is desired doneness. Remove from skillet. Add remaining beef to skillet; cook and stir until beef is desired doneness. Return all of the beef to the skillet; sprinkle flour and pepper over beef. Stir to coat.

4. Stir in broth, tomato paste, and Worcestershire sauce. Cook and stir until bubbly. Cook and stir for 1 minute more. Divide noodle mixture among 4 bowls. Spoon beef mixture on noodle mixture. Top with sour cream mixture. **MAKES 4 SERVINGS.**

Per serving: 413 cal., 16 g total fat (6 g sat. fat), 103 mg chol., 504 mg sodium, 33 g carbo., 3 g fiber, 33 g pro.

Mediterranean Mostaccioli

Start to Finish: 25 minutes

  4 ounces dried mostaccioli or gemelli pasta
  2 cups sliced zucchini
  8 ounces ground beef
$^1/_2$ of a medium eggplant, peeled and cubed (about 2$^1/_2$ cups)
  1 14.5-ounce can diced tomatoes with basil, oregano, and garlic, undrained
  2 tablespoons tomato paste
$^1/_2$ cup shredded carrot (1 medium)
$^1/_4$ cup snipped fresh basil
  2 tablespoons raisins (optional)
$^1/_4$ teaspoon ground cinnamon
  1 tablespoon balsamic vinegar (optional)
$^1/_2$ cup shredded mozzarella cheese (2 ounces)

1. Cook pasta according to package directions, adding zucchini during the last 2 minutes of cooking. Drain; keep warm.

2. Meanwhile, for the sauce, in a large skillet cook beef and eggplant over medium heat until beef is brown; drain off fat. Stir in undrained tomatoes, tomato paste, carrot, basil, raisins (if desired), and cinnamon. Bring to boiling; reduce heat. Simmer, uncovered, about 2 minutes, or to desired consistency, stirring occasionally. Remove from heat. If desired, stir in vinegar. Serve sauce over pasta mixture. Sprinkle with cheese.

MAKES 4 TO 6 SERVINGS.

Per serving: 334 cal., 11 g total fat (5 g sat. fat), 47 mg chol., 672 mg sodium, 38 g carbo., 4 g fiber, 21 g pro.

Quick Tip Choose an eggplant that is firm, smooth-skinned, and heavy for its size; avoid those with soft or brown spots. Store eggplants in a cool, dry place and use within 1 to 2 days of purchase. For longer storage (up to 5 days), place them in a plastic bag and store in the vegetable drawer of the refrigerator.

Mediterranean
Mostaccioli

Grilled Chili
Burgers

Grilled Chili Burgers

Prep: 20 minutes **Grill:** 10 minutes

- 1 recipe Chimichurri Sauce
- 1 pound 95% lean ground beef
- 8 ounces ground pork
- 1 tablespoon chili powder
- 1/2 teaspoon onion powder
- 1/4 teaspoon ground cumin
- 1/8 teaspoon salt
- 3 whole wheat pita bread rounds, quartered and toasted
- 3/4 cup bottled roasted red sweet peppers, drained and cut into strips

1. Prepare Chimichurri sauce; set aside. In a large bowl combine beef, pork, chili powder, onion powder, cumin, and salt. Mix well. Shape into six 1/2-inch-thick patties.

2. For a charcoal grill, grill patties on the rack of an uncovered grill for 10 to 13 minutes or until done (160°F)*, turning once halfway through grilling. (For a gas grill, preheat grill. Reduce heat to medium. Place patties on grill rack over heat. Cover and grill as above.)

3. Place each patty on two of the pita quarters. Top with roasted peppers and Chimichurri Sauce. **MAKES 6 SANDWICHES.**

Chimichurri Sauce In a small bowl combine 1/2 cup finely snipped fresh parsley; 1/2 cup finely snipped fresh cilantro; 2 tablespoons red wine vinegar; 1 tablespoon olive oil; 2 cloves garlic, minced; 1/4 teaspoon salt; 1/4 teaspoon black pepper; and 1/8 teaspoon cayenne pepper.

Per sandwich: 325 cal., 15 g total fat (5 g sat. fat), 74 mg chol., 407 mg sodium, 21 g carbo., 4 g fiber, 26 g pro.

*Note The internal color of ground meat patties is not a reliable doneness indicator. Regardless of color, a beef, lamb, pork, or veal burger cooked to an internal temperature of 160°F is safe to eat. Ground turkey or chicken burgers must be cooked to 165°F.

Double-Beef Burgers

Double-Beef Burgers

Prep: 15 minutes **Grill:** 14 minutes

- 1 egg, lightly beaten
- 1 2 1/2-ounce package very thinly sliced corned beef, chopped
- 1/3 cup finely chopped cabbage
- 1/4 cup soft rye bread crumbs (about 1/2 slice)
- 1/2 teaspoon caraway seeds
- 1/4 teaspoon salt
- 1 pound lean ground beef
- 1 large red onion, sliced
- 4 kaiser rolls, split
- 3 tablespoons horseradish mustard

1. In a medium bowl combine egg, corned beef, cabbage, bread crumbs, caraway seeds, and salt. Add ground beef; mix well. Shape mixture into four 3/4-inch-thick patties.

2. For a charcoal grill, place patties on the rack of an uncovered grill directly over medium coals. Grill for 14 to 18 minutes or until done (160°F; see note at left), turning once halfway through grilling. Add onion slices to the grill during the last 10 to 12 minutes or until tender, turning once halfway through grilling. Toast kaiser rolls on the grill. (For a gas grill, preheat grill. Reduce heat to medium. Place patties, then onion slices and kaiser rolls on grill rack over heat. Cover and grill as above.)

3. Spread kaiser rolls with horseradish mustard. Serve burgers in rolls with onion slices. **MAKES 4 SERVINGS.**

Per sandwich: 479 cal., 22 g total fat (7 g sat. fat), 138 mg chol., 861 mg sodium, 36 g carbo., 2 g fiber, 33 g pro.

Quick Tip To make soft bread crumbs, simply whirl bread in a food processor. For finer crumbs, remove the crust first.

Italian Pizza Burgers

Italian Pizza Burgers

Start to Finish: 30 minutes

- 4 4-ounce uncooked beef patties
- 4 ³/₄-inch slices sourdough bread
- 1 cup mushroom pasta sauce
- 1 cup shredded provolone or mozzarella cheese (4 ounces)
- 2 tablespoons thinly sliced fresh basil

1. Preheat broiler. Place beef patties on the unheated rack of a broiler pan. Broil 3 to 4 inches from heat for 10 to 12 minutes or until an instant-read thermometer inserted in centers registers 160°F (see note, page 103),

turning once halfway through cooking. Add the bread slices to the broiler pan the last 2 to 3 minutes of broiling; turn once to toast evenly.

2. Meanwhile, in a medium saucepan heat pasta sauce over medium heat until heated through, stirring occasionally. Place 1 patty on each bread slice. Spoon pasta sauce over patties; sprinkle with cheese. Broil for 1 to 2 minutes more or until cheese is melted. Top with basil. **MAKES 4 BURGERS.**

Per burger: 504 cal., 30 g total fat (13 g sat. fat), 96 mg chol., 815 mg sodium, 27 g carbo., 2 g fiber, 30 g pro.

Beef Patties au Poivre

Start to Finish: 25 minutes

- 1 tablespoon green peppercorns in brine, drained
- 1 tablespoon butter
- ¼ cup frozen chopped onion, thawed
- 2 tablespoons brandy
- 2 tablespoons all-purpose flour
- 1 cup beef broth
- ¼ cup whipping cream
- 4 4-ounce purchased uncooked beef patties
- ½ teaspoon salt
- ¼ teaspoon black pepper
- 4 hamburger buns (optional)
     Seasoned french-fried potatoes (optional)

1. On a clean work surface crush half the peppercorns with the back of a spoon.

2. For sauce, in a small saucepan melt butter over medium heat. Add onion and all the peppercorns; cook for 4 to 5 minutes or until browned. Carefully add brandy. Cook for 30 seconds, stirring to scrape up any browned bits from the bottom of the pan with a wooden spoon. Stir in flour; cook and stir for 2 minutes. Add beef broth; cook and stir until thickened and bubbly. Reduce heat; cook for 2 to 3 minutes. Add whipping cream; cook and stir for 1 to 2 minutes. Remove from heat; cover sauce to keep warm.

3. Heat a large nonstick skillet over medium heat. Sprinkle beef patties with salt and pepper. Add patties to skillet; cook for 1 to 2 minutes on each side or until an instant-read thermometer inserted in centers registers 160°F (see note, page 103).

4. If desired, serve patties on buns with sauce and seasoned fries. **MAKES 4 SERVINGS.**

Per serving: 322 cal., 22 g total fat (11 g sat. fat), 106 mg chol., 644 mg sodium, 4 g carbo., 0 g fiber, 24 g pro.

Beef Patties
au Poivre

Pork Medallions with Lemon-Dill Green Beans

Memphis-Style
Pork Chops

Pork Medallions with Lemon-Dill Green Beans ♡

Start to Finish: 20 minutes

- 1 1- to 1¹/₂-pound honey mustard-marinated pork tenderloin
- 1 tablespoon butter or margarine
- 1 9-ounce package frozen French-cut green beans, thawed
- 1 teaspoon dried dill
- 1 teaspoon lemon juice
   Fresh dill sprigs (optional)
   Lemon slices (optional)

1. Cut pork tenderloin into ¹/₄-inch slices. In a very large skillet cook pork in hot butter on medium heat for 4 to 6 minutes or until juices run clear, turning once. Remove meat from skillet; reserve drippings. Keep warm.

2. Add green beans and dill to drippings in skillet. Cook and stir for 3 to 4 minutes or until beans are tender. Stir in lemon juice. Transfer beans and pork slices to a serving platter. If desired, garnish with fresh dill and lemon slices. **MAKES 4 SERVINGS.**

Per serving: 189 cal., 8 g total fat (4 g sat. fat), 53 mg chol., 531 mg sodium, 8 g carbo., 2 g fiber, 21 g pro.

Quick Tip This recipe calls for dried dill for convenience, but if you have some fresh dill on hand, by all means use it. The general rule of substituting dried herbs for fresh is 1 tablespoon of fresh herb for every 1 teaspoon of dried (and vice versa), which is a three-to-one ratio.

Memphis-Style Pork Chops ♡

Prep: 15 minutes **Grill:** 12 minutes

- ¹/₂ cup bottled chili sauce
- 2 tablespoons molasses
- 2 tablespoons cider vinegar
- 1 teaspoon chili powder
- 4 boneless pork loin chops, cut ³/₄ to 1 inch thick (about 1¹/₄ pounds total)
- 1 teaspoon dried basil, crushed
- ¹/₂ teaspoon paprika
- ¹/₄ teaspoon salt
- ¹/₄ teaspoon onion powder
- ¹/₄ teaspoon cayenne pepper

1. In a small saucepan stir together chili sauce, molasses, vinegar, and chili powder. Bring to boiling; reduce heat. Simmer, uncovered, for 3 minutes. Remove from heat.

2. Trim fat from chops. In a small bowl stir together basil, paprika, salt, onion powder, and cayenne pepper. Sprinkle evenly over both sides of chops; rub in with your fingers.

3. For a charcoal grill, grill chops on the rack of an uncovered grill directly over medium coals for 12 to 15 minutes or until juices run clear (160°F), turning once and brushing with chili sauce mixture during the last 5 minutes of grilling. (For a gas grill, preheat grill. Reduce heat to medium. Place chops on grill rack over heat. Cover and grill as above.)

MAKES 4 SERVINGS.

Per serving: 260 cal., 7 g total fat (3 g sat. fat), 83 mg chol., 623 mg sodium, 16 g carbo., 2 g fiber, 31 g pro.

Cranberry- and Citrus-Glazed Pork Roast

Prep: 15 minutes **Roast:** 1¹/₂ hours
Stand: 15 minutes **Oven:** 325°F

- ¹/₄ teaspoon salt
- ¹/₄ teaspoon black pepper
- ¹/₂ teaspoon ground sage
- 1 2¹/₂- to 3-pound boneless pork top loin roast
- 1 16-ounce can whole or jellied cranberry sauce
- ¹/₂ teaspoon finely shredded orange peel
- ¹/₃ cup orange juice

1. Preheat oven to 325°F. For the rub, in a small bowl stir together salt, pepper, and ¹/₄ teaspoon of the sage. Sprinkle rub evenly over all sides of pork roast; rub in mixture with your fingers. Place roast on rack in a shallow roasting pan. Roast, uncovered, for 1 hour.
2. For the sauce, in a medium saucepan stir together cranberry sauce, orange peel, orange juice, and the remaining ¹/₄ teaspoon sage. Bring to boiling; reduce heat. Simmer, uncovered, about 10 minutes or until sauce has thickened slightly.
3. Spoon about ¹/₄ cup of the sauce over pork. Roast, uncovered, for 30 to 45 minutes more or until done (155°F). Remove from oven. Cover pork loosely with foil; let stand for 15 minutes before slicing. (The temperature of the pork will rise 5°F during standing.) Reheat remaining sauce. Serve warm sauce with pork. **MAKES 8 TO 10 SERVINGS.**

Per serving: 290 cal., 7 g total fat (2 g sat. fat), 77 mg chol., 132 mg sodium, 23 g carbo., 1 g fiber, 31 g pro.

Orecchiette with Pancetta and Broccoli Rabe ♡

Prep: 20 minutes **Cook:** 15 minutes

- 4 ounces pancetta, coarsely chopped
- 6 ounces dried orecchiette or gemelli pasta
- 2 teaspoons olive oil
- 4 cloves garlic, minced (2 teaspoons)
- ¹/₄ teaspoon crushed red pepper
- 3 cups cut-up broccoli rabe or broccoli
- ¹/₃ cup reduced-sodium chicken broth
- ¹/₄ cup pitted Greek black olives or pitted ripe olives or 2 tablespoons drained capers
- ¹/₄ cup finely shredded Parmesan cheese

1. In a large skillet cook pancetta over medium heat about 10 minutes or until crisp. Drain on paper towels, reserving 1 tablespoon drippings in skillet. Set pancetta aside.
2. In a large saucepan cook pasta according to package directions. Drain; return pasta to pan. Toss with oil; keep warm.
3. In the same skillet heat reserved drippings over medium heat. Add garlic and crushed red pepper; cook and stir for 30 seconds. Add broccoli rabe and broth. Bring to boiling; reduce heat. Cover and simmer for 3 minutes or until broccoli rabe is tender. Stir in pancetta and olives; heat through. Add broccoli rabe mixture to pasta mixture in saucepan. Add half of the Parmesan cheese and toss to combine. Transfer pasta mixture to a serving dish and sprinkle with remaining Parmesan cheese. **MAKES 6 SERVINGS.**

Per serving: 211 cal., 9 g total fat (3 g sat. fat), 11 mg chol., 244 mg sodium, 25 g carbo., 2 g fiber, 8 g pro.

Pork Medallions with Cranberry and Fig Chutney ♡

Start to Finish: 20 minutes

- 1 cup fresh cranberries or ¹/₂ cup canned whole cranberry sauce
- ¹/₂ cup apple juice
- ¹/₄ cup snipped dried figs
- 2 tablespoons packed brown sugar or granulated sugar
- 1 teaspoon snipped fresh rosemary or ¹/₂ teaspoon dried rosemary, crushed Salt and black pepper
- 12 ounces pork tenderloin
- 4 teaspoons vegetable oil

1. For the chutney, in a small heavy saucepan stir together cranberries, apple juice, figs, brown sugar, and rosemary. Bring to boiling; reduce heat. Simmer, uncovered, for 5 to 8 minutes or until chutney is of desired consistency, stirring occasionally. Season to taste with salt and pepper. Set aside.
2. Meanwhile, trim fat from pork. Cut pork crosswise into 12 pieces. Press each piece with palm of hand to make an even thickness. In a large nonstick skillet heat oil over medium-high heat. Add pork; cook the pork for 2 to 3 minutes or until juices run clear, turning once.
3. To serve, spoon some of the warm chutney over pork and pass remaining chutney. **MAKES 4 SERVINGS.**

Per serving: 227 cal., 7 g total fat (1 g sat. fat), 55 mg chol., 185 mg sodium, 23 g carbo., 3 g fiber, 18 g pro.

A roast cooks itself: Put it in the oven when you get home, then go about your business until it's ready to serve.

Pork Medallions with Cranberry and Fig Chutney

Oven-Baked
Cassoulet

Oven-Baked Cassoulet ♡

Prep: 20 minute **Bake:** 40 minutes
Oven: 325°F

　　Nonstick cooking spray
12　ounces lean boneless pork, cut into
　　¹/₂-inch cubes
1　teaspoon vegetable oil
1　cup chopped onion (1 large)
1　cup chopped carrots (2 medium)
3　cloves garlic, minced
2　15-ounce cans cannellini beans (white
　　kidney beans), rinsed and drained
4　plum tomatoes, chopped
²/₃　cup reduced-sodium chicken broth
²/₃　cup water
2　ounces smoked turkey sausage, halved
　　lengthwise and cut into ¹/₄-inch slices
1　teaspoon dried thyme, crushed
¹/₄　teaspoon dried rosemary, crushed
¹/₄　teaspoon black pepper
2　tablespoons snipped fresh thyme or Italian
　　(flat-leaf) parsley

1. Preheat oven to 325°F. Lightly coat an unheated Dutch oven with cooking spray. Preheat over medium-high heat. Add pork to Dutch oven; cook and stir until pork is browned. Remove pork from Dutch oven. Reduce heat. Carefully add oil to hot Dutch oven. Add onion, carrots, and garlic; cook until onion is tender. Stir in pork, beans, tomatoes, broth, the water, turkey sausage, thyme, rosemary, and pepper.

2. Bake, covered, for 40 to 45 minutes or until pork and carrots are tender. To serve, spoon into serving bowls or individual casseroles; sprinkle with thyme.

MAKES 5 SERVINGS.

Per serving: 263 cal., 6 g total fat (2 g sat. fat), 48 mg chol., 500 mg sodium, 33 g carbo., 10 g fiber, 28 g pro.

Dijon Pork Salad

Prep: 10 minutes **Roast:** 20 minutes
Oven: 425°F

1　1-pound pork tenderloin
　　Salt and black pepper
²/₃　cup bottled Dijon lime salad dressing or
　　oil and vinegar salad dressing
8　cups torn mixed salad greens
2　ounces Gouda or white Cheddar cheese,
　　cut into bite-size strips
12　cherry tomatoes, quartered

1. Preheat oven to 425°F. Trim fat from pork. Place pork on a rack in a shallow roasting pan. Sprinkle with salt and pepper. Brush pork with 2 tablespoons of the salad dressing. Roast, uncovered, for 20 to 30 minutes or until done (160°F).

2. Meanwhile, arrange salad greens on 4 salad plates. Top with cheese and tomatoes. Thinly slice pork; arrange pork slices on salads. Serve with remaining salad dressing. **MAKES 4 SERVINGS.**

Per serving: 336 cal., 24 g total fat (5 g sat. fat), 71 mg chol., 535 mg sodium, 5 g carbo., 2 g fiber, 23 g pro.

Oregano and Pork Chop Skillet

Start to Finish: 30 minutes.

1　pound boneless pork sirloin chops, cut
　　¹/₂ inch thick
2　tablespoons all-purpose flour
¹/₂　teaspoon salt
¹/₂　teaspoon black pepper
2　tablespoons olive oil
1　1-pound whole winter squash (such as
　　butternut or banana), peeled, seeded, and
　　cut into 1-inch cubes (2 cups)
1　medium onion, cut into thin wedges
1　tablespoon snipped fresh oregano or
　　1 teaspoon dried oregano, crushed
¹/₄　cup chicken broth
¹/₄　cup orange juice
2　medium zucchini, quartered lengthwise and
　　cut into 1-inch pieces (about 2¹/₂ cups)

1. Trim fat from pork; if necessary, cut meat into four serving-size portions. Sprinkle both sides of meat with some of the flour, salt, and pepper.

2. In a large skillet heat oil over medium-high heat. Add chops and brown for 4 minutes, turning once. Add winter squash and onion; sprinkle with dried oregano (if using). Pour broth and orange juice over vegetables and pork. Bring to boiling; reduce heat. Cover and simmer for 10 minutes.

3. Add zucchini. Cover and cook about 5 minutes more or until chops are tender and no longer pink. Transfer chops to a serving platter. Stir fresh oregano (if using) into vegetables. Serve vegetables with chops.

MAKES 4 SERVINGS.

Per serving: 276 cal., 11 g total fat (3 g sat. fat), 71 mg chol., 417 mg sodium, 17 g carbo., 2 g fiber, 26 g pro.

Fast French

Cassoulet is a rich French-style casserole of white beans, pork, sausages, tomatoes, and duck legs confit that is traditionally slow-baked in the oven for hours. This version is not only healthier than traditional cassoulet (only 6 grams of fat and 263 calories per serving!), but you can also make it on a weeknight. While it bakes for 40 minutes in the oven, you can go through the mail, fold a load of laundry—or simply sit down and put your feet up.

Classic Schnitzel

all-purpose flour, and $^1/_2$ teaspoon dried dill. Stir into hot broth in skillet. Cook and stir until thickened and bubbly. Cook and stir for 1 minute more. Makes about 2 cups.

Cornmeal-Crusted Pork

Start to Finish: 20 minutes

$^1/_2$ cup yellow cornmeal
$^1/_2$ teaspoon salt
$^1/_2$ teaspoon black pepper
1 egg, lightly beaten
1 tablespoon water
1 pound pork tenderloin, cut into $^1/_2$-inch slices
2 tablespoons olive oil or vegetable oil
12 ounces fresh green beans
2 medium zucchini and/or yellow summer squash, thinly bias-sliced
2 tablespoons fresh oregano leaves

1. In a shallow bowl combine cornmeal, salt, and pepper. In another shallow bowl combine egg and the water. Dip pork into egg mixture and then into cornmeal mixture to coat.
2. In an extra-large skillet heat oil over medium-high heat. Add pork; cook about 2 minutes on each side or until no pink remains. Transfer pork to a serving platter. Add beans and zucchini to skillet; cook and stir for 6 to 8 minutes or until crisp-tender. Season to taste with salt and pepper. Serve alongside pork. Sprinkle with oregano leaves. **MAKES 4 SERVINGS.**

Per serving: 310 cal., 13 g total fat (3 g sat. fat), 127 mg chol., 385 mg sodium, 21 g carbo., 5 g fiber, 29 g pro.

Quick Tip The cornmeal breading in the Cornmeal-Crusted Pork recipe is incredibly versatile. Tailor it to your liking by adding dried herbs and spices, such as cayenne pepper, oregano, basil, marjoram, paprika, and cumin. Try it on fish fillets or skinless, boneless chicken breasts as well.

Classic Schnitzel

Start to Finish: 35 minutes

$^1/_2$ cup all-purpose flour
$^1/_4$ teaspoon garlic salt
$^1/_4$ teaspoon celery salt
$^1/_4$ teaspoon seasoned salt
$^1/_4$ teaspoon paprika
$^1/_8$ teaspoon black pepper
1 egg, lightly beaten
$^1/_2$ cup milk
6 4-ounce pork sirloin cutlets, about $^1/_2$ inch thick
2 to 3 tablespoons vegetable oil
Lemon wedges (optional)
1 recipe Sour Cream-Dill Sauce (optional)

1. In a shallow dish combine flour, garlic salt, celery salt, seasoned salt, paprika, and pepper. In another shallow dish stir together egg and milk. Coat each cutlet with flour

mixture, then dip in egg mixture and again in flour mixture.
2. In a large skillet heat oil over medium heat. Cook cutlets in hot oil for 12 to 15 minutes or until browned and meat is thoroughly cooked, turning once. (Remove meat from skillet and keep warm while preparing Sour Cream-Dill Sauce, if using.) If desired, serve with lemon wedges and/or Sour Cream-Dill Sauce. **MAKES 6 SERVINGS.**

Per serving: 254 cal., 12 g total fat (3 g sat. fat), 108 mg chol., 242 mg sodium, 9 g carbo., 0 g fiber, 27 g pro.

Sour Cream-Dill Sauce Pour 1$^1/_4$ cups chicken broth into the skillet used for cooking cutlets. Heat over medium heat, scraping up browned bits in skillet. Bring mixture to boiling. Meanwhile, in a small bowl stir together $^1/_2$ cup sour cream, 2 tablespoons

Cornmeal-Crusted Pork

Pork Chops
Provençal

Pork Chops Provençal

Prep: 15 minutes **Cook:** 14 minutes

- 8 ounces orzo (rosamarina)
- 1 tablespoon olive oil
- 4 boneless pork chops, ³/₄ inch thick
- ¹/₈ teaspoon salt
- ¹/₄ teaspoon black pepper
- 1 cup dry white wine
- 2 cloves garlic, minced
- 3 plum tomatoes, seeded and chopped
- 1 tablespoon grainy Dijon mustard
- ¹/₃ cup pitted and coarsely chopped niçoise olives
- 1 tablespoon capers
- 2 tablespoons snipped fresh parsley

1. Cook orzo following package directions.

2. Meanwhile, in a large nonstick skillet heat oil over medium-high heat. Trim fat from pork chops. Sprinkle chops with salt and pepper. Add chops to skillet; reduce heat to medium. Cook for 8 to 12 minutes or until temperature registers (160°F), turning once halfway through cooking. Transfer chops to a plate; cover to keep warm.

3. For sauce, add wine and garlic to skillet, stirring to scrape up browned bits. Cook over medium heat for 3 minutes. Stir in tomatoes, mustard, olives, and capers. Cook for 3 minutes, stirring occasionally. Stir in parsley. To serve, spoon sauce over chops. Serve orzo on the side. **MAKES 4 SERVINGS.**

Per serving: 583 cal., 19 g total fat (4 g sat. fat), 78 mg chol., 468 mg sodium, 51 g carbo., 4 g fiber, 39 g pro.

Maple Pork and Apples

Maple Pork and Apples

Start to Finish: 20 minutes

- 4 pork loin chops, ¹/₂ inch thick
  Salt and black pepper
- 2 tablespoons butter or margarine
- 12 baby carrots with tops (not baby-cut carrots), halved lengthwise
- 1 medium apple, sliced crosswise and seeds removed
- ¹/₃ cup pure maple syrup

1. Trim fat from chops. Sprinkle chops lightly with salt and pepper. In a large skillet melt butter over medium heat; add chops. Brown for 2 minutes, turning once. Reduce heat to medium-low. Add carrots, apple slices, and maple syrup. Simmer, covered, about 8 minutes or until chops are done (160°F).

2. Using a slotted spoon, transfer chops, carrots, and apples to platter. Bring syrup mixture to boiling. Boil gently, uncovered, for 1 to 2 minutes or until thickened. Pour over chops. **MAKES 4 SERVINGS.**

Per serving: 451 cal., 19 g total fat (8 g sat. fat), 124 mg chol., 447 mg sodium, 25 g carbo., 1 g fiber, 44 g pro.

Pork Chops Dijon

Pork Chops Dijon

Start to Finish: 30 minutes

- 3 tablespoons Dijon mustard
- 2 tablespoons bottled reduced-calorie Italian salad dressing
- ¼ teaspoon black pepper Nonstick cooking spray
- 4 pork loin chops, cut ½ inch thick (about 1½ pounds total)
- 1 medium onion, halved and sliced

1. In a small bowl combine mustard, Italian dressing, and pepper; set aside. Trim fat from the chops. Coat an unheated large skillet with cooking spray. Preheat the skillet on medium-high heat; add the chops; cook until brown on both sides, turning once. Remove chops from skillet.

2. Add onion to skillet. Cook and stir on medium heat for 3 minutes. Push onion aside; return chops to skillet. Spread mustard mixture on chops. Cover and cook on medium-low heat about 15 minutes or until done (160°F). Spoon onion mixture over chops. **MAKES 4 SERVINGS.**

Per serving: 163 cal., 5 g total fat (2 g sat. fat), 53 mg chol., 403 mg sodium, 2 g carbo., 0 g fiber, 22 g pro.

Pork and Pumpkin Noodle Bowl ♡

Start to Finish: 30 minutes

- 8 ounces whole wheat linguine
- 1 small red onion, thinly sliced
- 1 tablespoon olive oil
- 1 pound pork loin, cut into ½-inch-thick slices
- 3 tablespoons reduced-sodium soy sauce Black pepper
- 12 fresh sage leaves
- 2 cloves garlic, minced, or ½ teaspoon garlic powder
- 1 cup canned or frozen pureed pumpkin or butternut squash
- 1 cup water
- ¼ cup blue cheese crumbles (optional)

1. Cook pasta according to package directions, adding onion during last 5 minutes of cooking time. Drain and keep warm.

2. Meanwhile, in an extra-large skillet heat oil. Brush pork with some soy sauce and generously sprinkle with pepper. Cook sage leaves in hot oil until crisp. Drain on paper towels. Add pork to skillet and cook for 2 minutes on each side or until golden outside and slightly pink inside. Remove pork from skillet; cover to keep warm.

3. In the same skillet combine remaining soy sauce, garlic, ¼ cup of the pumpkin, and the water. Bring to boiling; reduce sauce slightly. Add pasta and onions to skillet; heat through. In a small skillet heat remaining pumpkin.

4. Divide pasta among 4 bowls. Serve pork with pasta, pumpkin, sage leaves, and blue cheese. **MAKES 4 SERVINGS.**

Per serving: 414 cal., 9 g total fat (2 g sat. fat), 71 mg chol., 645 mg sodium, 51 g carbo., 2 g fiber, 34 g pro.

Stuffed Shells
with Eggplant
Sauce

Stuffed Shells with Eggplant Sauce

Prep: 45 minutes **Bake:** 33 minutes
Oven: 375°F

- 30 jumbo pasta shells, cooked and drained
- 3 links hot or sweet Italian sausage, casings removed
- 8 ounces fresh mushrooms, finely chopped
- 1/2 cup finely chopped onion (1 medium)
- 1 egg, lightly beaten
- 1 cup ricotta cheese
- 1 3/4 cups shredded Italian blend cheese (7 ounces)
- 1 cup baby spinach leaves
- 3/4 teaspoon kosher salt
- 1 small eggplant (12 ounces), trimmed and chopped
- 1 26- to 28-ounce jar garden-style pasta sauce

1. In a nonstick large skillet cook sausage, mushrooms, and onion over medium heat until sausage is browned and vegetables are tender. Remove mixture from skillet; set aside. In a large bowl combine egg, ricotta cheese, 1/2 cup of the Italian cheese blend, the spinach, and 1/4 teaspoon of the salt. Stir in sausage mixture.
2. For eggplant sauce, in the same skillet cook eggplant until tender. Add pasta sauce and the remaining 1/2 teaspoon salt. Bring to boiling; remove from heat.
3. Preheat oven to 375°F. Spoon two-thirds of the eggplant sauce into a 3-quart rectangular baking dish. Fill each pasta shell with 2 tablespoons of the sausage mixture and arrange in dish. Spoon remaining sauce over filled shells.
4. Bake, covered, about 25 minutes or until sauce is bubbly. Sprinkle with the remaining 1 1/4 cups Italian cheese blend. Bake, uncovered, 8 to 10 minutes more or until cheese is melted. **MAKES 10 SERVINGS.**

Per serving: 350 cal., 13 g total fat (5 g sat. fat), 60 mg chol., 920 mg sodium, 40 g carbo., 3 g fiber, 20 g pro.

Pork and Noodle Salad Bowls

Start to Finish: 15 minutes

- 1 3-ounce package ramen noodles (any variety)
- 1 17-ounce package cooked pork roast au jus, unheated
- 1 cup fresh pea pods, strings and tips removed
- 1/4 cup cider vinegar
- 3 tablespoons salad oil
- 1 tablespoon soy sauce
- 8 butterhead (Boston or Bibb) lettuce leaves
- 1/3 cup butter toffee glaze-flavor sliced almonds

1. Cook noodles according to package directions, except discard seasoning packet; drain. Meanwhile, remove pork roast from au jus; discard au jus. Cut pork into large chunks and place in a large bowl. Add hot noodles and pea pods to pork in bowl.
2. In a screw-top jar combine vinegar, oil, and soy sauce; cover and shake well. Pour over pork mixture; toss to combine.
3. Place lettuce leaves on 4 dinner plates. Spoon pork mixture into lettuce leaves. Sprinkle with almonds. **MAKES 4 SERVINGS.**

Per serving: 409 cal., 24 g total fat (5 g sat. fat), 72 mg chol., 832 mg sodium, 19 g carbo., 2 g fiber, 30 g pro.

Spicy Orange-Glazed Pork Chops

Prep: 10 minutes **Grill:** 12 minutes

- 1/4 cup orange marmalade
- 2 teaspoons Dijon mustard
- 1 teaspoon lemon juice
- 1/8 to 1/4 teaspoon cayenne pepper
- 4 boneless pork loin chops, cut 3/4 inch thick
  Salt and black pepper

1. For the glaze, in a small bowl stir together orange marmalade, mustard, lemon juice, and cayenne pepper. Set glaze aside.
2. Trim fat from chops. Sprinkle chops with salt and black pepper. For a charcoal grill, grill chops on the greased rack of an uncovered grill directly over medium coals for 12 to 15 minutes or until done (160°F), turning once and brushing frequently with glaze during the last few minutes of grilling. (For a gas grill, preheat grill. Reduce heat to medium. Place chops on grill rack over heat. Cover and grill as above.) **MAKES 4 SERVINGS.**

Per serving: 263 cal., 10 g total fat (3 g sat. fat), 92 mg chol., 126 mg sodium, 5 g carbo., 0 g fiber, 37 g pro.

Pork has the delightful quality of being crisp-cooked on the outside while remaining juicy on the inside.

Pork and Hominy Skillet

Start to Finish: 20 minutes

    1 tablespoon vegetable oil
    1 large sweet onion, cut into wedges
    2 medium carrots, thinly sliced
    1 17-ounce package refrigerated cooked
       pork roast au jus
    2 8.8-ounce pouches cooked whole grain
       brown rice
    1 15-ounce can yellow hominy, rinsed and
       drained
  2/3 cup water
       Black pepper

1. In a very large skillet heat oil over medium heat. Add onion and carrots to hot oil; cook for 5 minutes.
2. Add pork with juices, breaking up meat with the back of a wooden spoon. Add rice, drained hominy, and the water. Cook, covered, about 5 minutes, stirring occasionally, until heated through. Season to taste with pepper. **MAKES 4 SERVINGS.**

Per serving: 503 cal., 14 g total fat (3 g sat. fat), 72 mg chol., 742 mg sodium, 63 g carbo., 5 g fiber, 32 g pro.

Easy Skillet Lasagna

Start to Finish: 25 minutes

    1 pound bulk Italian sausage
    1 8-ounce package sliced fresh mushrooms
  3/4 cup chopped green sweet pepper
       (1 medium)
  1/2 cup chopped onion (1 medium)
    8 ounces dried campanelle or mafalda pasta
    1 26-ounce jar mushroom pasta sauce
    1 cup shredded Italian cheese blend
       (4 ounces)
       Snipped fresh parsley (optional)

1. In an extra-large skillet cook sausage, mushrooms, sweet pepper, and onion on medium heat until sausage is no longer pink and vegetables are tender. Drain off fat.
2. Meanwhile, cook pasta according to package directions; drain.
3. Stir pasta and pasta sauce into mixture in skillet. Return to a simmer. Sprinkle with cheese. Cook, covered, over low heat until cheese melts. If desired, sprinkle with parsley. **MAKES 4 TO 6 SERVINGS.**

Per serving: 892 cal., 49 g total fat (19 g sat. fat), 106 mg chol., 1,881 mg sodium, 78 g carbo., 8 g fiber, 36 g pro.

Apple-Glazed Pork Loaf

Start to Finish: 30 minutes **Oven:** 425°F

  1/2 cup apple jelly
    1 tablespoon Dijon mustard
    2 small apples
    2 eggs, lightly beaten
    1 pound ground pork
  1/2 teaspoon salt
  1/2 teaspoon black pepper
    1 medium sweet potato, chopped
    1 tablespoon olive oil
       Salt and black pepper
  1/8 teaspoon cayenne pepper (optional)
    2 ciabatta sandwich rolls, split and toasted

1. Preheat oven to 425°F. Grease a 15×10×1-inch baking pan; set aside. For apple glaze, in a small microwave-safe bowl microwave jelly on high about 30 seconds or until jelly melts. Stir in mustard. Set aside. Chop 1 apple; set aside.
2. In a large bowl combine eggs, ground meat, half of the chopped apple, the 1/2 teaspoon salt, and the 1/2 teaspoon pepper. Form into four 6×2-inch loaves. Place in prepared baking pan. Spoon a small amount of apple glaze over each loaf. Bake for 10 minutes.
3. Meanwhile, thinly slice the remaining apple. Top loaves with some of the apple slices; drizzle loaves with a little more apple glaze. Bake for 5 to 10 minutes more or until an instant-read thermometer inserted in centers registers 160°F (see note, page 103).
4. Place sweet potato in a large microwave-safe bowl. Microwave, uncovered, on high about 4 minutes or until nearly tender.
5. Meanwhile, in a large skillet heat oil over medium-high heat. Add sweet potato and the remaining chopped apple. Season with salt, black pepper, and, if desired, cayenne pepper. Cook and stir for 3 to 4 minutes or until potato and apple are tender and golden.
6. Place a pork loaf on each roll half. Serve with the sweet potato mixture. Drizzle with any remaining apple glaze. **MAKES 4 SERVINGS.**

Per serving: 697 cal., 32 g total fat (11 g sat. fat), 187 mg chol., 842 mg sodium, 74 g carbo., 5 g fiber, 28 g pro.

Skillet suppers—tasty and quick melanges of meat, vegetables, and pasta or grains—are fun to make and satisfying to eat.

Quick
Pepperoni
Pasta

Quick Pepperoni Pasta

Start to Finish: 30 minutes

    6 ounces dried spaghetti pasta, broken
       in half
    3 cups sliced fresh mushrooms (8 ounces)
  2/3 cup cubed pepperoni (3 ounces)
    1 tablespoon butter
    8 ounces fresh spinach, torn (6 cups)
  1/4 cup grated Parmesan cheese
    2 tablespoons snipped fresh basil
    1 teaspoon lemon juice
       Breadsticks (optional)

1. Cook pasta according to package
directions; drain.

2. Meanwhile, in a very large skillet cook
mushrooms and pepperoni in butter over
medium heat for 5 minutes or until
mushrooms are just tender. Drain off fat. Stir
in spinach. Cook and stir for 1 minute or until
spinach begins to wilt. Remove from heat.

3. In a large bowl toss together pasta,
pepperoni mixture, 3 tablespoons of the
Parmesan cheese, the basil, and lemon juice.
Sprinkle with remaining Parmesan cheese.
If desired, serve with breadsticks.

MAKES 4 SERVINGS.

Per serving: 344 cal., 14 g total fat (5 g sat. fat), 32 mg
chol., 604 mg sodium, 39 g carbo., 2 g fiber, 15 g pro.

Rotini-
Kielbasa
Skillet

Rotini-Kielbasa Skillet

Start to Finish: 35 minutes

    2 cups dried rotini or rotelle pasta (about
       6 ounces)
    1 tablespoon olive oil
    1 medium onion, cut into wedges
    2 cloves garlic, minced
    1 pound cooked kielbasa, halved lengthwise
       and sliced diagonally
    1 small zucchini, cut into matchstick-size
       strips

    1 yellow or orange sweet pepper, cut into
       thin bit-size strips
    1 teaspoon dried Italian seasoning, crushed
  1/8 teaspoon cayenne pepper
    8 plum tomatoes, cored and chopped (about
       1 pound)

1. Cook pasta according to package
directions; drain. Meanwhile, in a very large
skillet heat oil over medium-high heat. Add
onion and garlic and cook for 1 minute. Add
kielbasa; cook until onion is tender, stirring
frequently.

2. Add zucchini, sweet pepper, Italian
seasoning, and cayenne pepper; cook and
stir for 5 minutes. Stir in tomatoes and
cooked pasta. Heat through, stirring
occasionally. If desired, garnish with fresh
herbs. **MAKES 6 SERVINGS.**

Per serving: 400 cal., 26 g total fat (11 g sat. fat),
33 mg chol., 622 mg sodium, 29 g carb., 3 g dietary
fiber, 14 g pro.

Greek-Style Pasta Skillet

Greek-Style Pasta Skillet

Start to Finish: 30 minutes

- 12 ounces ground lamb or ground beef
- 1/2 cup chopped onion (1 medium)
- 1 14.5-ounce can diced tomatoes, undrained
- 1 5.5-ounce can tomato juice
- 1/2 cup water
- 1/2 teaspoon instant beef bouillon granules
- 1/2 teaspoon ground cinnamon
- 1/8 teaspoon garlic powder
- 1 cup packaged dried medium shell macaroni or elbow macaroni
- 1 cup frozen cut green beans
- 1/2 cup crumbled feta cheese (2 ounces)

1. In a large skillet cook ground meat and onion until meat is no longer pink. Drain off fat. Stir in undrained tomatoes, tomato juice, the water, bouillon granules, cinnamon, and garlic powder. Bring to boiling.

2. Stir uncooked macaroni and green beans into meat mixture. Return to boiling; reduce heat. Simmer, covered, about 15 minutes or until macaroni and green beans are tender. Sprinkle with feta cheese. **MAKES 4 SERVINGS.**

Per serving: 362 cal., 16 g total fat (7 g sat. fat), 70 mg chol., 647 mg sodium, 33 g carbo., 2 g fiber, 22 g pro.

Herbed Lamb Steak Salad

Start to Finish: 20 minutes

- 1 pound lamb arm steaks, 1/2 inch thick
- 1 tablespoon olive oil
  Salt and black pepper
- 1 5-ounce package mixed salad greens with herbs
- 2/3 cup sliced fresh radishes
- 1 6-ounce container plain yogurt
- 1 to 2 tablespoons snipped fresh mint
  Herbed feta cheese

1. Heat a grill pan over medium-high heat. Trim fat from steaks. Brush steaks with oil; sprinkle lightly with salt and pepper. Place steaks on a grill pan. Cook steaks for 8 to 12 minutes for medium (160°F), turning once halfway through cooking. Transfer steaks to a cutting board. Cover; let stand for 2 minutes.

2. Meanwhile, divide salad greens and radishes among 4 plates. For dressing, in a small bowl combine yogurt and mint; season with salt and pepper.

3. Remove bones from lamb. Cut lamb into strips; place meat on salad greens. Sprinkle with feta cheese; pass dressing.

MAKES 4 SERVINGS.

Per serving: 344 cal., 26 g total fat (10 g sat. fat), 82 mg chol., 258 mg sodium, 5 g carbo., 1 g fiber, 22 g pro.

Poultry

Chicken Caribbean with Coconut-Orange Sauce

Chicken-Pineapple Fajitas ♡

Start to Finish: 20 minutes **Oven:** 350°F

- 8 6-inch flour tortillas
  Nonstick cooking spray
- 4 1-inch slices peeled fresh pineapple
- 1 pound skinless, boneless chicken breast halves
- 2 small red and/or orange sweet peppers, cut into thin bite-size strips
- 2 teaspoons Jamaican jerk seasoning
- 1/8 teaspoon black pepper
- 1 tablespoon vegetable oil
  Fresh cilantro (optional)
  Lime wedges (optional)

1. Preheat oven to 350°F. Wrap tortillas in foil. Place foil packet in the oven. Meanwhile, lightly coat an extra-large nonstick skillet with cooking spray; heat over medium-high heat. Add pineapple. Cook for 4 to 6 minutes or until light brown, turning once. Transfer pineapple to a cutting board; set aside.
2. Meanwhile, cut chicken into thin strips. In a large bowl toss chicken and sweet peppers with jerk seasoning and black pepper.
3. In the same skillet heat the oil over medium-high heat; add chicken mixture. Cook and stir for 4 to 6 minutes or until chicken is no longer pink.
4. Meanwhile, core and coarsely chop pineapple slices. Divide pineapple and chicken mixture among the warm tortillas. If desired, serve with cilantro and lime wedges.
MAKES 4 SERVINGS.

Per serving: 393 cal., 10 g total fat (2 g sat. fat), 66 mg chol., 633 mg sodium, 43 g carbo., 4 g fiber, 32 g pro.

Chicken Caribbean with Coconut-Orange Sauce

Start to Finish: 25 minutes

- 1/2 teaspoon Jamaican jerk seasoning
- 4 skinless, boneless chicken breast halves (1 1/4 to 1 1/2 pounds total)
- 1/2 cup canned unsweeteend coconut milk
- 1/2 teaspoon finely shredded orange peel (optional)
- 1/4 cup fresh orange juice
- 1 tablespoon snipped fresh basil
- 2 cups hot cooked rice
- 1 tablespoon thinly sliced basil
  Orange slices (optional)

1. Rub jerk seasoning evenly over both sides of chicken. For a charcoal grill, grill chicken on the rack of an uncovered grill directly over medium coals for 12 to 15 minutes or until no longer pink (170°F), turning once halfway through grilling. (For a gas grill, preheat grill. Reduce heat to medium. Place chicken on grill rack over heat. Cover and grill as above.)
2. Meanwhile, for sauce, in a small saucepan combine coconut milk, orange peel (if desired), orange juice, and the snipped basil. Bring to boiling; reduce heat. Simmer, uncovered, about 5 minutes or until sauce is reduced to 1/2 cup.
3. Serve chicken with sauce and rice; sprinkle with sliced basil. If desired, garnish with orange slices. **MAKES 4 SERVINGS.**

Per serving: 294 cal., 8 g total fat (6 g sat. fat), 66 mg chol., 108 mg sodium, 25 g carbo., 0 g fiber, 29 g pro.

Chicken-
Pineapple
Fajitas

Chicken
Piccata

Chicken Piccata

Start to Finish: 20 minutes

- 4 small skinless, boneless chicken breast halves (1¼ pounds total)
- 1 tablespoon Dijon mustard
  Salt and black pepper
- ¼ cup seasoned fine dry bread crumbs
- ¼ cup olive oil
- 2 small lemons
- 8 ounces haricots verts, trimmed if desired, or green beans, trimmed and halved lengthwise
- 1 tablespoon capers
  Hot buttered pasta (optional)

1. Place a chicken breast half between 2 sheets of plastic wrap. Using the flat side of a meat mallet lightly pound to an even thickness; discard plastic wrap. Repeat with remaining chicken breast halves. Brush chicken lightly with Dijon mustard; sprinkle with salt and pepper. Place chicken on a waxed paper-lined baking sheet. Sprinkle chicken with crumbs to coat.

2. Heat 2 tablespoons of the oil in an extra-large skillet over medium-high heat; add chicken breast halves; cook 4 minutes per side or until no pink remains.

3. Meanwhile, slice 1 lemon. Transfer chicken to serving plates. Add remaining oil to skillet. Cook haricots verts in hot oil for 4 to 5 minutes or until crisp-tender, adding the lemon slices the last minute of cooking. Using a slotted spoon, remove beans to plates. Juice remaining lemon. Add lemon juice and capers to skillet; cook for 30 seconds. Drizzle on chicken and beans. Serve with pasta. **MAKES 4 SERVINGS.**

Per serving: 362 cal., 16 g total fat (3 g sat. fat), 99 mg chol., 546 mg sodium, 13 g carbo., 4 g fiber, 42 g pro.

Sautéed Chicken with Garlicky Pasta

Sautéed Chicken with Garlicky Pasta

Start to Finish: 20 minutes

- 1 pound dried angel hair pasta
- 4 skinless, boneless chicken breast halves (1¼ to 1½ pounds total)
- 2 teaspoons snipped fresh thyme
- ¼ cup olive oil
- 8 ounces mushrooms, sliced
- 1 large red onion, sliced
- 3 cloves garlic, minced
- 1 14-ounce can chicken broth
- 1 tablespoon all-purpose flour
- 1 teaspoon Dijon mustard
- 6 plum tomatoes, thinly sliced
- ¼ cup snipped fresh parsley

1. Cook pasta according to package directions. Drain and return to pot.

2. Meanwhile, combine 1 teaspoon of the thyme, ¼ teaspoon salt, and ⅛ teaspoon black pepper. Sprinkle over chicken. In a large skillet cook chicken in 1 tablespoon hot oil until no longer pink (170°F), turning once. Remove from skillet; keep warm.

2. In same skillet cook mushrooms, onion, and garlic in 1 tablespoon of the oil until tender. Remove and set aside. In a bowl whisk together broth, flour, and mustard. Add to skillet; cook until thickened and bubbly. Add tomatoes, parsley, and remaining 1 teaspoon thyme. Reduce heat; simmmer for 1 minute.

3. Toss pasta with remaining 2 tablespoons oil, ½ teaspoon salt, and ⅛ teaspoon black pepper. Add mushroom mixture and tomato mixture; toss to mix. Serve with chicken.

MAKES 4 SERVINGS.

Per serving: 595 cal., 15 g total fat (2 g sat. fat), 53 mg chol., 790 mg sodium, 79 g carbo., 4 g fiber, 36 g pro.

Spicy Chinese Chicken with Eggplant

12 ounces skinless, boneless chicken breast halves
6 cups torn mixed greens
1/2 of a medium cantaloupe, seeded, peeled, and cut into 1-inch chunks
1 cup raspberries
1 small apple, cored and sliced
1 recipe Mango Vinaigrette
1/4 cup thinly sliced green onions (2)

1. Seed, peel, and cube the mangoes. Measure 1 cup mango cubes for use in the vinaigrette; set remaining mango cubes aside for salad.
2. In a small bowl stir together curry powder, pepper, and salt. Sprinkle chicken evenly with curry mixture; rub in with your fingers.
3. For charcoal grill, grill chicken on the rack of an uncovered grill directly over medium coals for 12 to 15 minutes or until tender and no longer pink (170°F), turning once halfway through grilling. (For gas grill, preheat grill. Reduce heat to medium. Place chicken on grill rack over heat. Cover and grill as above.) (Or preheat broiler. Place chicken on the unheated rack of a broiler pan. Broil 4 to 5 inches from the heat for 10 to 12 minutes or until tender and no longer pink [170°F], turning once.) Cool chicken slightly; slice into 1/4-inch-wide strips.
4. Arrange greens on 4 serving plates. Top greens with chicken strips, cantaloupe, raspberries, apple slices, and reserved mango cubes. Drizzle salads with Mango Vinaigrette. Sprinkle with green onions.

Mango Vinaigrette In a blender or food processor combine the 1 cup mango cubes, 3 tablespoons orange juice, 2 tablespoons rice vinegar or white wine vinegar, 2 teaspoons honey, and 1 teaspoon Dijon mustard. Cover and blend or process until smooth. Cover and chill until serving time (up to 2 hours). **MAKES 4 SERVINGS.**

Per serving: 253 cal., 2 g total fat (0 g sat. fat), 49 mg chol., 173 mg sodium, 39 g carbo., 7 g fiber, 22 g pro.

Spicy Chinese Chicken with Eggplant ♡

Start to Finish: 30 minutes

4 cups eggplant cut into thin bite-size strips
2 tablespoons soy sauce
1 tablespoon cornstarch
1 tablespoon dry sherry or water
8 ounces cooked chicken, cut into bite-size strips
2 tablespoons vegetable oil
4 or 5 fresh jalapeños, seeded and thinly sliced (see note, page 12)
1/2 cup chicken broth
1 clove garlic, minced
1 tablespoon very finely chopped fresh ginger
3 cups hot cooked rice or cellophane noodles

1. In a large bowl cover eggplant strips with boiling water; let stand for 5 minutes. Drain and set aside. (Eggplant may darken.)

2. Meanwhile, in a large bowl combine soy sauce, cornstarch, and sherry. Add chicken, stirring to coat; set aside.
3. In a large saucepan heat oil; add jalapeños. Cook and stir about 4 minutes or until tender. Remove jalapeños from pan. Add chicken mixture to pan; cook and stir for 3 to 4 minutes or until chicken is heated through and sauce has thickened. Stir in eggplant, jalapeños, broth, garlic, and ginger. Heat through. Serve with rice. **MAKES 6 SERVINGS.**

Per serving: 340 cal., 8 g total fat (2 g sat. fat), 50 mg chol., 655 mg sodium, 42 g carbo., 4 g fiber, 22 g pro.

Chicken and Fruit Salad with Mango Vinaigrette ♡

Prep: 20 minutes **Grill:** 12 minutes

2 medium mangoes
1/2 teaspoon curry powder
1/4 teaspoon coarsely ground black pepper
1/8 teaspoon salt

Chicken and Fruit Salad with Mango Vinaigrette

Papaya and Coconut Chicken Salad

Papaya and Coconut Chicken Salad

Start to Finish: 30 minutes **Oven:** 450°F

- 1 pound skinless, boneless chicken breast halves
- ¹/₂ teaspoon salt
- 1¹/₂ cups flaked coconut
- 1 medium papaya
- ¹/₄ cup cider vinegar
- ¹/₄ cup vegetable oil
- 1 tablespoon honey
- ¹/₄ teaspoon salt
  Dash cayenne pepper
- 1 5-ounce package mixed salad greens
- ³/₄ cup blueberries

1. Heat oven to 450°F. Line a baking sheet with foil; set aside. Cut chicken into strips; season with salt. Place coconut in shallow dish. Roll chicken in coconut to coat, pressing lightly to adhere. Transfer to prepared baking sheet. Bake about 12 minutes or until coconut is golden and chicken is no longer pink.

2. Meanwhile, peel, seed, and cut papaya into cubes. For dressing, place ¹/₄ cup papaya cubes in blender or food processor; add vinegar, oil, honey, the ¹/₄ teaspoon salt, and cayenne pepper. Process until smooth. Toss ¹/₄ cup dressing with greens; divide among 4 plates.

3. Top greens with chicken, remaining papaya, and blueberries. Pass remaining dressing. **MAKES 4 SERVINGS.**

Per serving: 526 cal., 30 g total fat (15 g sat. fat), 66 mg chol., 639 mg sodium, 35 g carbo., 6 g fiber, 30 g pro.

Grilled Greek Chicken Salad

Prep: 30 minutes **Marinate:** 4 to 24 hours
Grill: 12 minutes

- 4 skinless, boneless chicken breast halves (1¹/₄ to 1¹/₂ pounds total)
- 1 tablespoon lemon juice
- 1 tablespoon olive oil
- 1 tablespoon snipped fresh oregano or 1 teaspoon dried oregano, crushed
- 2 cloves garlic, minced

Grilled Greek Chicken Salad

- ¹/₄ teaspooon black pepper
- 3 medium cucumbers, seeded and coarsely chopped
- 2 medium red and/or yellow tomatoes, coarsely chopped
- ¹/₂ cup sliced red onion
  Mixed salad greens (optional)
- ¹/₃ cup bottled reduced-calorie creamy cucumber salad dressing
- ¹/₂ cup crumbled feta cheese (2 ounces)
- ¹/₄ cup pitted kalamata olives or ripe olives

1. Put chicken in a resealable plastic bag set in a shallow dish. For marinade, in a small bowl combine lemon juice, olive oil, oregano, garlic, and pepper. Pour marinade over chicken. Seal bag; turn to coat chicken. Marinate in the refrigerator for 4 to 24 hours, turning bag occasionally.

2. Meanwhile, in a medium bowl toss together cucumbers, tomatoes, and onion.

3. Drain chicken, discarding marinade. For a charcoal grill, grill on the rack of an uncovered grill directly over medium coals for 12 to 15 minutes or until tender and no longer pink (170°F), turning once. (For a gas grill, preheat grill. Reduce heat to medium. Place chicken on grill rack over heat. Cover; grill as above.)

4. Transfer chicken to a cutting board; cut into bite-size pieces. Toss chicken with cucumber mixture. If desired, serve on salad greens. Drizzle with salad dressing. Sprinkle with cheese and olives. **MAKES 4 SERVINGS.**

Per serving: 328 cal., 13 g total fat (3 g sat. fat), 95 mg chol., 626 mg sodium, 15 g carbo., 3 g fiber, 37 g pro.

Tarragon
Chicken
Linguine

Tarragon Chicken Linguine

Start to Finish: 25 minutes

- 6 ounces dried linguine or fettuccine pasta
- 2 cups broccoli florets
- 1/2 cup reduced-sodium chicken broth
- 2 teaspoons cornstarch
- 1/4 teaspoon lemon-pepper seasoning or black pepper
- 3 skinless, boneless chicken breast halves (12 ounces total), cut into bite-size strips
- 2 teaspoons olive oil or vegetable oil
- 1 tablespoon snipped fresh tarragon or dill or 1/2 teaspoon dried tarragon or dill, crushed

1. Cook pasta according to directions, adding broccoli the last 4 minutes. Drain; keep warm.

2. Combine broth, cornstarch, and seasoning; set aside.

3. In a large nonstick skillet cook chicken in hot oil 4 minutes or until no longer pink, stirring often.

4. Stir cornstarch mixture; add to skillet. Cook and stir until thickened. Stir in tarragon; cook for 2 minutes. Serve over pasta.

MAKES 4 SERVINGS.

Per serving: 293 cal., 4 g total fat (1 g sat. fat), 49 mg chol., 153 mg sodium, 36 g carbo., 2 g fiber, 27 g pro.

Tip If you don't have cornstarch on hand, you may substitute 4 teaspoons all-purpose flour for the 2 teaspoons of cornstarch.

Chicken-Tortilla Bake ♡

Prep: 15 minutes **Bake:** 45 minutes
Oven: 350°F

- 2 10.75-ounce cans reduced-sodium condensed cream of chicken soup
- 1 10-ounce can diced tomatoes with green chiles, undrained
- 12 6- or 7-inch corn tortillas, cut into thin bite-size strips
- 3 cups cubed cooked chicken (1 pound)
- 1 cup shredded taco cheese (4 ounces)

1. Preheat oven to 350°F. In a medium bowl stir together soup and undrained tomatoes; set aside.

2. Sprinkle one-third of the tortilla strips over the bottom of an ungreased 3-quart rectangular baking dish. Layer half of the chicken over tortilla strips; spoon half of the soup mixture on top. Repeat layers. Sprinkle with remaining tortilla strips.

3. Bake, covered, about 40 minutes or until bubbly around edges and center is hot. Uncover and sprinkle with cheese. Bake about 5 minutes more or until cheese is melted.

MAKES 8 SERVINGS.

Per serving: 291 cal., 10 g total fat (4 g sat. fat), 64 mg chol., 658 mg sodium, 28 g carbo., 2 g fiber, 22 g pro.

Chicken-
Tortilla Bake

Asian
Chicken
Salad

Chicken, Goat Cheese, and Greens

Prep: 15 minutes **Bake:** 15 minutes
Oven: 350°F

1¹/₂ pounds Swiss chard, beet greens, and/or
mustard greens, trimmed and washed
1 2- to 2¹/₂-pound purchased deli-roasted
chicken
3 tablespoons olive oil
2 tablespoons lemon juice
2 tablespoons snipped fresh dill, oregano,
and/or sage
¹/₄ teaspoon sea salt, kosher salt, or salt
¹/₈ teaspoon cracked black pepper
1 3- to 4-ounce log goat cheese (chèvre),
sliced into rounds or coarsely crumbled
¹/₈ teaspoon cracked black pepper

1. Preheat oven to 350°F. Reserve 1 or
2 small leaves of Swiss chard. Tear remaining
chard and place in a 3-quart rectangular
baking dish. Remove string from chicken; use
the string to tie the chicken legs together.
Place chicken on chard in dish.
2. In a small bowl combine oil and lemon
juice. Drizzle oil mixture over chicken and
chard in baking dish. Sprinkle 1 tablespoon
of the dill, oregano, and/or sage over the
chicken and chard. Sprinkle the salt and
¹/₈ teaspoon pepper only over the torn chard.
3. Loosely cover baking dish with foil. Bake
for 15 to 20 minutes or until torn chard is
tender. Meanwhile, sprinkle cheese with
remaining 1 tablespoon snipped dill and
¹/₈ teaspoon pepper.

4. Transfer chicken to a serving platter. Place
some of the goat cheese on top of chicken.
Add reserved chard leaves. Toss cooked
chard in dish to evenly coat with cooking
liquid. Serve cooked chard and remaining
cheese with chicken. **MAKES 4 SERVINGS.**

Per serving: 542 cal., 36 g total fat (10 g sat. fat), 143 mg
chol., 620 mg sodium, 7 g carbo., 3 g fiber, 48 g pro.

Tip This recipe doubles easily to serve
8. Double the ingredients and prepare as
directed, except place all the greens and both
chickens in a large shallow roasting pan.

Asian Chicken Salad ♡

Start to Finish: 15 minutes

1 10-ounce package torn mixed salad
greens
8 ounces cooked chicken, cut into bite-size
pieces
¹/₃ cup bottled Asian vinaigrette salad
dressing
1 11-ounce can mandarin orange sections,
drained
3 tablespoons sliced almonds, toasted

1. In a large bowl combine greens and
chicken. Add salad dressing; toss to coat.
Divide greens mixture among 4 salad plates.
Top with mandarin orange sections and
almonds. Serve immediately.
MAKES 4 SERVINGS.

Per serving: 218 cal., 9 g total fat (1 g sat. fat), 50 mg
chol., 502 mg sodium, 15 g carbo., 2 g fiber, 19 g pro.

Lemon-Dill Butter Chicken and Cucumbers

over medium heat for 3 to 4 minutes or just until cucumber is tender. Spoon sauce over chicken. **MAKES 4 SERVINGS.**

Per serving: 244 cal., 11 g total fat (6 g sat. fat), 107 mg chol., 477 mg sodium, 2 g carbo., 0 g fiber, 33 g pro.

Tip Choose lemons with smooth, bright color skin with no tinge of green. They should be firm, plump, and heavy for their size. Refrigerate lemons in a plastic bag for 2 to 3 weeks.

Mediterranean Chicken and Pasta ♡

Start to Finish: 20 minutes

    1 6-ounce jar marinated artichoke hearts
    1 tablespoon olive oil
   12 ounces skinless, boneless chicken
       breasts, cut into bite-size pieces
    3 cloves garlic, thinly sliced
  ¹/₄ cup chicken broth
  ¹/₄ cup dry white wine
    1 teaspoon dried oregano, crushed
    1 cup roasted red sweet peppers, drained
       and cut into strips
  ¹/₄ cup pitted kalamata olives
    3 cups hot cooked campanelle or penne
       pasta
  ¹/₄ cup crumbled feta cheese (optional)

1. Drain artichokes, reserving marinade. Cut up any large pieces. Set aside. In a large skillet heat oil over medium-high heat. Add chicken and garlic. Cook and stir until chicken is brown. Add the reserved artichoke marinade, broth, wine, and oregano.
2. Bring to boiling; reduce heat. Simmer, covered, for 10 minutes. Stir in artichokes, peppers, and olives. Heat through.
3. To serve, spoon the chicken mixture over pasta. If desired, sprinkle with feta cheese. **MAKES 4 SERVINGS.**

Per serving: 347 cal., 9 g total fat (1 g sat. fat), 49 mg chol., 323 mg sodium, 38 g carbo., 3 g fiber, 26 g pro.

Lemon-Dill Butter Chicken and Cucumbers

Prep: 10 minutes **Broil:** 12 minutes

    4 skinless, boneless chicken breast halves
       (1¹/₄ to 1¹/₂ pounds total)
    1 medium lemon
    3 tablespoons butter
  ¹/₂ teaspoon dried dill
  ¹/₄ teaspoon salt
  ¹/₄ teaspoon black pepper
 1¹/₂ cups coarsely chopped cucumber or
       zucchini

1. Preheat broiler. Place chicken on the unheated rack of a broiler pan. Broil 4 to 5 inches from heat for 12 to 15 minutes or until tender and no longer pink (170°F), turning once halfway through broiling.
2. Meanwhile, finely shred ¹/₂ teaspoon peel from the lemon. Cut lemon in half; squeeze lemon to get 2 tablespoons juice.
3. In a small skillet melt butter over medium heat. Stir in lemon peel, lemon juice, dill, salt, and pepper. Stir in cucumber. Cook and stir

Mediterranean
Chicken and
Pasta

Asian Chicken and Vegetables

Asian Chicken and Vegetables ♡

Prep: 10 minutes **Bake:** 40 minutes
Oven: 400°F

- 8 chicken drumsticks and/or thighs, skinned (about 2 pounds total)
- 1 tablespoon vegetable oil
- 1½ teaspoons five-spice powder
- ⅓ cup bottled plum sauce or sweet-and-sour sauce
- 1 14-ounce package frozen baby whole potatoes, broccoli, carrots, baby corn, and red pepper mix or one 16-ounce package frozen stir-fry vegetables (any combination)

1. Preheat oven to 400°F. Arrange the chicken pieces in a 13×9×2-inch baking pan, making sure pieces do not touch. Brush chicken pieces with vegetable oil; sprinkle with 1 teaspoon of the five-spice powder. Bake, uncovered, for 25 minutes.

2. Meanwhile, in a large bowl combine plum sauce and the remaining ½ teaspoon five-spice powder. Add frozen vegetables; toss to coat.

3. Move chicken pieces to one side of the baking pan. Add vegetable mixture to the other side of the baking pan. Bake for 15 to 20 minutes more or until chicken is no longer pink (180°F), stirring vegetables once during baking. Using a slotted spoon, transfer chicken and vegetables to a serving platter.
MAKES 4 SERVINGS.

Per serving: 277 cal., 9 g total fat (2 g sat. fat), 98 mg chol., 124 mg sodium, 21 g carbo., 2 g fiber, 30 g pro.

Zesty Chicken with Black Beans and Rice

Zesty Chicken with Black Beans and Rice

Start to Finish: 30 minutes

- 2 tablespoons vegetable oil
- 1 pound skinless, boneless chicken breast halves, cut into 2-inch pieces
- 1 6- to 7.4-ounce package Spanish rice mix
- 1¾ cups water
- 1 15-ounce can black beans, rinsed and drained
- 1 14.5-ounce can diced tomatoes, undrained
  Sour cream, sliced green onions, and lime wedges (optional)

1. In a 12-inch skillet heat 1 tablespoon of the oil over medium-high heat. Add chicken pieces; cook in hot oil until chicken is lightly browned. Remove chicken from skillet and keep warm.

2. Add rice mix and remaining 1 tablespoon oil to skillet; cook and stir for 2 minutes over medium heat. Stir in seasoning packet from rice mix, the water, drained beans, and undrained tomatoes; add chicken. Bring to boiling; reduce heat. Cover and simmer for 15 to 20 minutes, or until rice is tender and chicken is no longer pink. Remove from heat and let stand, covered, for 5 minutes.

3. If desired, serve with sour cream, green onions, and lime wedges. **MAKES 4 SERVINGS.**

Per serving: 424 cal., 9 g total fat (2 g sat. fat), 66 mg chol., 1,080 mg sodium, 52 g carbo., 6 g fiber, 37 g pro.

Grilled Lime Chicken with Pineapple Salsa

Pear and Chicken Salad ♡

Prep: 20 minutes **Grill:** 12 minutes

12 ounces fresh asparagus spears
 2 small pears, halved lengthwise and cored
     (remove stems, if desired)
     Fresh lemon juice
 4 skinless, boneless chicken breast halves
     (1¼ to 1½ pounds total)
 6 cups torn mixed salad greens
     Milk (optional)
 1 recipe Blue Cheese Dressing

1. Snap off and discard woody bases from asparagus. In a large saucepan cook asparagus, covered, in a small amount of boiling lightly salted water for 3 to 5 minutes or until crisp-tender. Drain; set aside.
2. Meanwhile, brush cut sides of pears with lemon juice; set aside. Sprinkle chicken with salt and black pepper.
3. For a charcoal grill, grill chicken on the rack of uncovered grill directly over medium heat for 5 minutes. Turn chicken. Add pears to grill rack, cut sides down. Grill chicken and pears for 7 to 10 minutes more or until chicken is no longer pink (170°F) and pears are tender. If desired, add asparagus the last 3 minutes of grilling. (For a gas grill, preheat grill. Reduce heat to medium. Place chicken, pears, and asparagus on grill rack over heat; grill as above.)
4. Transfer chicken to a cutting board; slice chicken. Cut pear halves in half making 8 quarters. Arrange greens, chicken, and asparagus on serving plates. If necessary, stir milk into Blue Cheese Dressing to reach desired consistency. Spoon dressing over salad. Add pear pieces. **MAKES 4 SERVINGS.**

Blue Cheese Dressing In a small bowl combine ½ cup plain fat-free yogurt, ¼ cup chopped red onion, 2 tablespoons crumbled blue cheese, 1 tablespoon snipped fresh chives, and ⅛ teaspoon ground white pepper. Cover and chill until ready to serve. **MAKES ⅔ CUP.**

Per serving: 243 cal., 3 g total fat (1 g sat. fat), 86 mg chol., 314 mg sodium, 16 g carbo., 4 g fiber, 38 g pro.

Grilled Lime Chicken with Pineapple Salsa ♡

Prep: 20 minutes **Grill:** 12 minutes

½ teaspoon finely shredded lime peel
¼ cup fresh lime juice
 1 tablespoon vegetable oil
¼ teaspoon salt
¼ teaspoon coarsely ground black pepper
 6 skinless, boneless chicken breast halves
     (about 1¾ pounds total)
 3 cups fresh pineapple chunks (1 pound)
 1 cup chopped, seeded tomato (1 large)
½ cup chopped red onion (1 medium)
½ cup chopped green or red sweet pepper
 1 4-ounce can diced green chiles, drained
 2 tablespoons snipped fresh cilantro
½ teaspoon finely shredded lime peel
 2 tablespoons fresh lime juice
 1 clove garlic, minced

1. In a small bowl stir together ½ teaspoon lime peel, the ¼ cup lime juice, the oil, salt, and black pepper. Brush chicken with the lime mixture.
2. For a charcoal grill, grill chicken on the rack of uncovered grill directly over medium coals for 12 to 15 minutes or until chicken is no longer pink (170°F), turning and brushing once with lime mixture. (For a gas grill, preheat grill. Reduce heat to medium. Place chicken on grill rack. Cover; grill as above.) Discard any remaining lime mixture.
3. Meanwhile, for salsa, place pineapple in a food processor or blender. Cover and process or blend until coarsely chopped. Transfer pineapple to a large bowl. Stir in tomato, red onion, sweet pepper, green chiles, cilantro, ½ teaspoon lime peel, the 2 tablespoons lime juice, and the garlic. Cover and refrigerate until serving time. Serve with chicken. **MAKES 6 SERVINGS.**

Per serving: 226 cal., 4 g total fat (1 g sat. fat), 77 mg chol., 240 mg sodium, 15 g carbo., 2 g fiber, 32 g pro.

Chicken with
Green Pumpkin
Seed Mole

Chicken with Green Pumpkin Seed Mole ♡

Start to Finish: 25 minutes

Nonstick cooking spray
4 skinless, boneless chicken breast halves (1¼ to 1½ pounds total)
2 teaspoons vegetable oil
½ cup chopped onion (1 medium)
1 clove garlic, minced
1 13-ounce can tomatillos, rinsed and drained
⅓ cup shelled raw pumpkin seeds (pepitas), toasted*
1 4-ounce can diced green chiles, undrained
¼ cup chicken broth
3 tablespoons snipped fresh cilantro
¼ teaspoon salt
Shelled raw pumpkin seeds (pepitas), toasted* (optional)
Cilantro (optional)

1. Coat an unheated large skillet with cooking spray. Heat skillet over medium heat. Cook chicken in hot skillet for 10 to 12 minutes or until no longer pink (170°F), turning once halfway through cooking. Remove chicken; cover to keep warm.
2. For the mole, in the same skillet heat oil over medium heat. Add onion and garlic; cook about 5 minutes or until onion is tender. In a blender or food processor combine onion mixture, tomatillos, the ⅓ cup toasted pumpkin seeds, the undrained chiles, chicken broth, cilantro, and salt. Cover and blend or process with several on-off turns to a coarse mixture. Transfer mole to the skillet; stir and cook until heated through.
3. To serve, spoon mole on chicken breasts. If desired, sprinkle with additional toasted pumpkin seeds, and cilantro.
MAKES 4 SERVINGS.

Per serving: 202 cal., 7 g total fat (1 g sat. fat), 60 mg chol., 846 mg sodium, 11 g carbo., 3 g fiber, 24 g pro.

*Note To toast pumpkin seeds, spread them in a shallow baking pan. Bake in a 350°F oven about 10 minutes or until toasted, stirring once or twice. Store toasted pumpkin seeds, tightly covered, in the refrigerator for 1 week. For longer storage, freeze them, raw or toasted, up to 1 year.

Lebanese Chicken

Lebanese Chicken

Prep: 10 minutes **Cook:** 16 minutes

1 tablespoon butter or margarine
8 skinless, boneless chicken thighs (about 1½ pounds)
⅓ cup chopped onion (1 small)
1 clove garlic, minced
2 teaspoons finely shredded orange peel
½ cup fresh orange juice
¼ teaspoon salt
¼ teaspoon ground cinnamon
⅛ teaspoon ground allspice
2 tablespoons honey
Orange wedges (optional)
Fresh mint leaves (optional)

1. In a large skillet melt butter over medium heat. Add chicken, onion, and garlic. Cook about 6 minutes or until chicken is browned, turning once.
2. Add orange peel, orange juice, and salt to skillet. Bring to boiling; reduce heat. Simmer, covered, for 5 minutes. Sprinkle chicken with cinnamon and allspice; drizzle with honey. Simmer, uncovered, for 5 to 7 minutes more or until chicken is no longer pink (180°F). If desired, serve with orange wedges and fresh mint. **MAKES 4 SERVINGS.**

Per serving: 408 cal., 11 g total fat (3 g sat. fat), 69 mg chol., 238 mg sodium, 49 g carbo., 8 g fiber, 26 g pro.

Bow Tie Pasta with Chicken and Broccoli

3. Add chicken to drained pasta and broccoli in Dutch oven. Stir in mayonnaise and pepper. Cook over low heat for 1 minute or until heated through, stirring occasionally. Top servings with Parmesan cheese.
MAKES 6 SERVINGS.

Per serving: 309 cal., 9 g total fat (1 g sat. fat), 48 mg chol., 399 mg sodium, 30 g carbo., 4 g fiber, 26 g pro.

Fast Chicken and Rice

Start to Finish: 10 minutes

- $^1/_2$ cup frozen peas
- 1 8.8-ounce package cooked brown or white rice
- 1 tablespoon vegetable oil
- 1 pound chicken breast tenderloins, halved crosswise
- $^1/_4$ cup bottled stir-fry sauce
  Packaged oven-roasted sliced almonds (optional)

1. Stir frozen peas into rice package. Heat rice mixture in microwave following package directions for rice.
2. Meanwhile, in a large skillet heat oil over medium-high heat. Add chicken; cook and stir for 2 to 3 minutes or until no longer pink. Stir rice mixture into skillet. Stir in stir-fry sauce; heat through. If desired, sprinkle with almonds. **MAKES 4 SERVINGS.**

Per serving: 311 cal., 9 g total fat (1 g sat. fat), 66 mg chol., 453 mg sodium, 25 g carbo., 2 g fiber, 31 g pro.

Bow Tie Pasta with Chicken and Broccoli ♡

Start to Finish: 30 minutes

- 8 ounces dried multigrain or regular bow tie or penne pasta (about 2$^1/_2$ cups)
- 3 cups fresh broccoli florets
- 4 skinless, boneless chicken breast halves (1$^1/_4$ to 1$^1/_2$ pounds total), cut into bite-size pieces
- 1 teaspoon adobo seasoning
- 2 tablespoons olive oil, butter, or margarine
- 1 clove garlic, minced
- $^1/_4$ cup light mayonnaise or salad dressing
- $^1/_8$ teaspoon black pepper
- 2 tablespoons finely shredded Parmesan cheese

1. In a Dutch oven cook pasta following package directions, adding broccoli the last 5 minutes of cooking. Drain well. Return to the Dutch oven.
2. Meanwhile, in a medium bowl sprinkle chicken with adobo seasoning; toss to coat. In a large skillet heat olive oil over medium-high heat. Add garlic; cook for 30 seconds. Add chicken; cook for 3 to 4 minutes or until chicken is no longer pink, stirring occasionally.

Nice spice

Adobo seasoning is a blend of dried spices that is used widely in Latin and Spanish Caribbean cuisines. Exact blends vary from brand to brand, but basic ingredients are salt, garlic, oregano, black pepper, turmeric, and onion powder. Adobo also refers to a wet paste or sauce for marinating meat that often contains dried chiles, vinegar, and olive oil as well.

Fast Chicken
and Rice

Chicken Burgers with Ranch Coleslaw

Chicken Burgers with Ranch Coleslaw

Prep: 15 minutes **Grill:** 10 minutes

   3 cups packaged shredded cabbage with
     carrot (coleslaw mix)
 1/2 cup bottled ranch salad dressing
 1/4 teaspoon finely shredded lemon peel
   1 tablespoon butter or margarine
 1/2 cup finely chopped onion (1 medium)
1 1/4 pounds uncooked ground chicken
 1/2 cup shredded zucchini
 1/2 cup shredded Swiss cheese (2 ounces)
 1/2 teaspoon salt
 1/4 teaspoon freshly ground black pepper
     Nonstick cooking spray
   4 kaiser rolls, split

1. For ranch coleslaw, in a large bowl combine shredded cabbage with carrot, salad dressing, and lemon peel. Cover and chill until needed.

2. In a small skillet melt butter over medium-high heat. Add onion; cook until tender. Remove skillet from heat.

3. In a large bowl combine ground chicken, zucchini, cheese, salt, pepper, and cooked onion; mix well. Line a baking sheet with plastic wrap. Drop chicken mixture in 4 mounds on prepared baking sheet. Cover with another piece of plastic wrap and shape each mound into a 1/2-inch-thick patty.

4. For a charcoal grill, grill patties on the greased rack of an uncovered grill directly over medium coals for 10 to 13 minutes or until done (170°F)*, turning once halfway through grilling. (For a gas grill, preheat grill. Reduce heat to medium. Place patties on greased grill rack over heat. Cover and grill as above.) Place burgers with coleslaw in rolls. **MAKES 6 BURGERS.**

Per burger: 645 cal., 39 g total fat (11 g sat. fat), 146 mg chol., 1,088 mg sodium, 38 g carbo., 2 g fiber, 36 g pro.

*Note The internal color of a ground chicken or turkey patty is not a reliable doneness indicator. Regardless of color, a chicken or turkey burger cooked to an internal temperature of 170°F is safe to eat.

BBQ Chicken Burgers

BBQ Chicken Burgers ♥

Prep: 15 minutes **Grill:** 10 minutes

 1/3 cup chopped onion (1 small)
   1 teaspoon canola oil
   7 hamburger buns
   1 egg, lightly beaten
   3 tablespoons bottled barbecue sauce
 1/2 teaspoon salt
 1/4 teaspoon black pepper
   1 pound uncooked ground chicken or turkey
   1 cup fresh corn kernels or frozen whole
     kernel corn, thawed
     Sliced red onion (optional)
     Bottled barbecue sauce (optional)

1. In a small nonstick skillet cook onion in oil until tender but not browned.

2. Tear 1 hamburger bun into pieces; place in blender. Cover and blend for fine crumbs.

3. In a large bowl combine egg, the 3 tablespoons barbecue sauce, salt, pepper, cooked onion, and bread crumbs. Add chicken and corn; mix well. Shape chicken mixture into six 1/2-inch-thick patties.

4. For a charcoal grill, grill patties on the greased grill rack of an uncovered grill directly over medium coals for 10 to 13 minutes or until done (170°F; see Note, far left), turning once halfway through grilling. (For a gas grill, preheat grill. Reduce heat to medium. Place patties on the greased grill rack over heat. Cover and grill as above.) Serve on hamburger buns. If desired, top with red onion slices and additional barbecue sauce. **MAKES 6 BURGERS.**

Per burger: 287 cal., 6 g total fat (1 g sat. fat), 77 mg chol., 583 mg sodium, 35 g carbo., 2 g fiber, 22 g pro.

Soft Shell
Chicken Tacos

Green Chile and Chicken Enchiladas

Start to Finish: 28 minutes

1¼ pounds chicken breast tenders
1½ cups bottled green salsa
 1 4-ounce can diced green chiles
1½ cups shredded Mexican blend cheese
    (6 ounces)
 8 6- to 7-inch flour tortillas
    Refrigerated fresh salsa (optional)
    Lime wedges (optional)

1. Preheat broiler. Cut chicken into 1-inch pieces and place in a microwave-safe bowl. Microwave, covered, on high about 7 minutes or until no pink remains, stirring twice. Drain liquid. Break up chicken slightly in a bowl with the back of a wooden spoon. Add salsa and chiles. Cook about 3 minutes more or until heated through, stirring once. Stir in 1 cup of the cheese.
2. Spoon chicken mixture evenly down center of tortillas. Roll tortillas around filling and place in a 13×9×2-inch baking pan. Sprinkle remaining ½ cup cheese over enchiladas. Broil 3 to 4 inches from heat for 1 to 2 minutes or until cheese is melted.
3. To serve top enchiladas with salsa and lime wedges, if desired. **MAKES 4 SERVINGS.**

Per serving: 569 cal., 24 g total fat (8 g sat. fat), 120 mg chol., 1,081 mg sodium, 33 g carbo., 1 g fiber, 49 g pro.

Quick Tip Refrigerated salsa has a fresher taste and chunkier texture than most of the jarred varieties—close to that of pico de gallo. You can usually find it in both mild and hot versions in the produce section.

Soft Shell Chicken Tacos

Start to Finish: 20 minutes

 1 2¼- to 2½-pound purchased roasted chicken
 4 7- to 8-inch flour tortillas
½ cup sour cream salsa- or Mexican-flavor dip
 1 large red, green, or yellow sweet pepper, cut into bite-size strips
1½ cups shredded lettuce

1. Remove skin and bones from chicken and discard. Coarsely shred 2 cups of the chicken. Reserve remaining chicken for another use.
2. Spread 1 side of each tortilla with dip. Top with shredded chicken, sweet pepper, and lettuce. Fold each tortilla in half.
MAKES 4 SOFT-SHELL TACOS.

Per taco: 284 cal., 13 g total fat (5 g sat. fat), 82 mg chol., 479 mg sodium, 19 g carbo., 1 g fiber, 23 g pro.

Green Chile
and Chicken
Enchiladas

Layered Turkey Enchiladas

Start to Finish: 20 minutes **Oven:** 450°F

- 1 tablespoon vegetable oil
- 1 pound turkey breast tenderloin, cut into bite-size strips
- 1 16-ounce package frozen (yellow, green, and red) peppers and onion stir-fry vegetables
- 1 10-ounce can enchilada sauce
- 1/2 cup canned whole-berry cranberry sauce
- Salt and black pepper
- 9 6-inch corn tortillas, halved
- 1 8-ounce package shredded Mexican-blend cheese (2 cups)
- Lime wedges (optional)
- Cilantro sprigs (optional)

1. Position oven rack in the top third of the oven. Preheat oven to 450°F. In an extra-large skillet heat oil over medium heat. Add turkey; cook about 4 minutes or until no longer pink. Add frozen vegetables, enchilada sauce, and cranberry sauce. Bring to boiling. Remove skillet from heat. Sprinkle with salt and pepper.

2. In a 2-quart baking dish layer one-third of the tortillas, then one-third of the cheese. Using a slotted spoon, layer half the turkey and vegetables. Layer one-third of the tortillas, one-third of the cheese, the remaining turkey and vegetables (with slotted spoon), and the remaining tortillas. Spoon on remaining sauce from skillet; sprinkle with remaining cheese.

3. Bake about 5 minutes or until cheese is melted. Cut in squares. If desired, serve with lime and cilantro. **MAKES 4 SERVINGS.**

Per serving: 615 cal., 25 g total fat (11 g sat. fat), 120 mg chol., 1,171 mg sodium, 52 g carbo., 6 g fiber, 45 g pro.

Turkey Steaks with Apple and Maple Sauce

Turkey Steaks with Apple and Maple Sauce ♡

Start to Finish: 20 minutes

- 1 turkey tenderloin steak or 2 skinless, boneless chicken breast halves (8 to 10 ounces total)
- 1 tablespoon butter or margarine
- 2 tablespoons pure maple or maple-flavor syrup
- 1 tablespoon cider or wine vinegar
- 1 teaspoon Dijon mustard
- 1/2 teaspoon instant chicken bouillon granules
- 1 medium tart red apple, cored and thinly sliced
- Fresh sage (optional)

1. If using turkey, cut tenderloin horizontally in half to make 2 steaks. In a medium skillet melt butter over medium heat. Add turkey or chicken; cook for 8 to 10 minutes or until no longer pink (170°F), turning once halfway through cooking. Transfer to 2 plates, reserving drippings in the skillet. Cover to keep warm.

2. Stir maple syrup, vinegar, mustard, and bouillon granules into drippings in the skillet. Add the apple slices. Cook and stir over medium heat for 2 to 3 minutes or until the apple is tender. To serve, spoon the apple mixture over the turkey. If desired, garnish with sage. **MAKES 2 SERVINGS.**

Per serving: 264 cal., 7 g total fat (4 g sat. fat), 65 mg chol., 376 mg sodium, 23 g carbo., 2 g fiber, 26 g pro.

Turkey and Peppers ♥

Start to Finish: 25 minutes

4   ¹/₄- to ³/₈-inch turkey breast slices (about 12 ounces)
    Salt and black pepper
1   tablespoon olive oil
2   medium red, yellow, and/or green sweet peppers, cut into thin strips
1   medium onion, halved lengthwise and sliced
1   fresh jalapeño, seeded and thinly sliced (see note, page 12)
³/₄ cup chicken broth
1   tablespoon all-purpose flour
1   teaspoon paprika
    Hot cooked rice (optional)

1. Sprinkle turkey lightly with salt and black pepper. In a large nonstick skillet cook turkey in hot oil over medium-high heat for 4 to 5 minutes or until turkey is tender and no longer pink (170°F), turning once. (If necessary, reduce heat to medium to prevent overbrowning.) Transfer turkey to a serving platter; cover and keep warm.

2. Add sweet peppers, onion, and jalapeño to skillet. Cook, covered, for 4 to 5 minutes or until vegetables are crisp-tender, stirring occasionally.

3. In a screw-top jar combine broth, flour, and paprika; shake well. Add to sweet pepper mixture. Cook and stir over medium heat until thickened and bubbly. Cook and stir for 1 minute more. If desired, serve turkey on hot cooked rice. Spoon the sweet pepper mixture over turkey and rice. **MAKES 4 SERVINGS.**

Per serving: 167 cal., 5 g total fat (1 g sat. fat), 51 mg chol., 260 mg sodium, 8 g carbo., 2 g fiber, 22 g pro.

Turkey-Potato Bake

Prep: 15 minutes **Bake:** 30 minutes
Stand: 10 minutes **Oven:** 400°F

2¹/₄ cups water
1   4.5- to 5-ounce package dry julienne potato mix
2   cups chopped cooked turkey or chicken breast (10 ounces)
1   cup shredded Cheddar cheese (4 ounces)
1   teaspoon dried parsley flakes
²/₃ cup milk

1. Preheat oven to 400°F. In a medium saucepan bring the water to boiling. Meanwhile, in a 2-quart square baking dish combine dry potatoes and sauce mix from potato mix. Stir in turkey, ¹/₂ cup of the Cheddar cheese, and the parsley flakes. Stir in the boiling water and the milk.

2. Bake, uncovered, for 30 to 35 minutes or until potatoes are tender. Sprinkle with the remaining ¹/₂ cup cheese. Let stand for 10 minutes before serving (mixture will thicken on standing). **MAKES 4 SERVINGS.**

Per serving: 370 cal., 15 g total fat (8 g sat. fat), 87 mg chol., 1,050 mg sodium, 27 g carbo., 1 g fiber, 32 g pro.

Parmesan-Sesame-Crusted Turkey

Start to Finish: 20 minutes

¹/₂ cup finely shredded Parmesan cheese
¹/₄ cup sesame seeds
1   egg, lightly beaten
4   turkey breast tenders, ¹/₂ inch thick
¹/₄ teaspoon salt
¹/₄ teaspoon black pepper
1   tablespoon olive oil or vegetable oil

1. In a shallow dish combine Parmesan cheese and sesame seeds. Place egg in another shallow dish. Dip turkey slices into egg; coat with Parmesan cheese mixture. Sprinkle turkey slices with salt and pepper.

2. In a large skillet heat oil over medium-high heat. Add turkey; cook turkey in hot oil for 8 to 10 minutes or until turkey is no longer pink (170°F), turning once halfway through cooking. **MAKES 4 SERVINGS.**

Per serving: 498 cal., 28 g total fat (13 g sat. fat), 171 mg chol., 1,336 mg sodium, 3 g carbo., 1 g fiber, 57 g pro.

Chicken may be America's favorite bird, but turkey is a close second. It cooks quickly and is every bit as versatile as its smaller cousin.

Turkey and Peppers

Turkey
Tetrazzini

Turkey Tetrazzini ♡

Prep: 30 minutes **Bake:** 10 minutes
Oven: 400°F

- 4 ounces dried whole wheat spaghetti pasta
- 2 cups sliced fresh cremini, button, or stemmed shiitake mushrooms
- ³/₄ cup chopped red and/or green sweet pepper (1 medium)
- ¹/₂ cup cold water
- 3 tablespoons all-purpose flour
- 1 12-ounce can evaporated fat-free milk
- ¹/₂ teaspoon instant chicken bouillon granules
- ¹/₈ teaspoon salt
- ¹/₈ teaspoon black pepper
  Dash ground nutmeg
- 1 cup chopped cooked turkey breast or chicken breast (5 ounces)
- ¹/₄ cup finely shredded Parmesan cheese (1 ounce)
- 2 tablespoons snipped fresh parsley
  Nonstick cooking spray

1. Preheat oven to 400°F. Cook the spaghetti according to package directions. Drain well and return to warm pan.

2. Meanwhile, in a covered large saucepan cook the mushrooms and sweet pepper in a small amount of boiling water for 3 to 6 minutes or until the vegetables are tender. Drain well; return to saucepan.

3. In a screw-top jar combine the ¹/₂ cup cold water and the flour; cover and shake until well mixed. Stir flour mixture into the vegetable mixture in saucepan. Stir in evaporated milk, bouillon granules, salt, black pepper, and nutmeg. Cook and stir until thickened and bubbly. Stir in the cooked spaghetti, turkey, Parmesan cheese, and parsley.

4. Lightly coat a 2-quart square baking dish with cooking spray. Spoon spaghetti mixture into dish. Bake, covered, for 10 to 15 minutes or until heated through. **MAKES 6 SERVINGS.**

Per serving: 202 cal., 2 g total fat (1 g sat. fat), 24 mg chol., 253 mg sodium, 32 g carbo., 2 g fiber, 17 g pro.

Quick Tip If you don't have cooked turkey or chicken, poach raw chicken breasts to use in this recipe. In a medium skillet place 6 ounces skinless, boneless chicken breast halves and 1 cup water. Bring to boiling; reduce heat.

Smoked Turkey and Tortellini Salad

Simmer, covered for 12 to 14 minutes, or until chicken is no longer pink (170°F). Drain well; cool. Chop chicken.

Smoked Turkey and Tortellini Salad

Start to Finish: 25 minutes

- 1 7- to 8-ounce package dried cheese-filled tortellini
- 1 cup chopped cooked, smoked turkey, ham, or chicken (5 ounces)
- 8 cherry tomatoes, quartered
- ¹/₂ cup coarsely chopped green sweet pepper
- ¹/₄ cup sliced pitted ripe olives (optional)
- ¹/₄ cup bottled Italian vinaigrette or balsamic vinaigrette salad dressing
  Black pepper

1. Cook tortellini according to package directions; drain. Rinse with cold water; drain again.

2. In a large bowl combine tortellini, turkey, tomatoes, sweet pepper, and, if desired, olives. Drizzle salad dressing over mixture; toss to coat. Season to taste with black pepper. **MAKES 4 SERVINGS.**

Per serving: 330 cal., 15 g total fat (2 g sat. fat), 20 mg chol., 897 mg sodium, 32 g carbo., 1 g fiber, 17 g pro.

Quick Tip For a vegetarian salad, replace the turkey with 1 cup chopped fresh broccoli or cauliflower.

Turkey and
Sugar Snap Pea
Salad

Divide chopped romaine among serving plates. Top with sugar snap peas, turkey strips, and bacon pieces. Serve with dressing. **MAKES 4 SERVINGS.**

Per serving: 392 cal., 32 g total fat (9 g sat. fat), 68 mg chol., 1,363 mg sodium, 9 g carbo., 2 g fiber, 17 g pro.

Turkey and Artichoke Toss

Start to Finish: 25 minutes

1   12- to 14-ounce jar quartered marinated artichoke hearts
¼   cup bottled roasted garlic vinaigrette salad dressing or creamy Parmesan-basil salad dressing
1   tablespoon honey
1   5-ounce package baby spinach
10   ounces deli-roasted turkey, cubed (2¼ cups)
1   cup cherry tomatoes, halved
½   cup packaged coarsely shredded fresh carrots
¼   cup sliced almonds, toasted*

1. Drain artichokes, reserving ¼ cup of the marinade. For dressing, in a small bowl stir together reserved marinade, salad dressing, and honey; set aside.
2. In a large salad bowl combine artichokes, spinach, turkey, tomatoes, carrots, and almonds.
3. Add dressing to spinach mixture; toss to mix. Serve at once. **MAKES 4 SERVINGS.**

Per serving: 342 cal., 20 g total fat (2 g sat. fat), 54 mg chol., 459 mg sodium, 19 g carbo., 3 g fiber, 25 g pro.

*Note Spread nuts, seeds, or shredded coconut in a shallow baking pan. Bake in a 350°F oven for 5 to 10 minutes or until pieces are golden brown, watching carefully and stirring once or twice so they don't burn.

Turkey and Sugar Snap Pea Salad

Start to Finish: 18 minutes

5   slices bacon
2   cups sugar snap peas
½   cup light mayonnaise or salad dressing
1   tablespoon Dijon mustard
1   tablespoon cider vinegar
1   tablespoon snipped fresh dill
     Salt and black pepper
1   small head romaine, coarsely chopped or torn
8   ounces smoked turkey breast, cut into bite-size strips

1. Line a 9-inch microwave-safe pie plate with paper towels. Arrange bacon slices in a single layer on the paper towels. Cover with additional paper towels. Cook on high for 4 to 5 minutes or until bacon is crisp. Carefully remove the pie plate from the microwave. Set cooked bacon aside to cool.
2. Meanwhile, cook the peas, covered, in a small amount of boiling salted water for 2 to 4 minutes or until crisp-tender; drain. Crumble 1 bacon slice; set aside. Break remaining bacon slices into 1-inch pieces.
3. In a small bowl combine mayonnaise, mustard, vinegar, and dill; season to taste with salt and pepper. Stir in crumbled bacon.

Turkey and Artichoke Toss

Turkey
Pot Pies

Turkey Pot Pies

Start to Finish: 30 minutes **Oven:** 425°F

- 1/2 of a 15-ounce package rolled refrigerated unbaked piecrust (1 crust)
- 1 2.75-ounce envelope country gravy mix
- 2 6-ounce packages refrigerated cooked turkey breast strips
- 1 10-ounce package frozen mixed vegetables
- 1 cup milk
- 2 teaspoons onion powder

1. Preheat oven to 425°F. Let piecrust stand at room temperature while preparing filling. In a medium saucepan prepare gravy mix according to package directions. Stir in turkey, vegetables, milk, and onion powder. Cook and stir until heated through. Spoon filling into six 10-ounce ramekins or individual baking dishes; set aside.
2. Meanwhile, unroll piecrust. Using a pizza cutter, cut piecrust into 12 wedges. Place 2 wedges over turkey filling in each ramekin. Place ramekins in a shallow baking pan. Bake for 15 minutes or until crust is golden.
MAKES 6 SERVINGS.

Per serving: 333 cal., 14 g total fat (6 g sat. fat), 33 mg chol., 975 mg sodium, 34 g carbo., 3 g fiber, 17 g pro.

Quick Tip If you don't have ramekins, you can make one large pot pie in a 2-quart round casserole. Spoon the filling into the dish, then roll the piecrust to a circle about 1/2 inch larger diameter than the casserole. Roll the crust around a rolling pin, then gently unroll on the top of the dish. Pierce with a fork a few times to allow steam to escape. Bake in a 375°F oven for 20 to 25 minutes or until crust is golden.

Parmesan-Crusted Turkey with Mashed Cauliflower

Parmesan-Crusted Turkey with Mashed Cauliflower

Start to Finish: 20 minutes

- 3 cups coarsely chopped cauliflower (1/2 of a head)
- 1/4 cup water
- 2 8-ounce turkey breast tenderloins, halved horizontally
  Salt and black pepper
- 1/3 cup light mayonnaise or mayonnaise
- 1/3 cup finely shredded Parmesan cheese
- 3 tablespoons fine dry bread crumbs
- 2 tablespoons butter or margarine
  Chopped fresh flat-leaf parsley and/or paprika (optional)

1. Preheat broiler. In a microwave-safe 1 1/2-quart casserole combine cauliflower and the water. Cover and cook on high for 12 to 15 minutes or until very tender, stirring once.

2. Meanwhile, sprinkle turkey with salt and pepper. Place on unheated rack of a broiler pan. Broil 4 inches from heat for 5 minutes. Turn turkey; broil about 4 minutes more. Meanwhile, in a bowl combine mayonnaise, 1/4 cup of the Parmesan cheese, and the bread crumbs. Spread over turkey. Broil for 2 to 3 minutes more or until topping is golden and turkey is no longer pink (170°F).
3. Add butter and the remaining Parmesan cheese to cauliflower; mash until smooth. Serve mashed cauliflower with turkey. If desired, sprinkle with parsley and/or paprika.
MAKES 4 SERVINGS.

Per serving: 310 cal., 15 g total fat (6 g sat. fat), 97 mg chol., 574 mg sodium, 10 g carbo., 2 g fiber, 33 g pro.

Cajun Turkey Cutlets with Melon and Blueberries

Turkey and Sweet Potatoes ♥

Start to Finish: 40 minutes

- 1 pound sweet potatoes
- 2 turkey breast tenderloins
  (1 to 1 ¼ pounds total)
- ½ teaspoon salt
- ¼ teaspoon black pepper
- 1 tablespoon vegetable oil
- 1 cup purchased chunky salsa
- ¼ cup orange juice
  Snipped fresh cilantro or parsley (optional)

1. Peel sweet potatoes; cut into 1-inch pieces. In a saucepan cook sweet potatoes, covered, in enough boiling water to cover for 10 to 12 minutes or until potatoes are just tender; drain.

2. Meanwhile, cut turkey crosswise into ½-inch slices. Sprinkle with salt and pepper. In a large nonstick skillet heat oil over medium-high heat. Cook turkey in hot oil for 6 to 8 minutes or until tender and no longer pink, turning once.

3. Add salsa, orange juice, and sweet potatoes. Cook until heated through. If desired, sprinkle with snipped fresh cilantro.
MAKES 4 SERVINGS.

Per serving: 251 cal., 4 g total fat (1 g sat. fat), 70 mg chol., 775 mg sodium, 22 g carbo., 7 g fiber, 30 g pro.

Cajun Turkey Cutlets with Melon and Blueberries

Start to Finish: 20 minutes

- 2 turkey breast tenderloins, cut in half horizontally (about 1 pound)
- 1 tablespoon olive oil
- 1½ teaspoons Cajun seasoning
- 6 cups torn mixed greens
- 1½ cups sliced cantaloupe
- 1 cup fresh blueberries
  Crumbled farmer cheese (optional)
  Purchased salad dressing

1. Brush turkey with olive oil. Sprinkle with seasoning. For a charcoal grill, grill turkey portions on the rack of an uncovered grill directly over medium coals for 12 to 15 minutes or until turkey is tender and no longer pink (170°F), turning once. (For a gas grill, preheat grill. Reduce heat to medium. Place turkey on grill rack over heat. Cover; grill as above.) Slice turkey.

2. Arrange greens on a serving platter along with the turkey, cantaloupe, and blueberries. If desired, top with farmer cheese. Serve with salad dressing. **MAKES 4 SERVINGS.**

Per serving: 359 cal., 22 g total fat (4 g sat. fat), 68 mg chol., 161 mg sodium, 14 g carbo., 3 g fiber, 29 g pro.

Turkey and
Sweet Potatoes

CHAPTER 5

Fish & Seafood

Seared Tuna with Citrus Relish

California Tuna Parmesan

Start to Finish: 20 minutes **Oven:** 450°F

  4 4-ounce fresh or frozen tuna steaks
  2 lemons
$1/3$ cup olive oil
$1/2$ teaspoon freshly ground black pepper
$1/4$ teaspoon salt
12 ounces fresh asparagus spears, trimmed
  1 5-ounce package mixed baby greens
$1/3$ cup finely shaved Parmesan cheese

1. Thaw fish, if frozen. Rinse fish; pat dry with paper towels. Preheat oven to 450°F. Finely shred 2 teaspoons peel from 1 lemon. Squeeze juice from lemon. For dressing, in a small bowl whisk together olive oil, lemon peel and juice, pepper, and salt; set aside. Cut remaining lemon into wedges; set aside.
2. Place asparagus in a single layer in a shallow baking pan. Drizzle with 2 tablespoons of the dressing. Bake, uncovered, for 8 minutes.
3. Meanwhile, in a large skillet heat 1 tablespoon of the dressing. Add fish; cook for 8 to 12 minutes or until browned and center is slightly pink, turning once halfway through cooking.
4. Divide greens among 4 plates; top with tuna and asparagus. Drizzle with remaining dressing. Sprinkle with Parmesan cheese; pass lemon wedges. **MAKES 4 SERVINGS.**

Per serving: 377 cal., 26 g total fat (5 g sat. fat), 48 mg chol., 312 mg sodium, 9 g carbo., 4 g fiber, 31 g pro.

Seared Tuna with Citrus Relish ♡

Start to Finish: 30 minutes

  4 4-ounce fresh or frozen tuna steaks, cut $3/4$ inch thick
    Salt and black pepper
  2 teaspoons white wine vinegar
  2 teaspoons soy sauce
$1/2$ teaspoon grated fresh ginger
  1 tablespoon canola oil
  1 medium grapefruit, peeled and coarsely chopped
  1 medium orange, peeled and coarsely chopped
  2 tablespoons finely chopped red onion
  2 tablespoons snipped fresh cilantro
  2 teaspoons canola oil

1. Thaw fish, if frozen. Rinse fish; pat dry with paper towels. Sprinkle fish with salt and pepper; set aside.
2. For citrus relish, in a medium bowl combine vinegar, soy sauce, and ginger. Whisk in 1 tablespoon canola oil. Gently stir grapefruit, orange, red onion, and cilantro into the vinegar mixture. Set relish aside.
3. In a large skillet heat 2 teaspoons canola oil over medium heat. Add fish; cook for 6 to 9 minutes or until fish begins to flake when tested with a fork, carefully turning once halfway through cooking. Serve with citrus relish. **MAKES 4 SERVINGS.**

Per serving: 210 cal., 7 g total fat (1 g sat. fat), 51 mg chol., 342 mg sodium, 9 g carbo., 2 g fiber, 28 g pro.

California Tuna
Parmesan

Hawaiian Tuna Toss

Fresh Feta
Salmon Pasta

Hawaiian Tuna Toss

Start to Finish: 15 minutes

  5 cups packaged shredded broccoli
    (broccoli slaw mix)
  2 5-ounce pouches sweet and spicy
    marinated chunk light tuna
  1/2 cup bottled honey-dijon salad dressing
  1/2 of a small fresh pineapple, cut into 4 slices
  1/2 cup macadamia nuts, chopped

1. In a large bowl toss together broccoli slaw,
tuna, and salad dressing.
2. Arrange a quartered pineapple slice on
each of 4 plates. Spoon broccoli mixture over
pineapple. Sprinkle with nuts.
MAKES 4 SERVINGS.

Per serving: 399 cal., 25 g total fat (3 g sat. fat), 31 mg
chol., 480 mg sodium, 27 g carbo., 5 g fiber, 18 g pro.

Quick Tip If you don't have honey-dijon
salad dressing, any salad dressing that's on
the sweet side, including balsamic vinaigrette,
Asian-ginger vinaigrette, or poppy seed
dressing, works on this salad.

Fresh Feta Salmon Pasta

Start to Finish: 35 minutes

  6 ounces dried whole wheat penne or
    rotini pasta
    Nonstick cooking spray
  2 cloves garlic, minced
  4 large plum tomatoes, chopped
  1/2 cup sliced green onions (4)
  12 ounces cooked salmon, broken into
    chunks, or two 6-ounce cans water-pack,
    skinless, boneless salmon, drained
  1/8 teaspoon salt

  3 tablespoons snipped fresh basil
  1/2 teaspoon black pepper
  2 teaspoons olive oil
  3/4 cup crumbled feta cheese (3 ounces)
    Fresh basil sprigs

1. In a 4-quart Dutch oven cook pasta
according to package directions. Drain well.
Return pasta to Dutch oven; keep warm.
2. Lightly coat an unheated large nonstick
skillet with cooking spray. Heat skillet over
medium-high heat. Add garlic; cook and stir

for 15 seconds. Add tomatoes and green
onions to skillet; cook and stir just until
tender. Sprinkle salmon with salt. Add
salmon, snipped basil, and pepper to skillet.
Heat through.
3. Add oil to drained pasta; toss to mix. Add
salmon mixture and feta cheese to pasta;
toss gently to mix. Garnish with basil sprigs.
MAKES 4 SERVINGS.

Per serving: 442 cal., 20 g total fat (6 g sat. fat), 86 mg
chol., 384 mg sodium, 37 g carbo., 6 g fiber, 31 g pro.

Tuna-Potato Cakes

Basil-Buttered Salmon

Prep: 15 minutes **Broil:** 8 minutes

  4 fresh or frozen skinless salmon, halibut, or
      sea bass fillets (about 1 1/4 pounds)
1/2 teaspoon salt-free lemon-pepper
      seasoning
  2 tablespoons butter, softened
  1 teaspoon snipped fresh lemon basil or
      regular basil, or 1/4 teaspoon dried basil
  1 teaspoon snipped fresh parsley or cilantro
1/4 teaspoon finely shredded lemon peel
      Steamed asparagus (optional)
      Grated Parmesan cheese (optional)

1. Thaw fish, if frozen. Rinse fish; pat dry with paper towels. Sprinkle with lemon-pepper seasoning.

2. Place fish on the greased unheated rack of a broiler pan. Turn any thin portions under to make uniform thickness. Broil 4 inches from the heat for 5 minutes. Carefully turn fish over. Broil for 3 to 7 minutes more or until fish flakes easily when tested with a fork.

3. Meanwhile, in a small bowl stir together butter, basil, parsley, and lemon peel. To serve, spoon 1 teaspoon of the butter mixture on top of each fish piece. Cover and refrigerate remaining butter mixture for another use. Serve with steamed asparagus and Parmesan cheese, if desired.

Grilling Directions For a charcoal grill, grill fish on the greased rack of an uncovered grill directly over medium coals for 8 to 12 minutes or until fish flakes easily when tested with a fork, carefully turning once halfway through grilling. (For a gas grill, preheat grill. Reduce heat to medium. Place chicken on grill rack over heat. Cover and grill as above.) **MAKES 4 SERVINGS.**

Per serving: 294 cal., 19 g total fat (5 g sat. fat), 94 mg chol., 113 mg sodium, 0 g carbo., 0 g fiber, 28 g pro.

Tuna-Potato Cakes

Start to Finish: 20 minutes

  1 cup packaged refrigerated mashed
      potatoes with garlic
  1 12-ounce can tuna (water pack), drained
      and broken in chunks
1/3 cup seasoned fine dry bread crumbs
1/2 cup finely chopped celery (1 stalk)
1/4 teaspoon black pepper
  2 tablespoons vegetable oil
1/4 cup bottled tartar sauce

1. In a medium bowl combine mashed potatoes, tuna, bread crumbs, celery, and pepper; mix well.

2. In a large skillet heat oil over medium heat. Drop about 1/3 cup of the tuna-potato mixture into the hot oil; flatten to 1/2-inch-thick cake. Cook about 4 minutes or until browned. Carefully turn; cook about 4 minutes more. Serve with tartar sauce. **MAKES 4 SERVINGS.**

Per serving: 267 cal., 14 g total fat (2 g sat. fat), 22 mg chol., 621 mg sodium, 16 g carbo., 1 g fiber, 19 g pro.

Salmon with
Fresh Citrus
Salsa

Salmon with Fresh Citrus Salsa

Start to Finish: 20 minutes

    4   4- to 5-ounce fresh or frozen skinless
        salmon fillets, ³⁄₄ to 1 inch thick
        Salt and black pepper
    ¹⁄₃ cup red jalapeño jelly
    3   medium oranges, peeled, seeded, and
        coarsely chopped
    1   medium grapefruit, peeled and sectioned
    1   cup grape or cherry tomatoes, halved

1. Thaw fish, if frozen. Rinse fish; pat dry with paper towels. Preheat broiler. Sprinkle fish lightly with salt and pepper. Melt jelly in a small saucepan. Brush 2 tablespoons of the melted jelly on fish. Place fish on the unheated rack of a broiler pan. Broil 4 inches from heat for 8 to 10 minutes or until fish flakes easily when tested with a fork.

2. Meanwhile, for fresh citrus salsa, in a medium bowl combine oranges, grapefruit, tomatoes, and the remaining jelly. Season to taste with salt and pepper. Serve fish with citrus salsa. **MAKES 4 SERVINGS.**

Per serving: 362 cal., 13 g total fat (3 g sat. fat), 67 mg chol., 223 mg sodium, 40 g carbo., 4 g fiber, 24 g pro.

Coriander-Crusted Salmon with Tropical Rice

Coriander-Crusted Salmon with Tropical Rice

Prep: 15 minutes
Bake: 4 minutes per ¹⁄₂-inch thickness
Oven: 450°F

    1   1¹⁄₂-pound fresh or frozen salmon fillet
    2   tablespoons coriander seeds, coarsely
        crushed
    1   tablespoon packed brown sugar
    1   teaspoon lemon-pepper seasoning
    1   tablespoon butter or margarine, melted
    2   cups cooked rice
    1   medium mango, peeled, seeded, and
        chopped
    1   tablespoon snipped fresh cilantro
    1   teaspoon finely shredded lemon peel
        Finely shredded lemon peel (optional)
        Fresh cilantro sprigs (optional)

1. Thaw salmon, if frozen. Preheat oven to 450°F. Rinse fish; pat dry with paper towels. Measure thickness of fish. Place fish, skin side down, in a greased shallow baking pan. In a small bowl stir together coriander seeds, brown sugar, and lemon-pepper seasoning. Brush top and sides of fish with melted butter. Sprinkle fish with coriander mixture, pressing in slightly.

2. In a medium bowl stir together rice, mango, 1 tablespoon snipped cilantro, and 1 teaspoon lemon peel. Spoon rice mixture around fish.

3. Bake, uncovered, until fish begins to flake when tested with a fork. (Allow 4 to 6 minutes per ¹⁄₂-inch thickness.) To serve, cut fish in 4 pieces. Serve fish on rice mixture. If desired, garnish with additional lemon peel and cilantro sprigs. **MAKES 4 SERVINGS.**

Per serving: 336 cal., 9 g total fat (2 g sat. fat), 31 mg chol., 406 mg sodium, 36 g carbo., 1 g fiber, 27 g pro.

Quick Tip If you crush or grind spices from whole seeds, purchase an electric spice grinder or coffee mill designated for grinding spices. After you use the grinder, clean it by grinding torn bits of soft white bread, which will pick up the remaining ground spices. If there are residual ground spices, use a damp cloth to wipe out the grinder.

Dilly Salmon Fillets

Salmon Burgers

Prep: 20 minutes **Grill:** 10 minutes

1¼ pounds fresh or frozen salmon fillet
⅓ cup panko (Japanese-style) bread crumbs
¼ cup finely chopped green onions (2)
2 tablespoons snipped fresh dill
1 teaspoon finely shredded lemon peel
¼ teaspoon salt
¼ teaspoon black pepper
Nonstick cooking spray
Lettuce leaves
6 whole wheat hamburger buns, split and toasted
¼ cup tartar sauce

1. Thaw salmon, if frozen. Rinse fish; pat dry with paper towels. Using a sharp knife, cut a small corner of the skin away from flesh. Then gently pull and slice off the remaining skin, trying to keep as much flesh as possible intact to make the burgers. Discard skin; coarsely chop salmon.
2. In a food processor combine salmon, panko, green onions, 1 tablespoon of the dill, the lemon peel, salt, and pepper. Cover and process until the salmon is the consistency of ground beef and still has some shape. Do not over process.
3. Shape salmon mixture in four 3½-inch-diameter patties. Lightly coat both sides of patties with nonstick cooking spray.
4. For a charcoal grill, grill patties on rack of an uncovered grill directly over medium coals about 10 minutes or until done (160°F), carefully turning once halfway through grilling. (For a gas grill, preheat grill. Reduce heat to medium. Place patties on grill rack over heat. Cover and grill as above.)
5. Place lettuce and patties on buns; spread each burger with 1 tablespoon tartar sauce.
MAKES 4 BURGERS.

Per burger: 485 cal., 18 g total fat (3 g sat. fat), 95 mg chol., 720 mg sodium, 42 g carbo., 6 g fiber, 36 g pro.

Dilly Salmon Fillets

Prep: 15 minutes **Marinate:** 10 minutes
Grill: 5 minutes

4 5- to 6-ounce fresh or frozen skinless salmon fillets, ½ to ¾ inch thick
3 tablespoons fresh lemon juice
2 tablespoons snipped fresh dill
2 tablespoons mayonnaise or salad dressing
2 teaspoons Dijon mustard

1. Thaw fish, if frozen. Rinse fish; pat dry with paper towels. For marinade, in a shallow dish combine lemon juice and 1 tablespoon of the dill. Add fish; turn to coat. Marinate at room temperature for 10 minutes. Meanwhile, in a bowl stir together the remaining 1 tablespoon dill, the mayonnaise, and mustard; set aside.
2. For a charcoal grill, arrange medium-hot coals around a drip pan. Test for medium

heat above the pan. Place fish on greased grill rack over drip pan. Cover and grill for 3 minutes. Turn fish; spread with mayonnaise mixture. Cover and grill for 2 to 6 minutes more or until fish flakes easily when tested with a fork. (For a gas grill, preheat grill. Reduce heat to medium. Adjust for indirect cooking. Grill as above.) **MAKES 4 SERVINGS.**

Per serving: 211 cal., 11 g total fat (2 g sat. fat), 35 mg chol., 204 mg sodium, 1 g carbo., 0 g fiber, 25 g pro.

Quick Tip Marinating times for meat, poultry, and fish vary drastically, from minutes to hours, because each reacts differently to acids in the marinades. Acids—citrus juice, wine, and vinegar—start to cook the delicate fish when marinated too long. A brief time imparts plenty of flavor—and leaves the cooking to the grill.

Tuna with
Tuscan Beans

Tuna with Tuscan Beans ♡

Start to Finish: 20 minutes

1 pound fresh or frozen tuna or swordfish
  steaks, cut 1 inch thick
¼ teaspoon salt
¼ teaspoon black pepper
1 tablespoon olive oil
2 cloves garlic, minced
2 teaspoons olive oil
1 14.5-ounce can Italian-style stewed
  tomatoes, undrained and cut up
2 teaspoons snipped fresh sage or
  ¼ teaspoon ground sage
1 15-ounce can navy beans, rinsed and
  drained
  Lemon wedges
  Fresh sage sprigs (optional)

1. Thaw fish, if frozen. Rinse fish; pat dry with paper towels. Cut fish into 4 portions; sprinkle with salt and pepper. Heat 1 tablespoon oil in a large skillet over medium heat. Add the fish. Cook for 10 to 12 minutes or until fish flakes easily with a fork, turning once. (If using tuna, fish may still be pink in the center.)

2. Meanwhile, in a medium skillet cook garlic in 2 teaspoons hot oil for 15 seconds. Stir in the undrained tomatoes and the sage. Bring to boiling; reduce heat. Simmer, uncovered, for 5 minutes. Stir in beans; heat through.

3. To serve, remove the skin from fish, if present. Spoon some of the bean mixture onto 4 dinner plates. Place a fish portion on top of bean mixture on each plate. Serve with lemon wedges. If desired, garnish with sage sprigs. **MAKES 4 SERVINGS.**

Per serving: 339 cal., 8 g total fat (1 g sat. fat), 51 mg chol., 883 mg sodium, 30 g carbo., 6 g fiber, 36 g pro.

Flounder
with Roma
Tomatoes

Flounder with Roma Tomatoes ♡

Start to Finish: 25 minutes

1 pound fresh or frozen flounder fillets or
  other thin, mild fish fillets
1 tablespoon olive oil
1 cup finely chopped onions (2 medium)
½ cup chopped, seeded fresh Anaheim or
  other mild chile (see note, page 12)
2 cups chopped plum tomatoes (4 medium)
2 tablespoons capers, drained
¼ cup sliced, pitted imported black olives,
  such as kalamata or niçoise
¼ teaspoon salt
⅛ teaspoon black pepper

1. Thaw fish, if frozen. Rinse fish; pat dry with paper towels. Cut fish into 4 serving-size pieces, if necessary. Set fish aside.

2. In a large skillet heat oil over medium heat. Add onion and chile pepper; cook about 4 minutes or until tender. Stir in tomatoes, capers, olives, and ⅛ teaspoon of the salt. Arrange fish on the vegetable mixture. Sprinkle fish with the remaining ⅛ teaspoon salt and the black pepper. Cook, covered, over medium heat for 4 to 5 minutes or until fish begins to flake when tested with a fork. **MAKES 4 SERVINGS.**

Per serving: 188 cal., 6 g total fat (1 g sat. fat), 54 mg chol., 500 mg sodium, 10 g carbo., 2 g fiber, 23 g pro.

Seasoned Cod

layer (fish may be tight in the dish but do not overlap). Cover with vented plastic wrap. Microwave on high for 5 to 7 minutes or until fish flakes easily when tested with a fork, turning dish once halfway through cooking, if necessary. If desired, garnish with lemon wedges and/or parsley sprigs.

Parmesan-Crusted Fish ♥

Start to Finish: 20 minutes **Oven:** 450°F

  4 fresh or frozen skinless cod fillets
     Nonstick cooking spray
     Salt and black pepper
$^1/_3$ cup panko (Japanese-style) bread crumbs
$^1/_4$ cup finely shredded Parmesan cheese
     (1 ounce)
$^1/_2$ cup water
  1 10-ounce package shredded fresh carrots
     (3 cups)
  1 tablespoon butter or margarine
$^3/_4$ teaspoon ground ginger
     Mixed salad greens (optional)

1. Thaw fish, if frozen. Rinse fish; pat dry with paper towels. Preheat oven to 450°F. Lightly coat a baking sheet with cooking spray. Measure thickness of fish. Arrange fish on baking sheet. Sprinkle lightly with salt and pepper. In a small bowl stir together bread crumbs and Parmesan cheese. Sprinkle on fish.

2. Bake, uncovered, until crumbs are golden and fish begins to flake when tested with a fork. Allow 4 to 6 minutes per $^1/_2$-inch thickness of fish.

3. Meanwhile, in a large skillet bring the water to boiling. Add carrots; reduce heat to medium. Cook, covered, 5 minutes. Uncover and cook about 2 minutes or until water is evaporated. Add butter and ginger; toss until butter is melted and carrots are coated. Season with salt and pepper. Serve fish with carrot mixture and, if desired, salad greens. **MAKES 4 SERVINGS.**

Per serving: 233 cal., 6 g total fat (3 g sat. fat), 84 mg chol., 407 mg sodium, 11 g carbo., 2 g fiber, 34 g pro.

Seasoned Cod

Prep: 10 minutes
Broil: 4 to 6 minutes per $^1/_2$-inch thickness
Makes: 8 servings

  2 pounds fresh or frozen skinless cod fillets,
     $^3/_4$ to 1 inch thick
  1 teaspoon paprika
$^1/_2$ teaspoon black pepper
$^1/_2$ teaspoon seasoned salt
     Lemon wedges and/or fresh parsley sprigs
     (optional)

1. Preheat broiler. Thaw fish, if frozen. Rinse fish; pat dry with paper towels. In a small bowl combine paprika, pepper, and

seasoned salt. Sprinkle paprika mixture over both sides of each fish fillet. Measure thickness of fish.

2. Place fish on the greased unheated rack of a broiler pan. Broil 4 inches from the heat for 4 to 6 minutes per $^1/_2$-inch thickness of fish or until fish flakes easily when tested with a fork. If desired, garnish with lemon wedges and/or parsley sprigs. **MAKES 8 SERVINGS.**

Per serving: 93 cal., 1 g total fat (0 g sat. fat), 48 mg chol., 156 mg sodium, 0 g carbo., 0 g fiber, 20 g pro.

Microwave directions Prepare as directed through Step 1. In a microwave-safe 2-quart square baking dish, arrange fish in a single

Fish Tostadas with Chili-Lime Cream

Start to Finish: 20 minutes

  1 pound fresh or frozen tilapia or cod fillets
 ½ teaspoon chili powder
 ¼ teaspoon salt
  1 lime, halved
 ½ cup sour cream
 ½ teaspoon garlic powder
  8 6-inch tostada shells
  2 cups shredded cabbage mix
  1 avocado, halved, seeded, peeled, and sliced (optional)
  1 cup cherry tomatoes, quartered (optional)
     Bottled hot pepper sauce (optional)

1. Thaw fish, if frozen. Rinse fish; pat dry with paper towels. Preheat broiler. Sprinkle fish with ¼ teaspoon of the chili powder and salt. For chili-lime cream, in a small bowl squeeze 2 teaspoons juice from half of the lime. Stir in sour cream, garlic powder, and remaining chili powder; set aside. Cut remaining lime half in wedges for serving.

2. Place fish on the unheated greased broiler rack; tuck under thin edges. Place shells on baking sheet on lowest rack. Broil fish 4 inches from heat 4 to 6 minutes per ½-inch thickness until fish flakes when tested with fork. Break in chunks. Serve tostadas with cabbage, chili-lime cream, avocado, remaining lime half, and, if desired, tomatoes and hot pepper sauce. **MAKES 4 SERVINGS.**

Per serving: 278 cal., 14 g total fat (5 g sat. fat), 67 mg chol., 303 mg sodium, 17 g carbo., 2 g fiber, 25 g pro.

Crispy Almond Fish

Crispy Almond Fish

Start to Finish: 30 minutes

  1 pound fresh or frozen skinless white fish fillets, such as tilapia, cod, or flounder
 ⅓ cup all-purpose flour
  1 egg, slightly beaten
  2 tablespoons milk
 ⅓ cup fine dry bread crumbs
 ⅓ cup finely chopped almonds
 ½ teaspoon dried thyme, crushed
  2 to 3 tablespoons vegetable oil

1. Thaw fish, if frozen. Rinse fish; pat dry with paper towels. Cut into 4 serving-size pieces, if necessary. Measure thickness of fish.

2. Place flour in a shallow dish. In a second shallow dish whisk together egg and milk. In a third shallow dish combine bread crumbs, almonds, and thyme. Coat both sides of fillets with flour. Dip fillets in the egg mixture; dip in bread crumb mixture to coat.

3. In a large skillet heat 2 tablespoons oil over medium heat. Add fish fillets (if necessary, cook fish half at a time). Cook until golden and fish begins to flake when tested with a fork, turning once (allow 4 to 6 minutes per ½-inch thickness of fish).

MAKES 4 SERVINGS.

Per serving: 308 cal., 15 g total fat (3 g sat. fat), 110 mg chol., 145 mg sodium, 16 g carbo., 2 g fiber, 28 g pro.

Quick Tip Dredging is the process of coating food—such as a fish fillet—in flour and bread crumbs to create a crispy crust. The order in which you dredge is important. Flour comes first to give the egg something to adhere to—then the bread crumbs stick to the egg.

Fish Fillets
with Orange-
Ginger Sauce

Orange-Ginger Sauce In a small bowl stir together ¼ cup low-fat mayonnaise, 1 teaspoon orange marmalade, and ¼ teaspoon ground ginger. **MAKES 4 SERVINGS.**

Per serving: 319 cal., 10 g total fat (5 g sat. fat), 68 mg chol., 711 mg sodium, 31 g carbo., 2 g fiber, 25 g pro.

Maple-Hoisin Glazed Halibut

Prep: 10 minutes **Broil:** 8 minutes

```
4   5- to 6-ounce fresh or frozen halibut
    steaks, 1 inch thick
3   tablespoons hoisin sauce
2   tablespoons seasoned rice vinegar
2   tablespoons maple syrup
1   teaspoon grated fresh ginger
1   clove garlic, minced
¼   teaspoon crushed red pepper
¼   teaspoon black pepper
    Shredded leaf lettuce or napa cabbage
    (optional)
```

1. Thaw fish, if frozen. Preheat broiler. Rinse fish; pat dry with paper towels. In a small bowl stir together hoisin sauce, vinegar, maple syrup, ginger, garlic, and crushed red pepper. Set aside.

2. Sprinkle fish with black pepper. Place fish on the greased unheated rack of a broiler pan. Broil 4 inches from the heat for 5 minutes. Brush with glaze; turn fish. Brush with remaining glaze. Broil for 3 to 7 minutes more or until fish begins to flake when tested with a fork. If desired, serve on a bed of lettuce. **MAKES 4 SERVINGS.**

Per serving: 210 cal., 4 g total fat (1 g sat. fat), 45 mg chol., 285 mg sodium, 13 g carbo., 0 g fiber, 30 g pro.

Quick Tip After you purchase fresh fish, be sure to cook it as soon as possible. When you have to wait a couple days to use it, wrap the fish loosely in plastic wrap. Store it in the coldest part of your refrigerator for up to 2 days. Cover and refrigerate any leftover cooked fish and use within 2 days.

Fish Fillets with Orange-Ginger Sauce ♡

Start to Finish: 15 minutes Oven: 450°F

```
4   fresh or frozen fish fillets (such as cod,
    orange roughy, or pike), about ½ inch
    thick (about 1 pound total)
    Nonstick cooking spray
¼   cup fine dry bread crumbs
¼   teaspoon ground ginger
⅛   teaspoon salt
⅛   teaspoon cayenne pepper
2   tablespoons butter or margarine, melted
1   recipe Orange-Ginger Sauce
4   lettuce leaves (optional)
4   baguette-style rolls or kaiser rolls, split
    and toasted (optional)
```

1. Thaw fish, if frozen. Rinse fish; pat dry with paper towels. Preheat oven to 450°F. Lightly coat a shallow baking pan with cooking spray; set aside. In a small bowl combine bread crumbs, ginger, salt, and cayenne pepper; set aside. Place fish fillets on waxed paper. Brush tops and sides of the fish with melted butter; coat tops and sides with crumb mixture.

2. Arrange the fish fillets in a single layer, crumb sides up, in prepared baking pan. Bake for 4 to 6 minutes or until fish flakes easily when tested with a fork.

3. Top fish with Orange-Ginger Sauce. If desired, place fish onto a lettuce-lined roll to make a sandwich.

Maple-Hoisin Glazed Halibut

Halibut
Veracruz

Orange and Dill Sea Bass

Halibut Veracruz ♡

Prep: 20 minutes **Grill:** 4 minutes

- 4 fresh or frozen halibut, mahi mahi, grouper, or tuna steaks (about 1 1/2 pounds)
  Salt and black pepper
- 1 14 1/2-ounce can chopped tomatoes with green chiles, drained
- 1/4 cup sliced green onions (2)
- 1 tablespoon olive oil
- 2 cloves garlic, minced
- 1 teaspoon drained capers
- 1 teaspoon snipped fresh oregano or 1/2 teaspoon dried oregano, crushed
- 1/2 teaspoon snipped fresh thyme or 1/4 teaspoon dried thyme, crushed
  Cooked rice (optional)
  Flour tortillas (optional)

1. Thaw fish, if frozen. Rinse fish; pat dry with paper towels. Sprinkle fish evenly with salt and pepper. In a small bowl combine drained tomatoes with green chiles, green onions, oil, garlic, capers, oregano, and thyme; set aside.
2. Fold a 36×18-inch piece of heavy-duty foil in half to make an 18-inch square. Place fish steaks in center of foil. Top with tomato mixture. Bring up 2 opposite edges of foil; seal with a double fold. Fold remaining edges together to completely enclose fish, leaving space for steam to build.
3. For a charcoal grill, grill foil packet on the rack of an uncovered grill directly over medium coals for 4 to 6 minutes per 1/2-inch thickness of fish or until fish flakes easily when tested with a fork. (For a gas grill, preheat grill. Reduce heat to medium. Place foil packet on grill rack over heat. Cover and grill as above.) If desired, serve with rice and tortillas. **MAKES 4 SERVINGS.**

Per serving: 254 cal., 7 g total fat (1 g sat. fat), 54 mg chol., 651 mg sodium, 8 g carbo., 2 g fiber, 36 g pro.

Orange and Dill Sea Bass ♡

Prep: 15 minutes **Grill:** 6 minutes

- 4 5- to 6-ounce fresh or frozen sea bass or orange roughy fillets, cut 3/4 inch thick
- 2 tablespoons snipped fresh dill
- 2 tablespoons olive oil
- 1/4 teaspoon salt
- 1/4 teaspoon ground white pepper
- 4 large oranges, cut into 1/4-inch slices
- 1 orange, cut into wedges

1. Thaw fish, if frozen. Rinse fish; pat dry with paper towels. In a small bowl stir together dill, oil, salt, and white pepper. Brush both sides of fish fillets with dill mixture.
2. For a charcoal grill, arrange a bed of orange slices on a greased grill rack directly over medium coals. Arrange fish on orange slices. Cover and grill for 6 to 9 minutes or until fish begins to flake when tested with a fork (do not turn fish). (For a gas grill, preheat grill. Reduce heat to medium. Arrange orange slices and fish on greased grill rack over heat. Cover and grill as above.)
3. To serve, use a spatula to transfer fish and grilled orange slices to a serving platter. Squeeze the juice from orange wedges over the fish. **MAKES 4 SERVINGS.**

Per serving: 268 cal., 10 g total fat (2 g sat. fat), 58 mg chol., 242 mg sodium, 18 g carbo., 3 g fiber, 28 g pro.

Quick Tip White pepper has a distinctive flavor that is especially nice with fish. Like black pepper, it is best when freshly ground. If you can, keep one pepper grinder filled with black peppercorns and another with white peppercorns.

Pan-Seared Tilapia With Almond Browned Butter

Pan-Seared Tilapia with Almond Browned Butter

Start to Finish: 25 minutes

4   4- to 5-ounce fresh or frozen skinless tilapia or other white fish fillets
3   cups fresh pea pods, trimmed
      Salt and black pepper
1   teaspoon all-purpose flour
1   tablespoon olive oil
2   tablespoons butter
¼   cup coarsely chopped almonds
      Snipped fresh parsley (optional)

1. Thaw fish, if frozen. Rinse fish; pat dry with paper towels. Set aside. In a large saucepan bring a large amount of lightly salted water to boiling. Add pea pods; cook for 2 minutes. Drain and set aside.

2. Meanwhile, sprinkle 1 side of each fish fillet with salt, pepper, and flour. Heat a large skillet over medium-high heat. Add oil, tilting skillet to coat. Add fish, floured side up (if necessary, cook half the fish at a time). Cook fish for 4 to 5 minutes or until it is easy to lift with spatula. Gently turn fish and cook for 2 to 3 minutes more or until fish flakes when tested with a fork. Arrange pea pods on a platter; place fish on top of pea pods.

3. Reduce heat to medium. In same skillet melt butter; stir in almonds. Cook for 30 to 60 seconds or until nuts are lightly toasted (do not let butter burn). Spoon over fish fillets. If desired, sprinkle with snipped fresh parsley. **MAKES 4 SERVINGS.**

Per serving: 266 cal., 15 g total fat (5 g sat. fat), 71 mg chol., 210 mg sodium, 7 g carbo., 3 g fiber, 24 g pro.

Red Snapper with Carrots and Fennel ♡

Prep: 25 minutes **Bake:** 4 minutes
Oven: 450°F

1   pound fresh or frozen skinless red snapper fillets, about ½ inch thick
1   cup sliced fennel bulb
½   cup chopped onion (1 medium)
½   cup chopped carrot (1 medium)
2   cloves garlic, minced
1   tablespoon olive oil
1   tablespoon snipped fresh dill
¼   teaspoon salt
¼   teaspoon black pepper
¼   cup dry white wine or reduced-sodium chicken broth
      Fresh dill sprigs (optional)

1. Thaw fish, if frozen. Rinse fish; pat dry with paper towels. Preheat oven to 450°F. In a large skillet cook fennel, onion, carrot, and garlic in oil over medium heat for 5 to 7 minutes or until vegetables are tender and lightly browned. Remove from heat. Stir in dill, salt, and pepper. Stir in wine.

2. Spoon about 1 cup of the vegetable mixture into a 2-quart square baking dish. Place fish on top of vegetables, tucking under any thin edges. Spoon remaining vegetable mixture on fish.

3. Bake, uncovered, for 4 to 6 minutes or until fish flakes easily when tested with a fork. Transfer fish and vegetables to dinner plates. If desired, garnish with dill sprigs.

MAKES 4 SERVINGS.

Per serving: 182 cal., 6 g total fat (1 g sat. fat), 41 mg chol., 260 mg sodium, 6 g carbo., 7 g fiber, 24 g pro.

Red Snapper with Carrots and Fennel

Cajun Shrimp with Mango-Edamame Salsa

Start to Finish: 30 minutes

- 1 pound fresh or frozen large shrimp with tails
- 2 teaspoons purchased salt-free Cajun seasoning or Homemade Cajun Seasoning
- 1 tablespoon soybean cooking oil
- 1 recipe Mango-Edamame Salsa
  Belgian endive leaves (optional)

1. Thaw shrimp, if frozen. Peel and devein shrimp, leaving tails intact if desired. Rinse shrimp; pat dry with paper towels. Set aside.
2. In a large bowl toss shrimp with Cajun seasoning. In a large heavy skillet heat oil over medium-high heat. Add shrimp; cook and stir about 5 minutes or until shrimp are opaque.
3. Serve shrimp warm with Mango-Edamame Salsa and, if desired, Belgian endive leaves. **MAKES 4 SERVINGS.**

Per serving: 317 cal., 12 g total fat (2 g sat. fat), 129 mg chol., 287 mg sodium, 29 g carbo., 6 g fiber, 27 g pro.

Homemade Cajun Seasoning In a small bowl stir together $1/2$ teaspoon onion powder, $1/2$ teaspoon paprika, $1/4$ teaspoon ground white pepper, $1/4$ teaspoon garlic powder, $1/4$ teaspoon cayenne pepper, and $1/4$ teaspoon black pepper.

Mango-Edamame Salsa In a medium bowl combine 2 seeded, peeled, and chopped mangoes; 1 cup fresh or frozen shelled sweet soybeans (edamame), cooked and cooled; $3/4$ cup chopped red sweet pepper; $1/2$ cup finely chopped green onion; $1/4$ cup snipped fresh cilantro; 2 teaspoons soybean cooking oil; and $1/4$ teaspoon salt. Toss gently to mix. Cover and chill until serving time or up to 2 hours. **MAKES 3 CUPS.**

Buttery Garlic Shrimp with Red Pepper

Buttery Garlic Shrimp with Red Pepper

Start to Finish: 10 minutes

- $1 1/2$ pounds fresh or frozen medium shrimp, peeled and deveined
- 8 ounces dried angel hair pasta
- 2 tablespoons butter
- 2 cloves garlic, minced
  Salt
- $1/4$ teaspoon crushed red pepper

1. Thaw shrimp, if frozen. Rinse shrimp; pat dry with paper towels. Set shrimp aside. Cook pasta according to package directions. Drain pasta; keep warm.

2. Meanwhile, in a large skillet melt butter over medium heat. Add garlic; cook for 30 seconds. Add the shrimp; sprinkle with salt. Cook and stir the shrimp for 2 to 4 minutes or until shrimp are opaque. Sprinkle with crushed red pepper. Serve shrimp over hot cooked pasta. **MAKES 4 SERVINGS.**

Per serving: 444 cal., 10 g total fat (4 g sat. fat), 274 mg chol., 438 mg sodium, 44 g carbo., 1 g fiber, 42 g pro.

Quick Tip To thaw frozen shrimp, place in a bowl of cold water for 30 to 60 minutes.

Shrimp on Grits with Fresh Cilantro Sauce

5. Serve shrimp on grits; drizzle with fresh cilantro sauce. If desired, garnish with lemon wedges and additional cilantro sprigs.
MAKES 4 SERVINGS.

Per serving: 385 cal., 21 g total fat (5 g sat. fat), 185 mg chol., 423 mg sodium, 21 g carbo., 3 g fiber, 29 g pro.

Thai Shrimp and Fresh Vegetable Rice ♡

Start to Finish: 30 minutes

$^{3}/_{4}$ pound fresh or frozen peeled and deveined medium shrimp
 2 tablespoons lime juice
 4 teaspoons soy sauce
 1 fresh jalapeño, seeded and finely chopped (see note, page 12)
 1 teaspoon grated fresh ginger
 1 clove garlic, minced
 1 tablespoon vegetable oil
 1 pound fresh asparagus spears, bias-sliced into 1-inch pieces
 1 small red sweet pepper, cut into thin bite-size strips
 3 cups hot cooked rice
$^{1}/_{4}$ cup chopped peanuts

1. Thaw shrimp, if frozen. Rinse shrimp; pat dry with paper towels. Place shrimp in a medium bowl. For marinade, combine lime juice, soy sauce, jalapeño, ginger, and garlic. Pour over shrimp; toss to coat. Marinate at room temperature for 15 minutes, stirring occasionally. Drain shrimp well, reserving the marinade.
2. In a wok or large skillet heat oil over medium-high heat. (Add more oil if necessary during cooking.) Add shrimp; cook and stir for 2 to 3 minutes or until shrimp turn opaque. Remove from wok; cover and keep warm. Add asparagus and pepper strips to wok; cook and stir for 2 to 3 minutes or until crisp-tender. Add reserved marinade to wok; bring to boiling. Stir in rice and peanuts.
3. To serve, transfer rice mixture to serving bowls or plates. Spoon shrimp on top.
MAKES 4 SERVINGS.

Per serving: 331 cal., 9 g total fat (1 g sat. fat), 131 mg chol., 571 mg sodium, 41 g carbo., 2 g fiber, 11 g pro.

Shrimp on Grits with Fresh Cilantro Sauce

Start to Finish: 25 minutes

$1^{1}/_{2}$ pounds fresh or frozen medium shrimp
$1^{3}/_{4}$ cups water
$^{1}/_{2}$ cup quick cooking (hominy) grits
 2 small red and/or yellow sweet peppers, coarsely chopped
$^{1}/_{2}$ cup shredded Mexican-blend cheese (2 ounces)
 Salt and black pepper
$^{1}/_{4}$ cup olive oil
$^{1}/_{2}$ teaspoon chili powder
 1 cup cilantro sprigs
 1 tablespoon cider vinegar
 2 tablespoons water
 Lemon wedges (optional)
 Cilantro sprigs (optional)

1. Thaw shrimp, if frozen. Peel and devein shrimp, leaving tails intact. Rinse shrimp; pat dry with paper towels. Set aside.

2. For grits, in a medium saucepan bring the $1^{3}/_{4}$ cups water to boiling; stir in grits and sweet peppers. Return to boiling; reduce heat. Simmer, covered, about 5 minutes or until most of the water is absorbed and grits are tender. Stir in cheese. Season with salt and pepper. Cover and keep warm.
3. In a large skillet heat 1 tablespoon of the oil over medium heat. Toss shrimp with chili powder. Add shrimp to skillet. Cook and stir for 3 to 4 minutes or until shrimp are opaque.
4. For fresh cilantro sauce, in a food processor combine the remaining 3 tablespoons olive oil, the 1 cup cilantro sprigs, cider vinegar, and 2 tablespoons water. Cover and process until almost smooth. Season with salt and black pepper.

Thai Shrimp and Fresh Vegetable Rice

Greek Leeks
and Shrimp
Stir-Fry

Greek Leeks and Shrimp Stir-Fry ♡

Start to Finish: 30 minutes

1¼ pounds fresh or frozen peeled, deveined
    medium shrimp
⅔ cup water
⅓ cup lemon juice
1 tablespoon cornstarch
¼ teaspoon bouquet garni or dried oregano,
    crushed
1 cup couscous
½ teaspoon bouquet garni
¼ teaspoon salt
1½ cups boiling water
1 tablespoon olive oil
1⅓ cups thinly sliced leeks
½ cup crumbled feta cheese (2 ounces)
    Pita wedges (optional)

1. Thaw shrimp, if frozen. Rinse shrimp and
pat dry with paper towels; set aside.
2. In a small bowl combine the ⅔ cup water,
the lemon juice, cornstarch, and ¼ teaspoon
bouquet garni. Set aside.
3. In a small bowl combine couscous,
½ teaspoon bouquet garni, and salt. Pour
the boiling water over couscous. Cover and
let stand for 5 minutes.
4. Meanwhile, heat oil in wok or extra-large
skillet over medium-high heat. Cook and stir
leeks in hot oil for 2 to 3 minutes or until leeks
are tender. Remove leeks from wok; set
aside. Stir lemon juice mixture. Add to wok
and bring to boiling. Add shrimp and cook for
2 to 3 minutes or until opaque. Stir in cooked
leeks and half of the feta cheese.
5. To serve, fluff couscous with a fork.
Transfer couscous to a serving platter. Spoon
shrimp over couscous and sprinkle with
remaining feta cheese. If desired, serve with
pita wedges. **MAKES 4 SERVINGS.**

Per serving: 424 cal., 9 g total fat (3 g sat. fat), 228 mg
chol., 527 mg sodium, 45 g carbo., 3 g fiber, 37 g pro.

Shortcut
Shrimp Risotto

Shortcut Shrimp Risotto ♡

Start to Finish: 30 minutes

2 14.5-ounce cans reduced-sodium chicken
    broth
1⅓ cups Arborio rice or short grain white rice
½ cup finely chopped onion (1 medium)
1 tablespoon snipped fresh basil or
    ¾ teaspoon dried basil, crushed
1 10- to 12-ounce package frozen peeled
    cooked shrimp, thawed
1½ cups frozen peas
¼ cup grated Parmesan cheese

1. In a large saucepan combine broth, rice,
onion, and dried basil (if using). Bring mixture
to boiling; reduce heat. Cover and simmer for
18 minutes.

2. Stir in shrimp and peas. Cover and cook for
3 minutes more (do not lift lid). Stir in fresh
basil (if using). Divide among 4 plates. Sprinkle
servings with cheese. **MAKES 4 SERVINGS.**

Per serving: 305 cal., 3 g total fat (1 g sat. fat), 143 mg
chol., 767 mg sodium, 45 g carbo., 3 g fiber, 25 g pro.

Quick Tip Arborio rice is specified for
risotto because its high starch content gives
risotto classically creamy and luxurious
texture. Although it's the most common rice
used for risotto, it is not the only one. You can
also use Vialone Nano or Carnaroli.

Shrimp Celeste

Start to Finish: 25 minutes

- 1 pound fresh or frozen prawns or jumbo shrimp in shells (6 to 8)
- 3 tablespoons butter or margarine
- 1/2 cup sliced fresh mushrooms
- 1/2 cup chopped tomato (1 medium)
- 1/4 cup sliced green onions (2)
- 1 tablespoon minced garlic (6 cloves)
- 1 teaspoon curry powder
- 1/4 teaspoon salt
- 1/4 teaspoon black pepper
- 1/2 cup half-and-half or light cream
- 1 tablespoon all-purpose flour
- 1/4 cup brandy
- 1 1/2 cups hot cooked rice or couscous
  Snipped fresh parsley (optional)

1. Thaw prawns, if frozen. Peel and devein prawns. Rinse prawns; pat dry with paper towels. In a large skillet, melt butter over medium heat. Add prawns; cook for 5 minutes, turning once. Add mushrooms, tomato, green onions, garlic, curry powder, salt, and pepper. Cook and stir for 2 to 3 minutes more or until prawns turn opaque.

2. Meanwhile, in a small bowl whisk together half-and-half and flour until smooth. Add flour mixture and brandy to shrimp mixture in skillet. Cook and stir until thickened and bubbly; cook and stir for 1 minute more. Serve in shallow bowls with rice. If desired, sprinkle with parsley. **MAKES 2 SERVINGS.**

Per serving: 767 cal., 29 g total fat (16 g sat. fat), 413 mg chol., 781 mg sodium, 53 g carbo., 2 g fiber, 54 g pro.

Shrimp Capellini with Pesto Sauce

Start to Finish: 20 minutes

- 12 ounces fresh or frozen peeled and deveined shrimp
- 8 ounces dried tomato-flavor angel hair pasta (capellini), fettuccine, or linguine
  Nonstick cooking spray
- 2 medium yellow summer squash and/or zucchini, cut into 1/2-inch chunks (about 2 cups)
- 1/3 cup purchased pesto
- 1 medium plum tomato, chopped

1. Thaw shrimp, if frozen. Cook pasta according to package directions; drain and keep warm.

2. Meanwhile, spray an unheated large nonstick skillet with cooking spray (or brush it with a little oil drained from the pesto). Heat skillet over medium-high heat. Add shrimp; cook and stir for 2 minutes. Add squash; cook and stir about 2 minutes more or until shrimp turn opaque and squash is crisp-tender. Remove skillet from heat. Add pesto; toss gently to coat.

3. Serve shrimp mixture over pasta; sprinkle with tomato. **MAKES 4 SERVINGS.**

Per serving: 428 cal., 16 g total fat (0 g sat. fat), 134 mg chol., 316 mg sodium, 47 g carbo., 3 g fiber, 25 g pro.

Scallops with Tropical Salsa

Start to Finish: 25 minutes

- 1 cup finely chopped papaya or mango
- 1/2 cup seeded and chopped red sweet pepper
- 1/2 cup finely chopped, seeded cucumber
- 2 tablespoons chopped fresh cilantro
- 1 fresh jalapeño chile, seeded and finely chopped (see note, page 12)
- 4 teaspoons lime juice
- 1 teaspoon extra virgin olive oil
- 12 ounces fresh or frozen scallops
  Kosher salt
  Freshly ground black pepper
- 2 teaspoons extra virgin olive oil
- 1 clove garlic, minced
  Lime wedges (optional)

1. For salsa, in a small bowl stir together papaya, sweet pepper, cucumber, cilantro, jalapeño, lime juice, and 1 teaspoon olive oil. Let stand at room temperature for at least 15 minutes to allow flavors to blend.

2. Meanwhile, thaw scallops, if frozen. Rinse scallops; pat dry with paper towels. Halve any large scallops. Season lightly with kosher salt and black pepper.

3. In a large nonstick skillet, heat 2 teaspoons olive oil over medium heat. Add garlic; cook for 30 seconds. Add scallops. Cook and stir for 2 to 3 minutes or until scallops are opaque. Use a slotted spoon to remove scallops; drain on paper towels. Serve the scallops with the salsa. If desired, serve with lime wedges. **MAKES 4 SERVINGS.**

Per serving: 134 cal., 4 g total fat (1 g sat. fat), 28 mg chol., 262 mg sodium, 9 g carbo., 1 g fiber, 15 g pro.

Scallops with
Tropical Salsa

Spicy Shrimp Pasta

Spicy Shrimp Pasta

Start to Finish: 20 minutes

- 8 ounce dried angel hair pasta
- 3 cups fresh broccoli florets
- 1 6.5-ounce jar sun-dried tomato strips with Italian herbs packed in oil
- 2 shallots, finely chopped
- 1 pound frozen peeled and deveined shrimp with tails, thawed and drained
- 1/4 to 1/2 teaspoon crushed red pepper
  Salt and black pepper
- 1/4 cup snipped fresh basil

1. In a 4-quart Dutch oven cook pasta with broccoli according to pasta package directions. Drain; return to Dutch oven. Cover to keep warm.

2. Meanwhile, drain tomatoes, reserving oil. If necessary, add olive oil to equal 1/4 cup. In an extra-large skillet heat oil over medium-high heat. Add shallots; cook and stir 1 to 2 minutes or until tender. Add shrimp and crushed red pepper; cook and stir for 4 minutes. Add sun-dried tomatoes; cook and stir about 1 minute more or until shrimp are opaque.

3. Toss shrimp mixture with cooked pasta. Season with salt and pepper. Drizzle with additional olive oil. Transfer to serving bowls. Sprinkle with snipped fresh basil.

MAKES 4 SERVINGS.

Per serving: 526 cal., 19 g total fat (3 g sat. fat), 172 mg chol., 394 mg sodium, 55 g carbo., 5 g fiber, 34 g pro.

Tea-Sauced Scallops with Orange and Honey

Tea-Sauced Scallops with Orange and Honey

Start to Finish: 30 minutes

- 2 tablespoons olive oil
- 1 large clove garlic, minced
- 1 pound sea scallops
- 3/4 cup orange juice
- 4 teaspoons Chinese black tea leaves
- 4 teaspoons honey
- 2 teaspoons reduced-sodium soy sauce
- 6 ounces Chinese egg noodles, rice noodles, or angel hair pasta
- 1 medium orange sweet pepper, cut into bite-size strips
- 1 medium green onion, cut into thin strips
  Cilantro sprigs (optional)

1. Heat olive oil in a large nonstick skillet over medium-high heat. Add minced garlic; cook and stir for 30 seconds. Add scallops. Cook and stir for 4 to 6 minutes or until the scallops just turn opaque. Transfer scallops to a small bowl; cover and keep warm.

2. Carefully pour orange juice into skillet, stirring to dislodge any particles adhering to pan. Add tea leaves; cook and stir mixture for 30 seconds. Add honey, soy sauce, and any scallop liquid from the bowl. Reduce heat; simmer, uncovered, for 3 minutes or until sauce thickens slightly.

3. Cook Chinese noodles or pasta according to package directions, adding the sweet pepper the last 3 minutes of cooking. Drain; set aside.

4. Strain tea mixture through a fine-mesh sieve; return liquid to the pan, discarding solids. Transfer scallops from bowl to pan with a slotted spoon; toss gently to coat with the sauce. To serve, arrange noodles onto 4 warm dinner plates. Top with scallops and sauce. Garnish with green onion and, if desired, cilantro sprigs. **MAKES 4 SERVINGS.**

Per serving: 383 cal., 10 g total fat (2 g sat. fat), 73 mg chol., 286 mg sodium, 48 g carb., 2 g dietary fiber, 12 g sugar, 26 g protein.

Pan-Seared Scallops

Pan-Seared Scallops ♡

Start to Finish: 20 minutes

- 1 pound fresh or frozen sea scallops
- 2 tablespoons all-purpose flour
- 1 to 2 teaspoons blackened steak seasoning or Cajun seasoning
- 1 tablespoon vegetable oil
- 1 10-ounce package prewashed spinach
- 1 tablespoon water
- 2 tablespoons balsamic vinegar
- ¼ cup cooked bacon pieces

1. Thaw scallops, if frozen. Rinse scallops; pat dry. In a resealable plastic bag combine flour and steak seasoning. Add scallops; toss gently to coat. In a large skillet heat oil over medium heat. Add scallops; cook for 3 to 5 minutes or until browned and opaque, turning once halfway through cooking. Remove scallops.

2. Add spinach to skillet; sprinkle with the water. Cook, covered, over medium-high heat about 2 minutes or until spinach starts to wilt. Add vinegar; toss to coat evenly. Return scallops to skillet; heat through. Sprinkle with bacon. **MAKES 4 SERVINGS.**

Per serving: 158 cal., 6 g total fat (1 g sat. fat), 37 mg chol., 323 mg sodium, 9 g carbo., 2 g fiber, 18 g pro.

Quick Tip There are two types of scallops—sea scallops and bay scallops. Sea scallops are generally larger than bay scallops. Choose scallops that are plump and moist with translucent color and fresh, sweet smell. The best scallops are dry-packed. Scallops that are packed in liquid tend to steam in the pan rather than sear. Quick searing gives them a crust on the outside and creamy, tender centers.

Speedy Paella ♡

Start to Finish: 14 minutes

- 8 ounces fresh or frozen sea scallops
- 8 ounces fresh or frozen cooked peeled, deveined shrimp
- 1 10-ounce package frozen long grain white rice with vegetables (peas, corn, and carrots)
- 1 tablespoon vegetable oil
- 4 plum tomatoes, coarsely chopped
- ½ to 1 teaspoon ground turmeric
  Salt and black pepper
  Snipped fresh parsley (optional)

1. Thaw scallops and shrimp, if frozen. Rinse scallops; pat dry with paper towels. Cut any large scallops in half. Prepare the rice following the microwave package directions.
2. Meanwhile, in a large skillet heat oil over medium heat. Add scallops; cook about 3 minutes or until scallops are opaque. Add shrimp and tomatoes; heat through.
3. Transfer the rice to a bowl; stir in turmeric. Spoon seafood-tomato mixture over rice; lightly toss. Season with salt and pepper. If desired, sprinkle dish with snipped parsley.
MAKES 4 SERVINGS.

Per serving: 229 cal., 5 g total fat (1 g sat. fat), 129 mg chol., 374 mg sodium, 22 g carbo., 2 g fiber, 24 g pro.

Speedy Paella

Sides

Breads

Pasta, Rice, and Grains

Salads

Vegetable Sides

Insalata Mista

Orange-Asparagus Salad ♡
Start to Finish: 20 minutes

- 8 ounces fresh asparagus
- 1 medium orange, peeled and sliced crosswise
- 2 tablespoons orange juice
- 2 teaspoons olive oil
- 1/2 teaspoon Dijon mustard
- 1/8 teaspoon salt
  Dash black pepper

1. Snap off and discard woody bases from asparagus. If desired, scrape off scales. Cut stems into 2-inch-long pieces. In a covered small saucepan cook asparagus in a small amount of boiling water for 1 minute; drain. Cool immediately in a bowl of ice water. Drain on paper towels.

2. Cut orange slices into 2 section pieces; set aside.

3. For dressing, in a medium bowl whisk together orange juice, oil, mustard, salt, and pepper. Add asparagus and orange sections; stir gently to coat. Serve immediately. (Or cover and chill for up to 6 hours.)
MAKES 2 SERVINGS.

Per serving: 94 cal., 5 g total fat (1 g sat. fat), 0 mg chol., 177 mg sodium, 12 g carbo., 3 g fiber, 2 g pro.

Romaine with Creamy Garlic Dressing
Start to Finish: 5 minutes

- 1/2 cup plain yogurt
- 1/3 cup bottled Italian salad dressing
- 1 garlic clove, minced
- 4 cups torn romaine lettuce
- 1/4 cup finely shredded Parmesan cheese

1. For the dressing, in a small bowl stir together yogurt, salad dressing, and garlic.

2. Arrange lettuce on 4 salad plates. Drizzle each salad with 1 tablespoon of the dressing. Sprinkle with Parmesan cheese.
MAKES 4 SERVINGS.

Per serving: 257 cal., 19 g total fat (7 g sat. fat), 26 mg chol., 744 mg sodium, 7 g carbo., 1 g fiber, 15 g pro.

Insalata Mista
Start to Finish: 15 minutes

- 4 cups torn mixed greens (such as radicchio, spinach, arugula, and/or chicory)
- 1 cup yellow and/or red cherry tomatoes, halved
- 1/4 cup snipped fresh basil
- 1/2 cup Greek olives
- 1 recipe Italian Vinaigrette
- 3 ounces thinly sliced fresh mozzarella cheese

1. In a large bowl toss together the mixed greens, tomatoes, basil, and olives. Drizzle Italian Vinaigrette over salad; toss to coat. Top with mozzarella cheese. **MAKES 4 SERVINGS.**

Italian Vinaigrette In a screw-top jar combine 2 tablespoons olive oil or salad oil, 2 tablespoons balsamic vinegar, 2 teaspoons snipped fresh oregano or basil, 1/8 teaspoon salt, and 1/8 teaspoon black pepper. Cover the jar; shake well. Serve immediately or cover and store in the refrigerator up to 2 weeks. Shake before serving. **MAKES ABOUT 1/4 CUP.**

Per serving: 169 cal., 14 g total fat (4 g sat. fat), 16 mg chol., 255 mg sodium, 7 g carbo., 2 g fiber, 6 g pro.

Orange-
Asparagus
Salad

Caesar Salad

Napa Cabbage Slaw ♡

Start to Finish: 15 minutes

3 cups finely shredded napa cabbage
1 cup finely shredded bok choy
¼ of a small red sweet pepper, cut into thin strips (about ¼ cup)
¼ cup rice vinegar or white wine vinegar
1 tablespoon salad oil
½ teaspoon dark sesame oil

1. In a large bowl combine cabbage, bok choy, and sweet pepper strips.
2. For dressing, in a small bowl stir together vinegar, salad oil, and sesame oil. Pour dressing over cabbage mixture; toss gently to coat. If desired, cover and refrigerate up to 2 hours. **MAKES 6 SERVINGS.**

Per serving: 40 cal., 3 g total fat (0 g sat. fat), 0 mg chol., 81 mg sodium, 2 g carbo., 2 g fiber, 1 g pro.

Caesar Salad

Start to Finish: 20 minutes

1 whole clove garlic, peeled
2 tablespoons refrigerated or frozen egg product
3 anchovy fillets (optional)
½ teaspoon Dijon mustard
2 tablespoons grated Parmesan cheese
1 tablespoon lemon juice
½ cup olive oil
2 tablespoons olive oil
1 tablespoon butter
1 clove garlic, minced
2 cups ¾-inch cubes Italian bread
1 tablespoon snipped fresh parsley
1 tablespoon grated Parmesan cheese
1 head romaine, torn in 1½-inch pieces

1. For dressing, in a small saucepan cook the whole garlic clove in boiling water for 5 minutes. Drain. Place garlic in a food processor or blender. Add egg product, anchovies (if desired), mustard, 2 tablespoons Parmesan cheese, and lemon juice. Process or blend for 1 minute. With machine running, add ½ cup olive oil in a stream until blended.
2. For croutons, in a large nonstick skillet heat 2 tablespoons olive oil and butter over medium-low heat. Add minced garlic; cook for 2 minutes. Add bread cubes. Increase heat to medium-high; cook for 7 to 8 minutes or until bread is evenly browned, stirring frequently. Stir in parsley and the 1 tablespoon Parmesan cheese; toss to coat.

3. To assemble, in a large bowl toss together romaine, dressing, and croutons. Divide equally among 4 to 6 plates. **MAKES 4 TO 6 SERVINGS.**

Per serving: 292 cal., 26 g total fat (5 g sat. fat), 8 mg chol., 176 mg sodium, 10 g carbo., 1 g fiber, 5 g pro.

Quick Tip To make the Caesar dressing for this salad, emulsify the oil. Add the oil in a stream as other liquids blend at high speed for a thick, creamy texture. If the oil is simply stirred in, it separates from the other ingredients and the dressing becomes runny. Apply the same method to other homemade dressings.

Creamed Peas and New Potatoes ♡

Start to Finish: 30 minutes

     1 pound tiny new potatoes (10 to 12)
 1¹/₂ cups shelled peas or frozen peas
   ¹/₄ cup chopped onion
     1 tablespoon butter or margarine
     1 tablespoon all-purpose flour
   ¹/₂ teaspoon salt
        Dash black pepper
     1 cup milk
        Snipped fresh chives or dill (optional)

1. Scrub potatoes; cut any large potatoes in half. Peel a narrow strip from around the center of each whole potato. In a medium saucepan cook potatoes, covered, in a small amount of boiling salted water for 8 minutes. Add fresh peas and cook for 10 to 12 minutes more or until tender. (If using frozen peas, cook potatoes 14 minutes; add peas and cook 4 to 5 minutes more.) Drain; return vegetables to saucepan.
2. Meanwhile, in a small saucepan cook onion in hot butter until tender. Stir in flour, salt, and pepper. Add milk all at once. Cook and stir until thickened and bubbly. Cook and stir for 1 minute more. Stir into potatoes and peas; heat through. Season to taste. If desired, sprinkle with chives. **MAKES 4 SERVINGS.**

Per serving: 194 cal., 5 g total fat (3 g sat. fat), 13 mg chol., 358 mg sodium, 31 g carbo., 5 g fiber, 8 g pro.

Herb Salad with Creamy Lemon Dressing

Start to Finish: 20 minutes

     4 teaspoons finely shredded lemon peel
   ¹/₃ cup lemon juice
     3 cloves garlic, minced
     2 teaspoons Dijon mustard
   ¹/₄ teaspoon salt
   ¹/₄ teaspoon black pepper
   ¹/₂ cup olive oil
   ¹/₂ cup sour cream
     2 to 3 medium heads butterhead lettuce, torn, or 6 to 8 cups mixed baby salad greens
 1¹/₂ cups assorted fresh herbs, such as chives, basil, parsley, or mint; torn
    12 to 16 radishes, thinly sliced

1. For dressing, in a small bowl combine lemon peel, lemon juice, garlic, mustard, salt, and pepper. Slowly whisk in olive oil until thickened. Whisk in sour cream.
2. In a large bowl toss together lettuce and herbs; transfer to a platter. Top with sliced radishes; pass dressing. **MAKES 6 TO 8 SERVINGS.**

Per serving: 215 cal., 22 g total fat (5 g sat. fat), 7 mg chol., 161 mg sodium, 5 g carbo., 1 g fiber, 2 g pro.

Mixed Greens Salad with Pears ♡

Start to Finish: 15 minutes

     1 5-ounce bag spring mix salad greens
     2 medium pears, cored and sliced
     2 ounces Gruyère cheese, cubed
     1 recipe White Wine Vinaigrette
        Fresh pear, thinly sliced (optional)

1. In a large bowl combine salad greens, pear slices, and cheese. Drizzle with White Wine Vinaigrette and toss to coat. If desired, garnish with additional pear slices.

White Wine Vinaigrette In a screw-top jar combine 3 tablespoons salad oil; 2 tablespoons white wine vinegar; 1 tablespoon honey; ¹/₄ teaspoon dried basil or oregano, crushed; ¹/₈ teaspoon salt; ¹/₈ teaspoon dry mustard; and ¹/₈ teaspoon black pepper. Cover and shake to combine. **MAKES 6 SERVINGS.**

Per serving: 148 cal., 10 g total fat (3 g sat. fat), 10 mg chol., 85 mg sodium, 12 g carbo., 2 g fiber, 3 g pro.

Quick Tip This is a lovely salad to serve in the fall, when pears are in season. When buying pears, look for firm, unblemished skin. Pears are not usually ripe right from the store. Let them sit on the counter for a couple days until they are fragrant and yield to gentle pressure—then refrigerate until you are ready to use them.

●●

Although the main course may get more thought and attention, a stellar side dish makes a meal special.

Mixed Greens Salad with Pears

Prosciutto
with Asparagus
and New
Potatoes

Prosciutto with Asparagus and New Potatoes ♡

Prep: 15 minutes **Cook:** 15 minutes

1½ pounds fresh asparagus spears
1 20-ounce package refrigerated red potato wedges
¼ cup bottled Italian salad dressing
1 teaspoon finely shredded lemon peel
6 ounces thinly sliced prosciutto slices
    Parmesan cheese ribbons (optional)

1. Snap off and discard woody bases from the asparagus spears. If desired, scrape off scales. Cut into 2-inch pieces. Set aside.
2. In a large saucepan cook the potatoes, covered, in a small amount of lightly salted boiling water for 11 minutes. Add asparagus. Cook, covered, about 4 minutes more or until asparagus is crisp-tender and potatoes are tender; drain. Transfer to a platter.
3. Meanwhile, in a small bowl combine salad dressing and lemon peel. Drizzle salad dressing mixture over potatoes and asparagus. Arrange prosciutto next to vegetables. If desired, top with Parmesan cheese ribbons. Serve warm. **MAKES 8 SERVINGS.**

Per serving: 116 cal., 4 g total fat (1 g sat. fat), 15 mg chol., 770 mg sodium, 11 g carbo., 3 g fiber, 9 g pro.

Roasted Asparagus with Gruyère ♡

Prep: 15 minutes **Roast:** 20 minutes
Stand: 2 minutes **Oven:** 400°F

2 pounds fresh asparagus spears
1 small onion, cut into thin wedges
1 small red or yellow sweet pepper, cut into thin strips
1 tablespoon canola oil
¼ teaspoon salt
¼ teaspoon black pepper
¼ cup shredded Gruyère or Swiss cheese (1 ounce)

Roasted Asparagus with Gruyère

1. Preheat oven to 400°F. Snap off and discard woody bases from asparagus spears. Scrape off scales. In a 15×10×1-inch baking pan place asparagus, onion, and sweet pepper. Drizzle with oil; toss gently to coat. Spread in a single layer. Sprinkle with salt and black pepper.
2. Roast, uncovered, about 20 minutes or until asparagus is crisp-tender. Transfer to a platter; sprinkle with cheese. Let stand about 2 minutes or until cheese is melted.

MAKES 6 SERVINGS.

Per serving: 73 cal., 4 g total fat (1 g sat. fat), 5 mg chol., 127 mg sodium, 4 g carbo., 2 g fiber, 4 g pro.

It's a snap
The woody base of asparagus is fibrous and unpleasant to eat. To find the spot where the woody part starts, gently bend each stalk at about the bottom one-fourth of the stalk. The woody base will snap off right where it's supposed to. You can remove the tough skin with a sharp paring knife or vegetable peeler.

Lemony
Green Beans

Green Beans with Basil and Mint ♡

Start to Finish: 15 minutes

 6 cups water
 2 pounds fresh green beans, trimmed
   if desired
 2 cloves garlic, minced
 ¹/₂ cup chopped red sweet pepper (1 small)
 ¹/₂ cup shredded fresh basil
 ¹/₃ cup shredded fresh mint
 2 tablespoons olive oil
 ¹/₂ teaspoon salt

1. In a 4-quart Dutch oven bring the water to boiling. Add green beans and return to boiling; reduce heat. Simmer, uncovered, for 7 to 8 minutes or until beans are crisp-tender, adding garlic the last 1 minute of cooking. Drain well.

2. Meanwhile, in a large bowl combine sweet pepper, basil, mint, olive oil, and salt. Add drained green beans and garlic. Toss gently to combine. **MAKES 8 SERVINGS.**

Per serving: 71 cal., 4 g total fat (1 g sat. fat), 0 mg chol., 154 mg sodium, 9 g carbo., 4 g fiber, 2 g pro.

Lemony Green Beans ♡

Start to Finish: 20 minutes

1¹/₂ pounds green beans, trimmed, or three
   9-ounce packages frozen whole green
   beans
 3 tablespoons olive oil
 3 large shallots, cut into thin wedges
 6 cloves garlic, thinly sliced
 1 tablespoon finely shredded lemon peel
 ¹/₂ teaspoon salt
 ¹/₈ teaspoon black pepper
   Lemon wedges (optional)

1. In an extra-large skillet cook green beans in lightly salted boiling water for 2 to 5 minutes or until barely crisp-tender. Drain; rinse beans with cold water. Set aside.

2. In the same skillet heat olive oil over medium-high heat. Add shallots and garlic. Cook for 2 to 3 minutes or until shallots begin to brown, stirring occasionally. Add beans. Cook and toss for 1 to 2 minutes or until heated through. Remove from heat. Stir in lemon peel, salt, and pepper. If desired, serve with lemon wedges. **MAKES 8 SERVINGS.**

Per serving: 80 cal., 5 g total fat (1 g sat. fat), 0 mg chol., 152 mg sodium, 9 g carbo., 3 g fiber, 2 g pro.

Keep basil fresh

While you can refrigerate mint to keep it fresh, basil quickly browns and gets slimy in the refrigerator. To keep fresh basil at its best, place it, stems down, in a glass of cool water and keep it at room temperature. If you keep basil more than one day before using it, change the water.

Green Beans with Basil and Mint

Roasted Root
Vegetables

Roasted Root Vegetables ♥

Prep: 25 minutes **Roast:** 35 minutes
Oven: 425°F

 4 medium parsnips, peeled, halved
   lengthwise, and cut into 1-inch pieces
 4 medium turnips, peeled and cut into
   1-inch pieces, or 1 medium rutabaga,
   peeled and cut into 1-inch pieces
 2 small Yukon gold potatoes, peeled and cut
   into quarters, or 1 medium sweet potato,
   peeled and cut into 1-inch pieces
 3 medium carrots, halved lengthwise and
   cut into 1-inch pieces
 2 medium onions, cut into 1-inch wedges
 8 fresh sage leaves, slivered
 3 tablespoons olive oil
1½ teaspoons sea salt or kosher salt
 ½ teaspoon freshly ground black pepper
 ¼ cup honey
   Snipped fresh sage

1. Preheat oven to 425°F. In a large greased roasting pan combine parsnips, turnips, potatoes, carrots, onions, and 8 leaves of slivered sage. Combine oil, salt, and pepper; drizzle over vegetables in pan. Toss lightly.
2. Roast, uncovered, for 30 to 35 minutes until vegetables are lightly browned and tender, stirring occasionally. Drizzle honey over vegetables. Stir gently to coat. Roast for 5 minutes more. Sprinkle with the snipped sage. **MAKES 8 SERVINGS.**

Per serving: 168 cal., 5 g total fat (1 g sat. fat), 0 mg chol., 354 mg sodium, 30 g carbo., 5 g fiber, 2 g pro.

Quick Tip Although names are used interchangeably and both work equally well in most recipes, sweet potatoes and yams are different. Sweet potatoes have pale yellow flesh and a somewhat dry, mealy texture—similar to a baking potato. Yams have fairly dense, dark orange flesh and are generally sweeter than sweet potatoes. Either one works here.

Zucchini alla Romana

Zucchini alla Romana

Start to Finish: 15 minutes

 2 cloves garlic
 2 teaspoons olive oil
1½ pounds baby yellow summer squash
   and/or zucchini, halved lengthwise, or
   4 cups sliced yellow summer squash or
   zucchini
 1 teaspoon dried basil, crushed
 ¼ teaspoon salt
   Dash black pepper
 2 tablespoons finely shredded Romano or
   Parmesan cheese
 2 plum tomatoes, chopped (optional)

1. In a large skillet cook whole garlic cloves in oil until lightly brown; discard garlic.
2. Add squash, basil, salt, and pepper to oil in skillet. Cook, uncovered, over medium heat about 5 minutes or until squash is crisp-tender, stirring occasionally.
3. To serve, transfer mixture to a serving bowl. Sprinkle cheese and, if desired, tomatoes. **MAKES 6 SERVINGS.**

Per serving: 35 cal., 2 g total fat (1 g sat. fat), 2 mg chol., 130 mg sodium, 3 g carbo., 1 g fiber, 2 g pro.

Sweet-and-Sour
Cabbage

Butter-Glazed Carrots ♡

Start to Finish: 18 minutes

- 1 pound carrots, peeled and cut into
  $^1/_2$-inch diagonal slices
- 2 tablespoons butter, softened
- 1 to 2 teaspoons dried tarragon or basil,
  crushed
  Salt and black pepper

1. In a medium saucepan cook carrots,
covered, in $^1/_2$ cup boiling water for 8 to
10 minutes or just until carrots are tender;
drain off water.

2. Add butter and tarragon to the saucepan.
Stir until combined; if necessary heat over low
heat to melt butter completely. Season to taste
with salt and pepper. **MAKES 4 SERVINGS.**

Per serving: 98 cal., 6 g total fat (4 g sat. fat), 15 mg
chol., 261 mg sodium, 11 g carbo., 3 g fiber, 1 g pro.

Maple-Glazed Carrots Prepare as above,
except use 1 tablespoon butter, omit the
herb, and add 2 tablespoons pure maple
syrup and 1 tablespoon sesame seeds,
toasted.

Microwave directions In a microwave-safe
baking dish or casserole combine carrots and
$^1/_4$ cup water. Microwave, covered, on high
for 7 to 9 minutes or until carrots are tender,
stirring once. Drain off water. Add butter and
tarragon to the baking dish. Stir until
combined; if necessary, microwave for 10 to
20 seconds more to melt butter completely.
Season to taste with salt and pepper.

Sweet-and-Sour Cabbage ♡

Start to Finish: 15 minutes

- 3 tablespoons packed brown sugar
- 3 tablespoons vinegar
- 3 tablespoons water
- 4 teaspoons vegetable oil
- $^1/_4$ teaspoon caraway seeds
- $^1/_4$ teaspoon salt
  Dash black pepper
- 3 cups shredded red or green cabbage
- $^3/_4$ cup chopped apple

1. In a large skillet combine brown sugar,
vinegar, water, oil, caraway seeds, salt, and
pepper. Cook for 2 to 3 minutes or until hot
and brown sugar is dissolved, stirring
occasionally.

2. Stir in the cabbage and apple. Cook,
covered, over medium-low heat about
5 minutes or until cabbage is crisp-tender,
stirring occasionally. Serve with a slotted
spoon. **MAKES 4 SERVINGS.**

Per serving: 109 cal., 5 g total fat (1 g sat. fat), 0 mg
chol., 163 mg sodium, 17 g carbo., 2 g fiber, 1 g pro.

Quick Tip Shred the cabbage for this dish
on a box grater, with a good sharp chef's
knife—or in a food processor, which is easier.

Butter-Glazed
Carrots

Saucepan
Baked Beans

Saucepan Baked Beans ♡

Prep: 10 minutes **Cook:** 10 minutes

- 1 16-ounce can pork and beans in tomato sauce
- 1 15-ounce can navy or Great Northern beans, rinsed and drained
- ¼ cup ketchup
- 2 tablespoons maple syrup or packed brown sugar
- 2 teaspoons dry mustard
- ¼ cup chopped purchased cooked bacon, warmed

1. In a medium saucepan combine pork and beans, navy beans, ketchup, maple syrup, and dry mustard. Bring mixture to boiling; reduce heat. Simmer, uncovered, about 10 minutes or until desired consistency, stirring frequently. Top with bacon. **MAKES 6 SERVINGS.**

Per serving: 211 cal., 3 g total fat (1 g sat. fat), 5 mg chol., 870 mg sodium, 39 g carbo., 8 g fiber, 11 g pro.

Quick Tip If you like a little heat (of the tongue-tingling variety) in your baked beans, stir 1 finely chopped chipotle pepper in adobo sauce into the bean mixture before simmering.

Bacon bonanza

Buying precooked bacon adds pennies to each delicious strip. Instead, cook a pound by your favorite method to just under how you like it, then drain and cool on paper towels. Crumble it, divide it into portions, and wrap in clean paper towels. Store it in a sealed plastic bag in the freezer for up to 6 weeks. Before using, pop it in the micrwave for 30 seconds to 1 minute.

Garlicky Broccoli Rabe

Garlicky Broccoli Rabe ♡

Start to Finish: 20 minutes

- 2 pounds broccoli rabe
- 1 large red sweet pepper, cut into bite-size strips
- 1 teaspoon dried basil, crushed
- ¼ teaspoon salt
- 3 cloves garlic, minced
- 2 tablespoons olive oil
   Crushed red pepper
   Lemon wedges

1. Wash broccoli rabe; remove and discard woody stems. Coarsely chop the leafy greens; set aside florets and chopped leaves.

2. In a large skillet cook and stir sweet pepper, basil, salt, and garlic in hot oil over medium-high heat for 2 minutes. Add broccoli rabe. Using tongs, toss and cook vegetables for 4 to 6 minutes or until broccoli rabe is crisp-tender. Transfer to serving dish. Sprinkle with crushed red pepper. Serve with lemon wedges. **MAKES 6 SERVINGS.**

Per serving: 103 cal., 5 g total fat (1 g sat. fat), 0 mg chol., 178 mg sodium, 7 g carbo., 4 g fiber, 6 g pro.

Quick Tip Broccoli rabe, also known as rapini, is a pleasantly bitter green that is in peak season in the spring. When choosing broccoli rabe, look for slender, firm stalks; crisp, green leaves; and florets that are tightly closed.

Beet Greens
with Walnuts
and
Blue Cheese

Glazed Brussels Sprouts ♡

Start to Finish: 25 minutes

  3 tablespoons butter
  2 10-ounce packages frozen Brussels
     sprouts
  1 10-ounce package frozen whole small
     onions
 ⅓ cup pure maple syrup
     Salt and black pepper
 ¼ cup chopped walnuts, toasted

1. In a large skillet melt butter over medium heat. Add Brussels sprouts and onions. Cook, covered, about 10 minutes, stirring occasionally.

2. Drizzle vegetables with maple syrup. Cook, uncovered, for 1 to 2 minutes more, stirring occasionally. Season to taste with salt and pepper. Transfer vegetables to a serving bowl. Sprinkle with walnuts. **MAKES 8 SERVINGS.**

Per serving: 139 cal., 7 g total fat (3 g sat. fat), 12 mg chol., 83 mg sodium, 18 g carbo., 4 g fiber, 4 g pro.

Sweet Saucy Carrots and Pecans ♡

Start to Finish: 20 minutes

  1 1-pound package peeled baby carrots
  2 tablespoons orange marmalade
  1 tablespoon butter or margarine
 ½ teaspoon salt
  2 tablespoons pecan pieces, toasted

1. In a large covered saucepan cook the carrots in a small amount of boiling water for 8 to 10 minutes or until crisp-tender. Drain.

2. Return carrots to pan. Add orange marmalade, butter, and salt. Stir until carrots are coated. Top with the pecans. **MAKES 4 SERVINGS.**

Per serving: 124 cal., 6 g total fat (2 g sat. fat), 8 mg chol., 365 mg sodium, 19 g carbo., 4 g fiber, 2 g pro.

Beet Greens with Walnuts and Blue Cheese ♡

Start to Finish: 15 minutes

  8 ounces fresh beet greens
  2 teaspoons vegetable oil
  2 tablespoons chopped walnuts
  1 tablespoon crumbled blue cheese
 ¼ teaspoon black pepper

1. Thoroughly clean beet greens. Drain well. Cut beet greens into 1-inch strips. In a large skillet heat oil over medium-high heat. Add walnuts. Cook and stir for 2 minutes.

2. Add beet greens to skillet. Cook and stir, uncovered, about 1 minute or just until wilted. Top with crumbled blue cheese and pepper. **MAKES 4 SERVINGS.**

Per serving: 55 cal., 5 g total fat (1 g sat. fat), 0 mg chol., 109 mg sodium, 3 g carbo., 2 g fiber, 2 g pro.

Quick Tip This recipe can also be prepared with fresh spinach or Swiss chard. Whichever greens you choose to use, be sure to clean them well under cold running water to remove any dirt or sand. Drain well.

Glazed
Brussels
Sprouts

Hash Brown
Potato Cakes

Cauliflower with Lemon Dressing

Hash Brown Potato Cakes

Prep: 20 minutes **Cook:** 8 minutes per batch
Oven: 300°F

    1 pound russet or round red potatoes
 1/2 of a medium onion, very thinly sliced
    1 tablespoon olive oil
    2 teaspoons snipped fresh thyme or
       1/4 teaspoon dried thyme, crushed
 1/4 teaspoon salt
 1/8 teaspoon black pepper
       Nonstick cooking spray

1. Preheat oven to 300°F. Peel and coarsely shred potatoes; immediately rinse with cold water in a colander. Drain well, pressing lightly. Pat dry with paper towels; place in a large bowl. Quarter the onion slices. Stir onion, oil, thyme, salt, and pepper into shredded potatoes.
2. Lightly coat an unheated very large nonstick skillet or griddle with cooking spray. Heat skillet over medium heat.
3. For each cake, scoop a slightly rounded measuring tablespoon of potato mixture onto skillet. Using a spatula, press potato mixture to flatten evenly to 2 1/2- to 3-inch diameter. Cook for 5 minutes. Using a wide spatula, carefully turn potato cakes (avoid turning cakes too soon or they will not hold together). Cook for 3 to 5 minutes more or until golden brown. Remove cooked potato cakes from skillet; keep warm, uncovered, in oven while cooking remaining potato cakes. Repeat with remaining potato mixture, stirring mixture frequently. **MAKES 8 SERVINGS.**

Per serving: 59 cal., 2 g total fat (0 g sat. fat), 0 mg chol., 75 mg sodium, 9 g carbo., 1 g fiber, 1 g pro.

Cauliflower with Lemon Dressing

Start to Finish: 20 minutes

    2 small heads cauliflower
 1/2 cup water
    2 to 3 ounces thinly sliced Serrano ham,
       prosciutto, or cooked ham
    1 ounce Manchego cheese or Monterey
       Jack cheese, thinly shaved
 1/4 cup olive oil or vegetable oil
    2 tablespoons lemon juice
 1/2 teaspoon salt
    1 clove garlic, minced
 1/4 teaspoon sugar
 1/4 teaspoon dry mustard
 1/4 teaspoon freshly ground black pepper
    2 tablespoons pine nuts, toasted
    2 tablespoons capers, rinsed and drained

1. Remove heavy leaves and tough stems from cauliflower; cut cauliflower into wedges. Place cauliflower in a microwave-safe 3-quart casserole. Add the water. Microwave, covered, on high for 7 to 9 minutes or just until tender. Remove with a slotted spoon to serving plates. Top with ham and cheese.
2. Meanwhile, in a screw-top jar combine oil, lemon juice, salt, garlic, sugar, mustard, and pepper. Cover and shake well to combine; drizzle over cauliflower. Sprinkle with pine nuts and drained capers. **MAKES 4 SERVINGS.**

Per serving: 207 cal., 18 g total fat (3 g sat. fat), 10 mg chol., 848 mg sodium, 7 g carbo., 4 g fiber, 9 g pro.

Creamed
Spinach

Roasted Cheddar Potatoes

Prep: 10 minutes **Bake:** 25 minutes

- 1 24-ounce package frozen potato wedges (skins on)
- 2 tablespoons vegetable oil
- 4 cloves garlic, minced
- 1 teaspoon smoked paprika or paprika
- 1/4 teaspoon salt
   Nonstick cooking spray
- 1 cup shredded white or other cheddar cheese (4 ounces)
- 2/3 cup crushed croutons (about 1 cup croutons)
   Sour cream (optional)

1. Preheat oven following package directions for potatoes. Place frozen potatoes in a large resealable plastic bag. In a small bowl combine oil, garlic, paprika, and salt. Drizzle over potato wedges. Seal bag and shake to coat potatoes.

2. Lightly coat a 15×10×1-inch baking pan with cooking spray. Spread potato wedges in a single layer on prepared pan. Bake following package directions, turning once.

3. In a small bowl combine the cheese and crushed croutons. Sprinkle over the potatoes during the last 3 minutes of baking. Use a large spatula to transfer potato wedges to a platter or large plate, keeping potatoes in a single layer. If desired, serve with sour cream.
MAKES 8 SERVINGS.

Per serving: 165 cal., 8 g total fat (4 g sat. fat), 15 mg chol., 217 mg sodium, 19 g carbo., 1 g fiber, 5 g pro.

Creamed Spinach

Start to Finish: 30 minutes

- 2 10-ounce packages fresh spinach (large stems removed) or two 10-ounce packages frozen chopped spinach, thawed
- 2 tablespoons butter or margarine
- 1/2 cup chopped onion (1 medium)
- 2 to 3 cloves garlic, minced
- 1 cup whipping cream
- 1/2 teaspoon freshly ground black pepper
- 1/4 teaspoon salt
- 1/4 teaspoon ground nutmeg

1. In a large pot of rapidly boiling salted water cook fresh spinach (if using) for 1 minute. Drain well, squeezing out excess liquid. Pat dry with paper towels. Snip spinach with kitchen scissors to coarsely chop; set aside. If using frozen spinach, drain well, squeezing out excess liquid.

2. In a large skillet melt butter over medium heat. Add onion and garlic; cook about 5 minutes or until onion is tender. Stir in whipping cream, pepper, salt, and nutmeg. Bring to boiling; cook, uncovered, until cream begins to thicken. Add spinach. Simmer, uncovered, about 2 minutes or until thickened. Season with additional salt and pepper. **MAKES 4 SERVINGS.**

Per serving: 312 cal., 29 g total fat (17 g sat. fat), 98 mg chol., 347 mg sodium, 11 g carbo., 4 g fiber, 6 g pro.

Roasted
Cheddar
Potatoes

Beans, Barley, and Tomatoes

Beans, Barley, and Tomatoes ♡

Start to Finish: 30 minutes

- 1 14.5-ounce can vegetable broth or chicken broth
- 1 teaspoon Greek seasoning or garam masala
- 1 cup frozen green soybeans (shelled edamame)
- ¾ cup quick-cooking barley
- ½ cup shredded carrot (1 medium)
- 4 cups packaged prewashed fresh spinach
- 4 small to medium tomatoes, sliced

1. In a medium saucepan bring broth and Greek seasoning to boiling. Add soybeans and barley. Return to boiling; reduce heat. Simmer, covered, for 12 minutes. Stir carrot into barley mixture.

2. Meanwhile, arrange spinach on 4 salad plates; top with tomato slices. Using a slotted spoon, spoon barley mixture over tomatoes (or drain barley mixture; spoon over tomato slices). **MAKES 4 SERVINGS.**

Per serving: 171 cal., 3 g total fat (0 g sat. fat), 0 mg chol., 484 mg sodium, 33 g carbo., 10 g fiber, 9 g pro.

Quick Tip Store dried herbs in a cool, dark place for up to 6 months. To keep dried herbs tasting their best, be sure they are not exposed to air, light, or heat. The more airtight the storage container (screw-top glass jars work best), the longer the herbs will retain their flavor.

Corn and Bean Quinoa Pilaf ♡

Start to Finish: 30 minutes

- 1 teaspoon olive oil
- ½ cup chopped onion
- 2 cloves garlic, minced
- ½ cup quinoa
- 1 cup reduced-sodium chicken broth or vegetable broth
- ⅔ cup water
- ¾ cup Black Bean, Corn, and Jicama Salsa
  Fresh jalapeño slices (see note, page 12) (optional)

Corn and Bean Quinoa Pilaf

1. In a large saucepan heat oil over medium heat. Add onion and garlic; cook about 5 minutes or until onion is tender, stirring occasionally. Add quinoa; cook and stir about 3 minutes or until quinoa is lightly browned.

2. Add broth and the water. Bring to boiling; reduce heat. Cover and simmer for 15 to 20 minutes or until all of the liquid is absorbed and the quinoa is tender. Add Black Bean, Corn, and Jicama Salsa to quinoa mixture; heat through. If desired, garnish with jalapeño slices. **MAKES 4 SERVINGS.**

Black Bean, Corn, and Jicama Salsa In a medium bowl toss together one 15-ounce can black beans (rinsed and drained), 1 cup thawed frozen corn, 1 chopped large tomato, ½ cup chopped jicama, 2 thinly sliced green onions, 1 finely chopped jalapeño, 2 tablespoons snipped fresh cilantro, 2 tablespoons lime juice, ¼ teaspoon salt, and ¼ teaspoon ground cumin.

Per serving: 128 cal., 3 g total fat (0 g sat. fat), 0 mg chol., 227 mg sodium, 23 g carbo., 3 g fiber, 6 g pro.

Quick Tip Look for quinoa at health food stores or in the grains section of large supermarkets.

Pesto
Macaroni
Salad

Pasta with Pepper-Cheese Sauce

Start to Finish: 25 minutes

- 8 ounces dried medium shell macaroni, mostaccioli, or cut ziti pasta
- 1 0.9- to 1.25-ounce package hollandaise sauce mix
- 1 cup bottled roasted red sweet peppers, drained and chopped
- ½ cup shredded Monterey Jack cheese with jalapeño chile peppers (2 ounces)

1. Cook pasta according to package directions. Drain well and return pasta to pan.
2. Meanwhile, for sauce, prepare hollandaise sauce according to package directions, except use only 2 tablespoons butter. Stir in roasted red peppers. Remove pan from heat. Add cheese to sauce, stirring until cheese melts. Add sauce to pasta in pan; toss to coat. **MAKES 4 TO 6 SERVINGS.**

Per serving: 384 cal., 13 g total fat (8 g sat. fat), 36 mg chol., 407 mg sodium, 53 g carbo., 2 g fiber, 13 g pro.

Five-Minute Pilaf ♡

Start to Finish: 5 minutes

- 1 8.8-ounce pouch cooked brown rice (about 2 cups)
- 2 cups frozen Italian-blend vegetables or frozen zucchini and yellow summer squash
- ¼ cup refrigerated reduced-fat basil pesto
- 2 tablespoons pine nuts or chopped walnuts, toasted (see note, page 160)

1. In a large microwave-safe bowl combine brown rice and frozen vegetables. Cover bowl. Microwave on high for 4 to 5 minutes or until vegetables are crisp-tender and mixture is heated through, stirring once or twice during cooking. Stir in pesto. To serve, sprinkle with pine nuts. **MAKES 6 SERVINGS.**

Per serving: 136 cal., 6 g total fat (1 g sat. fat), 3 mg chol., 110 mg sodium, 17 g carbo., 2 g fiber, 4 g pro.

Pesto Macaroni Salad

Start to Finish: 30 minutes

- 3 cups dried bow tie and/or wagon wheel pasta
- 5 ounces fresh green beans, trimmed and cut into 1-inch pieces (about 1 cup)
- 1 pound small fresh mozzarella balls, drained and sliced
- 1 7-ounce container purchased refrigerated basil pesto
- ½ cup fresh basil leaves, torn
- ½ teaspoon fine sea salt

1. Cook macaroni according to package directions; drain. Rinse with cold water; drain again. In a saucepan cook beans, covered, in a small amount of boiling salted water for 10 to 15 minutes or until crisp tender; drain. Rinse with cold water; drain again.
2. In a large bowl combine macaroni, green beans, mozzarella, and pesto. Stir in basil and salt. Serve immediately or chill for up to 2 hours before serving. **MAKES 14 SERVINGS.**

Per serving: 249 cal., 14 g total fat (4 g sat. fat), 26 mg chol., 255 mg sodium, 20 g carbo., 1 g fiber, 11 g pro.

Five-Minute
Pilaf

Chive Batter
Rolls

Chive Batter Rolls

Prep: 30 minutes **Rise:** 20 minutes
Bake: 18 minutes **Stand:** 5 minutes
Oven: 350°F

- 1 tablespoon yellow cornmeal
- 2 cups all-purpose flour
- 1 package fast-rising active dry yeast
- 1/4 teaspoon black pepper
- 1 cup milk
- 2 tablespoons sugar
- 3 tablespoons butter or margarine
- 1/2 teaspoon salt
- 1 egg
- 1/2 cup snipped fresh chives or 1/4 cup finely chopped green onions (green tops only)
- 1/3 cup yellow cornmeal

1. Grease the bottoms and sides of twelve 2 1/2-inch muffin cups. Sprinkle bottoms with 1 tablespoon cornmeal; set aside. In a large mixing bowl stir together 1 1/4 cups of the flour, the yeast, and the pepper; set aside.
2. In a small saucepan combine milk, sugar, butter, and salt; heat and stir over medium heat just until mixture is warm (120°F to 130°F) and butter is almost melted. Add milk mixture and egg to flour mixture. Beat with an electric mixer on low to medium for 30 seconds, scraping bowl constantly. Beat on high for 3 minutes. Stir in the chives and 1/3 cup cornmeal. Stir in remaining flour. (The batter will be soft and sticky.) Cover and let rest in a warm place for 10 minutes.
3. Preheat oven to 350°F. Spoon batter into prepared muffin cups. Cover loosely. Let rise in a warm place for 20 minutes.
4. Bake, uncovered, about 18 minutes or until rolls sound hollow when tapped. Cool in muffin cups for 5 minutes; loosen edges and remove from muffin cups. Serve warm.

MAKES 12 ROLLS.

Per roll: 140 cal., 4 g total fat (2 g sat. fat), 28 mg chol., 144 mg sodium, 21 g carbo., 1 g fiber, 4 g pro.

Zucchini-Olive Couscous

Zucchini-Olive Couscous ♡

Start to Finish: 30 minutes

- 1 tablespoon olive oil
- 2 cloves garlic, minced
- 3 cups chicken broth
- 1 cup pimiento-stuffed green olives, pitted green olives, and/or pitted ripe olives, cut up
- 1 10-ounce package couscous
- 3 medium zucchini, halved lengthwise and thinly sliced (about 3 3/4 cups)
- 2 teaspoons finely shredded lemon peel
- 1/4 teaspoon freshly ground black pepper
- 1/2 cup sliced green onions (4)
- 2 tablespoons snipped fresh parsley
  Thin strips of lemon peel (optional)
  Lemon wedges (optional)

1. In a large saucepan heat olive oil over medium heat. Add garlic; cook and stir for 1 minute. Add chicken broth and olives; bring to boiling. Stir in couscous, zucchini, shredded lemon peel, and pepper. Cover; remove from heat. Let stand for 5 minutes.
2. To serve, gently stir in green onions and parsley. If desired, top with thin strips of lemon peel and serve with lemon wedges.

MAKES 8 SERVINGS.

Per serving: 190 cal., 5 g total fat (1 g sat. fat), 0 mg chol., 762 mg sodium, 31 g carbo., 3 g fiber, 6 g pro.

Broccoli Corn Bread

Speed baking

The term "quick breads" takes on a whole new meaning when you keep refrigerated breadsticks in your refrigerator and hot roll or biscuit mix and corn muffin mix in your pantry. With just a few stir-ins or toppings, such as dried herbs, vegetables, onion or garlic, or shredded cheese, you can put a basket of warm, flavorful bread on the table anytime.

Parmesan Rosettes

Prep: 15 minutes **Bake:** 15 minutes
Oven: 375°F

- 1 11-ounce package (12) refrigerated breadsticks
- 3 tablespoons grated Parmesan or Romano cheese
- 1 teaspoon sesame seeds
- $\frac{1}{2}$ teaspoon dried Italian seasoning, crushed
- $\frac{1}{4}$ teaspoon garlic powder
- 2 tablespoons butter, melted

1. Preheat oven to 375°F. Separate breadsticks and uncoil into 12 pieces. On a lightly floured surface, roll each piece into a 12-inch-long rope.
2. Tie each rope in a loose knot, leaving 2 long ends. Tuck the top end of the rope under roll. Bring bottom end up and tuck into center of roll.
3. In a shallow dish combine Parmesan cheese, sesame seeds, Italian seasoning, and garlic powder. Brush top and sides of each rosette with melted butter. Carefully dip the top and sides of each rosette into the cheese mixture. Place rosettes 2 to 3 inches apart on an ungreased baking sheet.
4. Bake for about 15 minutes or until golden. Serve warm. **MAKES 12 ROSETTES.**

Per rosette: 135 cal., 5 g total fat (2 g sat. fat), 6 mg chol., 334 mg sodium, 18 g carbo., 1 g fiber, 4 g pro.

Broccoli Corn Bread

Prep: 10 minutes **Bake:** 30 minutes
Oven: 350°F

- 1 8.5-ounce package corn muffin mix
- 3 eggs
- 1 8-ounce package shredded cheddar cheese (2 cups)
- 1 10-ounce package frozen chopped broccoli, thawed and well drained
- $\frac{1}{2}$ cup chopped onion (1 medium)

1. Preheat oven to 350°F. Grease a 9×9×2-inch baking pan; set aside.
2. In a large bowl combine the corn muffin mix and eggs. Stir in cheese, broccoli, and onion. Spoon batter into the prepared pan, spreading evenly.
3. Bake about 30 minutes or until a wooden toothpick inserted near the center comes out clean. Serve warm. **MAKES 16 SERVINGS.**

Per serving: 138 cal., 7 g total fat (3 g sat. fat), 55 mg chol., 209 mg sodium, 12 g carbo., 1 g fiber, 6 g pro.

Parmesan
Rosettes

Focaccia
Breadsticks

Focaccia Breadsticks

Prep: 15 minutes **Bake:** 12 minutes
Oven: 350°F

- ¼ cup oil-packed dried tomatoes
- ¼ cup grated Romano or Parmesan cheese
- 2 teaspoons water
- 1½ teaspoons snipped fresh rosemary or ½ teaspoon dried rosemary, crushed
- ⅛ teaspoon cracked black pepper
- 1 13.8-ounce package refrigerated pizza dough

1. Preheat oven to 350°F. Lightly grease a baking sheet; set aside.

2. Drain dried tomatoes, reserving oil; finely snip tomatoes. In a small bowl combine tomatoes, 2 teaspoons of the reserved oil, the Romano cheese, the water, rosemary, and pepper. Set aside.

3. On a lightly floured surface unroll the pizza dough. Roll the dough into a 10×8-inch rectangle. Spread the tomato mixture crosswise over half of the dough. Fold plain half of dough over filling; press lightly to seal edges. Cut the folded dough lengthwise into ten ½-inch strips. Fold each strip in half and twist two or three times. Place 1 inch apart on a prepared baking sheet.

4. Bake for 12 to 15 minutes or until golden brown. Serve warm or cool on a wire rack. **MAKES 10 BREADSTICKS.**

Per breadstick: 95 cal., 3 g total fat (1 g sat. fat), 2 mg chol., 157 mg sodium, 15 g carbo., 1 g fiber, 3 g pro.

Quick Tip Refrigerated pizza dough is a wonderful staple to keep on hand—a culinary blank slate. You can make it savory, as in this recipe, or you can make it sweet. Instead of the cheese and tomato mixture, spread the strips with a combination of a little melted butter, brown sugar, and cinnamon (maybe some chopped walnuts or pecans) for a pretty good approximation of a cinnamon roll.

Cheddar Garlic Biscuits

Start to Finish: 15 minutes **Oven:** 425°F

- 2 cups packaged biscuit mix
- ½ cup shredded cheddar cheese (2 ounces)
- ⅔ cup milk
- 2 tablespoons butter, melted
- ¼ teaspoon garlic powder

1. Preheat oven to 425°F. Grease a baking sheet; set aside.

2. In a large bowl combine biscuit mix and cheese; add milk. Stir to combine. Drop dough from rounded tablespoons onto prepared baking sheet. Bake for 8 to 9 minutes or until biscuits are golden.

3. Meanwhile, in a small bowl combine melted butter and garlic powder; brush over hot biscuits. Serve warm. **MAKES 10 BISCUITS.**

Per biscuit: 155 cal., 8 g total fat (4 g sat. fat), 14 mg chol., 367 mg sodium, 16 g carbo., 1 g fiber, 4 g pro.

Cheese-Garlic Crescents

Prep: 15 minutes **Bake:** 11 minutes
Oven: 375°F

- 1 8-ounce package (8) refrigerated crescent rolls
- ¼ cup semisoft cheese with garlic and herb
- 2 tablespoons finely chopped walnuts, toasted (see note, page 160)
  Nonstick cooking spray
  Milk
- 1 tablespoon seasoned fine dry bread crumbs

1. Preheat oven to 375°F. Unroll crescent rolls; divide into 8 triangles. In a small bowl stir together cheese and walnuts. Place a rounded measuring teaspoon of the cheese mixture near the center of the wide end of each crescent roll. Roll up, starting at the wide end.

2. Lightly coat a baking sheet with cooking spray. Place the rolls, point sides down, on the prepared baking sheet. Brush tops lightly with milk; sprinkle with bread crumbs.

3. Bake about 11 minutes or until bottoms are browned. Serve warm. **MAKES 8 ROLLS.**

Per roll: 141 cal., 10 g total fat (3 g sat. fat), 6 mg chol., 254 mg sodium, 12 g carbo., 0 g fiber, 3 g pro.

A basket of warm, fresh-from-the-oven bread on the table makes it look as if you've been cooking all day—even when you haven't.

CHAPTER 7

Desserts

Baked Fruit
Ambrosia

Baked Fruit Ambrosia ♡

Prep: 10 minutes **Bake:** 15 minutes
Oven: 350°F

- 2 medium oranges
- 1 8-ounce can pineapple tidbits
  (juice pack), drained
- 1/4 teaspoon ground cinnamon
- 2 tablespoons shredded coconut
  Fresh raspberries (optional)

1. Preheat oven to 350°F. Finely shred enough peel from 1 orange to make 1/2 teaspoon peel; set aside. Peel and section 2 oranges. Cut orange sections into bite-size pieces.
2. Divide orange pieces and pineapple among four 6-ounce custard cups. Sprinkle with orange peel and cinnamon. Top with coconut.

3. Bake about 15 minutes or until fruit is heated through and coconut is golden. If desired, garnish each serving with fresh raspberries. Serve warm. **MAKES 4 SERVINGS.**

Per serving: 66 cal., 1 g total fat (1 g sat. fat), 0 mg chol., 12 mg sodium, 14 g carbo., 2 g fiber, 1 g pro.

Quick Tip Purchase oranges that are firm and heavy for their size. Avoid any with spongy or moldy spots. A rough, brownish area called russeting occurs on the skin of some oranges and does not affect flavor or quality. Because oranges are sometimes dyed with food coloring, a bright color doesn't necessarily indicate quality.

Fluffy Cranberry Mousse

Start to Finish: 20 minutes

- 1/2 of an 8-ounce package cream cheese,
  softened
- 2 tablespoons sugar
- 1/2 teaspoon vanilla
- 1/2 cup frozen cranberry juice concentrate,
  thawed
- 1 16-ounce can whole cranberry sauce
- 1 1/2 cups whipping cream
- 1 recipe Sweetened Cranberries (optional)

1. In a large bowl beat cream cheese with an electric mixer on medium for 30 seconds. Beat in sugar and vanilla until smooth. Slowly add cranberry concentrate, beating until very smooth. In a small bowl stir the cranberry sauce to remove any large lumps; set aside.
2. In a large chilled bowl beat whipping cream with an electric mixer on low to medium until soft peaks form. Fold half the cranberry sauce and half the whipped cream into the cream cheese mixture. Fold in the remaining cranberry sauce and the remaining whipped cream.
3. Spoon cranberry mixture into 12 small chilled dishes or a large serving bowl. If desired, top with Sweetened Cranberries.
MAKES 12 SERVINGS.

Sweetened Cranberries In a medium skillet combine 1 cup fresh cranberries, 1/3 cup sugar, and 2 tablespoons water. Cook and stir over medium heat until sugar dissolves and cranberries just begin to pop. Remove from heat. Cover and chill until serving time.

Per serving: 223 cal., 14 g total fat (9 g sat. fat), 51 mg chol., 45 mg sodium, 23 g carbo., 1 g fiber, 1 g pro.

Fluffy
Cranberry
Mousse

Stovetop Peach-Raspberry Cobbler ♡

Start to Finish: 20 minutes **Oven:** 375°F

- 1 teaspoon sugar
  Dash ground cinnamon
- ½ of a sheet frozen puff pastry, thawed according to package directions
- 1 egg, lightly beaten
- 3 tablespoons sugar
- 1 tablespoon cornstarch
- ¼ teaspoon ground cinnamon
- 1 16-ounce package frozen unsweetened peach slices
- 1 cup fresh raspberries
- ½ cup water
  Vanilla ice cream (optional)

1. Preheat oven to 375°F. For puff pastry twists, in a small bowl combine 1 teaspoon sugar and dash cinnamon. Place puff pastry on a clean work surface. Brush pastry with beaten egg. Sprinkle with cinnamon-sugar mixture. Cut pastry lengthwise into 4 strips; cut each strip in half crosswise. Twist strips; place on a greased baking sheet. Bake about 15 minutes or until brown and puffed.

2. Meanwhile, in a large saucepan combine 3 tablespoons sugar, cornstarch, and ¼ teaspoon cinnamon. Add frozen peaches, half the raspberries, and the water. Cook over medium heat until mixture is thickened and bubbly. Cook and stir for 2 minutes more. Remove from heat. Stir in the remaining raspberries.

3. Divide fruit mixture among 4 dessert dishes. Top with puff pastry. If desired, serve with ice cream. **MAKES 4 SERVINGS.**

Per serving: 159 cal., 4 g total fat (1 g sat. fat), 53 mg chol., 34 mg sodium, 30 g carbo., 4 g fiber, 3 g pro.

Quick Apple Crisp

Quick Apple Crisp

Start to Finish: 15 minutes

- 1 21-ounce can apple pie filling
- ¼ cup dried cranberries
- ¼ teaspoon ground ginger or cinnamon
- ¼ teaspoon vanilla
- 1 cup granola
- 1 pint vanilla ice cream

1. In a medium saucepan combine pie filling, dried cranberries, and ginger; heat through over medium-low heat, stirring occasionally.

Remove from heat; stir in vanilla. Spoon into 4 bowls. Top each serving with granola. Serve with ice cream. **MAKES 4 SERVINGS.**

Per serving: 507 cal., 15 g total fat (8 g sat. fat), 68 mg chol., 113 mg sodium, 88 g carbo., 6 g fiber, 9 g pro.

Quick Tip If it's in your budget, buy real vanilla extract. It's more expensive than imitation, but one sniff of the real thing and you'll understand why it makes baked goods taste so much better than imitation.

Creamy Parfaits

Start to Finish: 20 minutes

- 1 4-serving-size package French vanilla instant pudding and pie filling mix
- 1 cup milk
- 1/2 cup mascarpone or cream cheese, softened
- 1/4 cup whipping cream
- 1 cup crushed biscotti or shortbread cookies (5 biscotti or 16 shortbread cookies)
- 1 cup fresh berries (such as blueberries, raspberries, and/or hulled, sliced strawberries)

1. Prepare pudding mix according to package directions using the 1 cup milk. Stir mascarpone cheese until smooth. Gradually stir 1/2 cup of the pudding into mascarpone cheese. Fold pudding-cheese mixture into the remaining pudding.

2. In a small chilled mixing bowl beat whipping cream with an electric mixer on medium until soft peaks form. Fold whipped cream into pudding mixture; set aside.

3. To assemble parfaits, arrange half the crushed biscotti in 4 parfait glasses or goblets. Add half of the berries to each glass. Spoon half the pudding mixture on top. Repeat with remaining crushed biscotti, berries, and pudding. Serve immediately or cover and chill for up to 4 hours. **MAKES 4 SERVINGS.**

Per serving: 492 cal., 25 g total fat (14 g sat. fat), 74 mg chol., 510 mg sodium, 61 g carbo., 2 g fiber, 12 g pro.

Caramel Apple Pastry

Prep: 10 minutes **Bake:** 15 minutes
Cool: 5 minutes **Oven:** 450°F

- 1/2 of a 15-ounce package rolled refrigerated unbaked piecrust (1 crust)
- 1 tablespoon butter
- 2 20-ounce cans sliced apples, well drained
- 1/2 cup packed brown sugar
- 1 tablespoon lemon juice
- 1 teaspoon apple pie spice or ground cinnamon
- 1 tablespoon purchased cinnamon-sugar
   Cinnamon or vanilla ice cream (optional)
   Caramel ice cream topping (optional)

1. Preheat oven to 450°F. Bring piecrust to room temperature according to package directions; set aside. In a large ovenproof skillet melt butter over high heat; stir in drained apple slices, brown sugar, lemon juice, and apple pie spice. Spread evenly in skillet. Cook until bubbly.

2. Meanwhile, on a lightly floured surface unroll piecrust. Sprinkle piecrust with cinnamon-sugar; rub into piecrust with your fingers. Carefully place the piecrust over bubbly apple mixture in skillet, cinnamon-sugar side up. Tuck in piecrust around the edge of the skillet, using a spatula to press edge down slightly.

3. Bake about 15 minutes or until piecrust is golden brown. Cool for 5 minutes. Carefully invert skillet onto a serving platter; remove skillet. Serve warm. If desired, serve with ice cream and caramel topping.

MAKES 6 SERVINGS.

Per serving: 381 cal., 12 g total fat (5 g sat. fat), 12 mg chol., 159 mg sodium, 69 g carbo., 3 g fiber, 1 g pro.

Quick Tip To make cinnamon-sugar, in a small bowl stir together 1 tablespoon sugar and 1/4 teaspoon ground cinnamon.

Individual Brownie Trifles

Start to Finish: 20 minutes

- 2/3 cup whipping cream
- 1 tablespoon sugar
- 1/4 teaspoon vanilla
- 8 2×2-inch purchased baked brownies, crumbled into pieces (about 2 cups)
- 2 cups fresh raspberries or dark sweet cherries, pitted
- 1 cup chocolate ice cream topping
   Unsweetened cocoa powder (optional)

1. In a large chilled mixing bowl combine whipping cream, sugar, and vanilla. Beat on medium until soft peaks form; set aside.

2. Divide half the crumbled brownies between 4 large parfait glasses or goblets. Layer half the raspberries, ice cream topping, and whipped cream among the glasses, creating layers. Repeat layers with the remaining brownies, raspberries, ice cream topping, and whipped cream. If desired, sprinkle with cocoa powder. Serve immediately or cover and chill up to 4 hours.

MAKES 4 SERVINGS.

Per serving: 627 cal., 29 g total fat (13 g sat. fat), 90 mg chol., 240 mg sodium, 88 g carbo., 7 g fiber, 9 g pro.

Quick Tip When a recipe calls for beating whipping cream until "soft peaks form," it means a peak will hold its shape but not appear stiff. Be careful not to beat beyond that or the cream will become stiff.

Soda Fountain
Ice Cream Pie

Soda Fountain Ice Cream Pie

Prep: 20 minutes **Freeze:** 9¹/₂ hours
Stand: 15 minutes

1¹/₂ cups crushed rolled sugar ice cream
    cones (12 cones)
¹/₄ cup sugar
¹/₂ cup butter, melted
3 cups fresh strawberries
1 quart vanilla ice cream
¹/₃ cup malted milk powder
¹/₂ cup finely chopped fresh strawberries
1 recipe Sweetened Whipped Cream
    (optional)
    Malted milk balls, coarsely chopped
    (optional)
    Fresh strawberries (optional)
    Hot fudge ice cream topping (optional)

1. For crust, in a medium bowl combine crushed cones and sugar. Drizzle with melted butter; toss gently to coat. Press mixture evenly onto bottom of an 8- or 9-inch springform pan. Cover and freeze about 30 minutes or until firm.

2. Meanwhile, place 3 cups strawberries in a blender. Cover and blend until smooth.

3. In a large chilled bowl stir ice cream with a wooden spoon until softened. Stir in ¹/₂ cup of the pureed strawberries and the malted milk powder. Spoon half the mixture on crust, spreading evenly. Cover and freeze for 30 minutes. (Cover and freeze remaining ice cream mixture.)

4. Spoon remaining pureed strawberries on ice cream layer. Cover and freeze for 30 minutes more. Stir remaining ice cream mixture to soften. Spoon over strawberry layer, spreading evenly. Top with the ¹/₂ cup chopped strawberries. Cover and freeze about 8 hours or until firm.

5. Let pie stand at room temperature for 15 minutes before serving. Cut into wedges. If desired, top with Sweetened Whipped Cream, chopped malted milk balls, and additional strawberries. If desired, serve with hot fudge topping. **MAKES 10 SERVINGS.**

Per serving: 307 cal., 17 g total fat (10 g sat. fat), 52 mg chol., 178 mg sodium, 37 g carbo., 2 g fiber, 4 g pro.

Blackberry Cream Pie

Sweetened Whipped Cream In a chilled mixing bowl beat 1 cup whipping cream, 2 tablespoons sugar, and ¹/₂ teaspoon vanilla with an electric mixer on medium until soft peaks form.

Blackberry Cream Pie

Prep: 10 minutes **Bake:** 5 minutes
Freeze: 4 to 24 hours **Oven:** 375°F

1 9-inch purchased graham cracker crumb
    pie shell
1 egg white, lightly beaten
1 cup whipping cream
1 8-ounce package cream cheese, softened
1 10-ounce jar blackberry or black raspberry
    spread
    Fresh blackberries or black raspberries,
    lemon peel twist, and/or mint leaves
    (optional)
    Whipped cream (optional)

1. Preheat oven to 375°F. Brush pie shell with beaten egg white. Bake for 5 minutes. Cool on a wire rack.

2. In a medium mixing bowl beat whipping cream with an electric mixer on medium until stiff peaks form; set aside.

3. In a large mixing bowl beat cream cheese on medium to high until smooth. Add blackberry spread. Beat on low just until combined. Fold in whipped cream. Spoon mixture into pie shell. Cover and freeze for 4 to 24 hours or until firm. If desired, garnish with fresh black berries, lemon peel twist, and/or mint, and whipped cream.

MAKES 8 SERVINGS.

Per serving: 294 cal., 21 g total fat (13 g sat. fat), 83 mg chol., 114 mg sodium, 23 g carbo., 0 g fiber, 7 g pro.

Mississippi
Mud Cake

Shortcut Malted Chocolate Cake

Prep: 10 minutes **Bake:** 30 minutes
Oven: 350°F

- 1 2-layer-size package dark chocolate fudge or devil's food cake mix
- 1/3 cup vanilla malted milk powder
- 1 12-ounce can whipped chocolate frosting
- 1/4 cup vanilla malted milk powder
- 1 1/2 cups coarsely chopped malted milk balls

1. Preheat oven to 350°F. Prepare cake mix according to package directions, adding 1/3 cup malted milk powder to batter. Pour batter into a greased 13×9×2-inch baking pan. Bake for 30 to 35 minutes or until a toothpick inserted near the center comes out clean. Place pan on a wire rack; cool completely.

2. In a medium bowl stir together frosting and 1/4 cup malted milk powder. Spread evenly over cake. Top with chopped malted milk balls. **MAKES 20 SERVINGS.**

Per serving: 231 cal., 7 g total fat (2 g sat. fat), 2 mg chol., 281 mg sodium, 41 g carbo., 1 g fiber, 3 g pro.

Mississippi Mud Cake

Prep: 15 minutes **Bake:** 30 minutes
Oven: 350°F

- 1 2-layer-size package chocolate cake mix
- 1 1/4 cups water
- 1/3 cup vegetable oil
- 1/3 cup creamy peanut butter
- 3 eggs
- 1 cup semisweet chocolate pieces (6 ounces)
- 1 16-ounce can chocolate fudge frosting
- 1 cup tiny marshmallows
- 1 cup chopped peanuts

1. Preheat oven to 350°F. Grease and lightly flour a 13×9×2-inch baking pan; set pan aside.

2. In a large mixing bowl combine cake mix, the water, oil, peanut butter, and eggs. Beat with an electric mixer on low until moistened. Beat on medium for 2 minutes. Stir in chocolate pieces. Pour into prepared pan. Bake for 30 to 35 minutes or until a wooden toothpick inserted in center comes out clean. Cool in pan on wire rack.

3. Drop spoonfuls of frosting over cake; spread evenly. Sprinkle with marshmallows and peanuts. **MAKES 12 TO 16 SERVINGS.**

Per serving: 591 cal., 30 g total fat (8 g sat. fat), 53 mg chol., 456 mg sodium, 76 g carbo., 3 g fiber, 9 g pro.

Malt magic

Malted milk powder adds a homey nutty-sweet flavor to Shortcut Malted Chocolate Cake. If you love it, there are all kinds of things you can do with this old-fashioned ingredient. Stir it into milk or malts (of course); sprinkle it on ice cream; stir it into pancake, biscuit, or brownie batter; or add it to chocolate chip cookie dough.

Shortcut
Chocolate Revel
Bars

Shortcut Chocolate Revel Bars

Prep: 20 minutes **Bake:** 25 minutes
Cool: 1 hour **Oven:** 350°F

1 1/2 cups semisweet chocolate pieces
1 14-ounce can sweetened condensed milk (1 1/4 cups)
2 tablespoons butter or margarine
1/2 cup chopped walnuts or pecans
2 teaspoons vanilla
2 18-ounce rolls refrigerated oatmeal chocolate chip cookie dough

1. Preheat oven to 350°F. In a small saucepan combine chocolate pieces, condensed milk, and butter. Cook and stir over low heat until chocolate is melted. Remove from heat. Stir in nuts and vanilla.
2. Press two-thirds (1 1/3 rolls) of the cookie dough into the bottom of an ungreased 15×10×1-inch baking pan. Spread the chocolate mixture evenly over the cookie dough. Dot the remaining cookie dough on top of chocolate mixture.
3. Bake about 25 minutes or until top is lightly browned (chocolate will still look moist). Cool on a wire rack. Cut into bars. To store, cover and refrigerate up to 3 days or freeze up to 1 month. **MAKES 30 BARS.**

Per bar: 255 cal., 13 g total fat (5 g sat. fat), 13 mg chol., 136 mg sodium, 33 g carbo., 1 g fiber, 3 g pro.

Molasses types

Molasses varies from light to dark, depending on the length of time it has been boiled or processed. Light molasses, from the first boil, has the most subtle, sweetest taste. Dark molasses, from the second boil, is more robust. Blackstrap molasses, from the third boil, has intense flavor, with a touch of bitterness. Choose one according to your taste.

Gingerbread Cupcakes

Gingerbread Cupcakes

Prep: 10 minutes **Bake:** 15 minutes
Cool: 10 minutes **Oven:** 350°F

1 cup all-purpose flour
1/2 teaspoon baking powder
1/2 teaspoon ground ginger
1/2 teaspoon ground cinnamon
1/4 teaspoon baking soda
Dash salt
1 egg white, lightly beaten
1/3 cup molasses
1/3 cup water
3 tablespoons vegetable oil
Powdered sugar (optional)

1. Preheat oven to 350°F. Line eight 2 1/2-inch muffin cups with paper bake cups; set aside. In a medium bowl stir together flour, baking powder, ginger, cinnamon, baking soda, and salt; set aside.
2. In a small bowl stir together egg white, molasses, the water, and oil. Stir molasses mixture into flour mixture just until blended. Spoon batter into prepared muffin cups.
3. Bake for 15 to 20 minutes or until cupcakes spring back when pressed lightly in centers. Cool in pans on wire racks for 10 minutes. Remove cupcakes from pans. Serve warm or cool. If desired, sift powdered sugar over cupcakes before serving.

MAKES 8 CUPCAKES.

Per cupcake: 137 cal., 5 g total fat (0 g sat. fat), 0 mg chol., 82 mg sodium, 20 g carbo., 1 g fiber, 2 g pro.

Ultimate
Chocolate
Sundaes

once. Add 2 tablespoons sugar. Cook and stir gently until sugar is dissolved and pears are glazed.

3. To assemble, place scoops of ice cream in 8 dessert bowls. Spoon a pear half and some butter mixture around the ice cream in each bowl. Top with the chocolate sauce. **MAKES 8 SERVINGS.**

Per serving: 538 cal., 33 g total fat (20 g sat. fat), 132 mg chol., 119 mg sodium, 56 g carbo., 3 g fiber, 7 g pro.

*Note If pears are large, cut into sixths or eighths.

Raspberry-Pecan Bars

Prep: 15 minutes **Bake:** 45 minutes
Oven: 350°F

      1 cup butter, softened
      1 cup sugar
      1 egg
  2¼ cups all-purpose flour
      1 cup chopped pecans
      1 10-ounce jar raspberry preserves

1. Preheat oven to 350°F. In a large mixing bowl beat butter with an electric mixer on medium to high for 30 seconds. Add sugar; beat until combined. Add egg; beat until combined. Beat in flour until crumbly. Stir in pecans. Measure 1½ cups of the mixture and set aside.

2. Press the remaining flour mixture into the bottom of an ungreased 8×8×2-inch baking pan. Spread preserves evenly over crust, leaving a ½-inch border around sides. Crumble reserved mixture over the top.

3. Bake for 45 to 50 minutes until top is browned. Cool in pan on a wire rack. Cut into bars. **MAKES 16 BARS.**

Per bar: 308 cal., 17 g total fat (8 g sat. fat), 44 mg chol., 92 mg sodium, 38 g carbo., 1 g fiber, 3 g pro.

Ultimate Chocolate Sundaes

Start to Finish: 30 minutes

      8 ounces semisweet or bittersweet
          chocolate, coarsely chopped
   ⅓ cup water
   ¼ cup sugar
   ¼ cup pear liqueur or pear nectar
      4 small Forelle or Bosc pears
          (1 pound total)
      3 tablespoons butter
      2 tablespoons sugar
      1 quart vanilla ice cream

1. For the chocolate sauce, in a small saucepan combine chocolate, the water, and ¼ cup sugar. Melt chocolate over low heat, stirring slowly and constantly. Stir in pear liqueur. Set aside to cool slightly.

2. If desired, peel pears cut into halves and remove cores.* If desired, leave stem on one portion. In a large skillet melt butter. Add pear halves; cook over medium heat about 12 minutes or until brown and tender, turning

Raspberry-Pecan Bars

Salted Peanut
Bars

Salted Peanut Bars

Prep: 20 minutes **Chill:** 2 hours

Nonstick cooking spray
4 cups dry-roasted or honey-roasted peanuts
1 10.5-ounce package tiny marshmallows
1/2 cup butter or margarine
1 12-ounce package peanut butter-flavor pieces (2 cups)
1 14-ounce can sweetened condensed milk (1 1/4 cups)
1/2 cup creamy peanut butter

1. Line a 13×9×2-inch baking pan with heavy foil. Coat foil with cooking spray. Spread half the peanuts in the pan.
2. In a 3-quart saucepan melt marshmallows and butter over low heat. Stir in peanut butter pieces, condensed milk, and peanut butter until smooth. Quickly pour over the peanuts in pan. Sprinkle remaining peanuts on top.
3. Chill until firm; cut into bars. Store in refrigerator. **MAKES 48 BARS.**

Per bar: 93 cal., 6 g total fat (2 g sat. fat), 4 mg chol., 82 mg sodium, 8 g carbo., 1 g fiber, 3 g pro.

Easy Lemon Tarts

Start to Finish: 15 minutes

1 cup powdered sugar
4 to 5 teaspoons milk
6 purchased small spongecake shells
6 tablespoons purchased lemon curd
Fresh raspberries (optional)
Fresh mint sprig (optional)

1. For icing, in a small bowl stir together powdered sugar and milk until drizzling consistency. Pour icing into a small plastic bag; snip off a small corner. Drizzle icing over spongecake shells. Place 1 rounded tablespoon of lemon curd into each center. If desired, garnish with fresh raspberries and mint sprigs. **MAKES 6 TARTS.**

Per tart: 255 cal., 4 g total fat (1 g sat. fat), 30 mg chol., 16 mg sodium, 55 g carbo., 2 g fiber, 1 g pro.

Pistachio-Lemon Gelato

Pistachio-Lemon Gelato

Prep: 30 minutes **Chill:** several hours
Freeze: following manufacturer's directions

1 medium lemon
12 egg yolks, lightly beaten
4 cups whole milk
1 1/3 cups sugar
1/2 cup frozen lemonade concentrate, thawed
1/3 cup chopped pistachios or almonds, toasted (see tip, page 160)

1. Using a vegetable peeler, cut long strips of peel from the lemon. In a large saucepan combine egg yolks, milk, sugar, and the lemon peel strips. Cook and stir over medium heat just until the mixture coats a metal spoon. Remove from heat. Remove lemon peel and discard.
2. Transfer the cooked egg mixture to a large bowl. Cover surface with plastic wrap. Refrigerate several hours or overnight until completely chilled.
3. Stir lemonade concentrate and nuts into cooled egg mixture. Freeze mixture in a 4- or 5-quart ice cream freezer following manufacturer's directions.
MAKES 14 (1/2-CUP) SERVINGS.

Per serving: 204 cal., 8 g total fat (3 g sat. fat), 192 mg chol., 41 mg sodium, 27 g carbo., 0 g fiber, 5 g pro.

Index

Note: Page references in bold indicate photographs.

In-a-Pinch Substitutions

It can happen to the best of cooks: Halfway through a recipe, you find you're completely out of a key ingredient. Here's what to do:

Recipe Calls For:	You May Substitute:
1 square unsweetened chocolate	3 Tbsp. unsweetened cocoa powder + 1 Tbsp. butter/margarine
1 cup cake flour	1 cup less 2 Tbsp. all-purpose flour
2 Tbsp. flour (for thickening)	1 Tbsp. cornstarch
1 tsp. baking powder	$\frac{1}{4}$ tsp. baking soda + $\frac{1}{2}$ tsp. cream of tartar + $\frac{1}{4}$ tsp. cornstarch
1 cup corn syrup	1 cup sugar + $\frac{1}{4}$ cup additional liquid used in recipe
1 cup milk	$\frac{1}{2}$ cup evaporated milk + $\frac{1}{2}$ cup water
1 cup buttermilk or sour milk	1 Tbsp. vinegar or lemon juice + enough milk to make 1 cup
1 cup sour cream (for baking)	1 cup plain yogurt
1 cup firmly packed brown sugar	1 cup sugar + 2 Tbsp. molasses
1 tsp. lemon juice	$\frac{1}{4}$ tsp. vinegar (not balsamic)
$\frac{1}{4}$ cup chopped onion	1 Tbsp. instant minced
1 clove garlic	$\frac{1}{4}$ tsp. garlic powder
2 cups tomato sauce	$\frac{3}{4}$ cup tomato paste + 1 cup water
1 Tbsp. prepared mustard	1 tsp. dry mustard + 1 Tbsp. water

How to Know What You Need

Making a shopping list based on a recipe can be tricky if you don't know how many tomatoes yields 3 cups chopped. Here are some handy translations:

When the Recipe Calls For:	You Need:
4 cups shredded cabbage	1 small cabbage
1 cup grated raw carrot	1 large carrot
$2\frac{1}{2}$ cups sliced carrots	1 pound raw carrots
4 cups cooked cut fresh green beans	1 pound beans
1 cup chopped onion	1 large onion
4 cups sliced raw potatoes	4 medium-size potatoes
1 cup chopped sweet pepper	1 large pepper
1 cup chopped tomato	1 large tomato
2 cups canned tomatoes	16 oz. can
4 cups sliced apples	4 medium-size apples
1 cup mashed banana	3 medium-size bananas
1 tsp. grated lemon rind	1 medium-size lemon
2 Tbsp. lemon juice	1 medium-size lemon
4 tsp. grated orange rind	1 medium-size orange
1 cup orange juice	3 medium-size oranges
4 cups sliced peaches	8 medium-size peaches
2 cups sliced strawberries	1 pint
1 cup soft bread crumbs	2 slices fresh bread
1 cup bread cubes	2 slices fresh bread
2 cups shredded Swiss or cheddar cheese	8 oz. cheese
1 cup egg whites	6 or 7 large eggs
1 egg white	2 tsp. egg white powder + 2 Tbsp. water
4 cups chopped walnuts or pecans	1 pound shelled